GW-BASIC®

Self-Teaching Guide

WILEY SELF-TEACHING GUIDES (STGs) are designed for first time users of computer applications and programming languages. They feature concept-reinforcing drills, exercises, and illustrations that enable you to measure your progress and learn at your own pace.

Other Wiley Self-Teaching Guides

PARADOX 3.5, Gloria Wheeler

MICROSOFT WORD 5.5 FOR THE PC, Ruth Ashley and Judi N. Fernandez

ALDUS PERSUASION FOR IBM PC'S AND COMPATIBLES, Karen Brown and Diane Stielstra

PERFORM, Peter Stephenson

QUARK XPress, Paul Kaitz and Luther Sperberg

WORDPERFECT 5.0/5.1, Neil Salkind

MICROSOFT WINDOWS 3.0, Keith Weiskamp and Saul Aguiar

TURBO C++, Bryan Flamig

MASTERING MICROSOFT WORKS, David Sachs, Babette Kronstadt, Judith Van Wormer, and Barbara Farrell

PC DOS 4, Ruth Ashley and Judi N. Fernandez

PC DOS – 3rd Edition, Ruth Ashley and Judi N. Fernandez

QUICKPASCAL, Keith Weiskamp and Saul Aguiar

To order our STGs, you can call Wiley directly at (201)469-4400 or check your local bookstores.

Mastering computers was never this easy, rewarding, and fun!

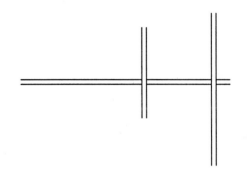

GW-BASIC®

Self-Teaching Guide

Ruth Ashley
Judi N. Fernandez

John Wiley & Sons, Inc.

New York • Chichester • Brisbane • Toronto • Singapore

Publisher: Therese A. Zak
Editor: Katherine Schowalter
Managing Editor: Ruth Greif
Production Services: DuoTech, Inc.

GW-BASIC, MS-DOS, and Microsoft are registered trademarks of the Microsoft Corporation.

Library of Congress Cataloging-in-Publication Data

Ashley, Ruth.
    GW-BASIC : self-teaching guide / Ruth Ashley, Judi N. Fernandez.
        p.   cm.
    Includes index.
    ISBN 0-471-53325-4 (pbk.)
    1. GW-BASIC (Computer program language)   I. Fernandez, Judi N., 1941-
II. Title.
QA76.73.G25A45   1991
005.13'3–dc20   91-7390
                                                                          CIP

Printed in the United States of America
  92 10 9 8 7 6 5 4 3 2
Printed and bound by Malloy Lithographing, Inc.

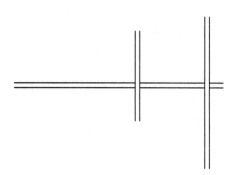

Contents

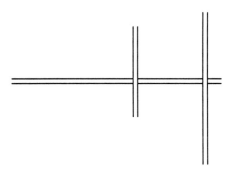

Preface

Welcome to the world of programming! The skills that you are about to develop may not turn you into a professional programmer, but they will help you to know what a computer can do and how it does it. You may want to go on to learn more sophisticated programming techniques and languages. Or you may want to apply the skills you learn here to making better use of your spreadsheet, word processor, or other application software. You'll be well prepared for any of these purposes.

The Purpose/Orientation of This Book

This book provides a comfortable introduction to programming using GW-BASIC. You'll learn to use the editor, to write simple programs using different basic features, and to fix your programs when they go wrong. You won't learn all there is to know about GW-BASIC, but you'll learn enough to write useful, interesting, and even fun programs to use many of the features of your computer.

The material you learn in the early chapters is used heavily throughout this book. Some later topics stand alone, such as using files, using graphics, and arrays. Throughout each chapter there are Self-Check sections that encourage you to try out the statements and options that have just been covered. Each chapter ends with a comprehensive program for you to write that incorporates most of the topics covered in that chapter.

What Is GW-BASIC?

The BASIC programming language was named for Beginners' All-purpose Symbolic Instructional Code; it is an easy way of giving instructions to the computer using symbols that most of us can readily understand. There are many forms of BASIC: some are easier to use, some have more statements, and others have different features.

GW-BASIC is a fairly generic form, distributed by several different companies. It is the form of BASIC often supplied with the operating system (DOS) when you get a new computer. Most of the statements and formats in GW-BASIC are exactly the same in other forms of BASIC.

Overview of Things to Come

You can't learn all of GW-BASIC to start with. You have to start with a few statements. As you learn to make the computer do what you want it to, you can add more statements and features until you can write programs to create quite complex effects.

In Chapter 1, you'll learn to set up your system and use GW-BASIC statements in direct mode; they'll be processed as soon as you press Enter. You'll learn to use half a dozen statements here, to give you a chance to get comfortable with GW-BASIC. You'll learn to use constants and variables and send output to either the screen or the printer.

In Chapter 2, you'll start writing and saving programs. You'll use all the statements you learned in Chapter 1. And you'll start documenting your programs so that they are easy for you to return to weeks or months later. This chapter deals heavily with the GW-BASIC Editor, since changing and correcting programs is the major task programmers have to do.

Chapter 3 introduces arithmetic, which is involved in almost every GW-BASIC program. You'll learn to perform simple arithmetic, use several built-in functions, and format output. You'll also learn to generate random numbers and to structure your programs so that they are easy to read.

Chapters 4 and 5 deal with program logic and statements that help you implement it. You'll learn to create branches, use conditions to let the program make decisions, and set up several types of loops to make programs repeat. In addition, you'll see how to debug programs to find errors, which none of us can avoid forever.

Chapter 6 shows you how to make your programs deal with the console; both input and output are covered. You'll learn to control the general screen mode and resolution, and how to use color on the screen. You'll also see how to detect the location of the cursor, specify where text is to be printed, and determine instantly when a key is pressed and which one it is.

Chapters 7 and 8 show you how to create and use files in your programs. Files let you store data on disk and access it at will in the same or other programs. Chapter 7 covers sequential files; Chapter 8 covers random files.

Chapter 9 deals with graphics. You'll learn to draw straight and curved lines, including boxes, rectangles, circles, and ellipses. You'll also learn to control individual pixels on the screen and to apply what you already know about color to your graphics.

Chapter 10 expands what you already know about using string data in programs. GW-BASIC has many functions and statements that help you manipulate strings in constant or variable form.

Chapter 11 introduces you to arrays and shows you how to define and manipulate them. Arrays make many programming tasks easier. They depend heavily on the use of loops for their processing. You'll see how to sort arrays and to use an array as an index for a random file.

Throughout the book, you'll find many hints for debugging and testing programs. Chapter 12 goes deeper into the subject, providing you with some more commands and techniques that will help you find program errors and straighten out your programs.

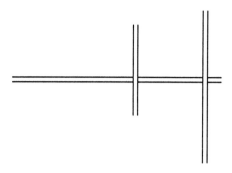

About This Book

We have used some standards to make reading this book and understanding GW-BASIC as easy as possible. This is a "learn-by-doing" book. We explain how something is done or a statement is used and show you at least one example. Usually, you'll see several examples.

A number of times each chapter, a Self-Check gives you a guided exercise covering topics just discussed. You can also try things on your own; that helps you learn. Just don't get discouraged by error messages. And do write the Exercise programs at the end of each chapter. Sample programs are shown for each Self-Check and end-of-chapter Exercise. Your programs won't be exactly the same. But you'll be able to compare yours to ours if you had problems getting your program to work correctly.

Any information in this book that represents how text appears on the screen is shown in type `like these words`. GW-BASIC words and statements are shown in uppercase characters. Statements and other GW-BASIC components often have relatively involved formats, that have required and optional parts, as well as parts you must supply. You'll see statement formats in most chapters. If they include several parts, they're generally explained in detail in the paragraph following their introduction. Upppercase words are required. Square brackets ([ ]) enclose optional parts of a format. Italics are used for parts that depend on the context and the effect you want; you have to replace these when you use the statement on your computer.

Enjoy the book while you are learning. Try things out at your computer as you read. In no time at all, you'll find that GW-BASIC is not only useful, but fun.

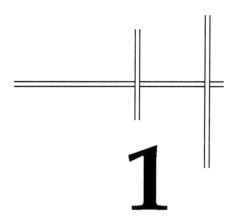

Getting Started

In this chapter, you'll start right out using GW-BASIC. You will learn the fundamentals of using the GW-BASIC editor as well as how to use several commands and statements for immediate response at the computer. In particular, you'll learn to:

- Start up and terminate GW-BASIC
- Use the KEY command
- Use the CLS command
- Use numeric and string constant values
- Assign values to numeric and string variables
- Use numeric and string variables in direct statements
- Display the date and time through GW-BASIC
- Use the BEEP statement
- Use the PRINT statement
- Use the LPRINT statement
- Use the INPUT statement

Getting GW-BASIC Ready

Before you can use GW-BASIC, it must be available on disk. GWBASIC.EXE and several other programs you can use with it were probably supplied as part of your MS DOS software. You'll want to set these programs up to work easily on your system. You don't have to know very many DOS commands to use GW-BASIC effectively. As long as you can use DIR to get a directory listing, TYPE to list a file's contents on the screen, and CD to change directories and change the current drive, you'll be all right. If you don't know any DOS commands yet, this guide will show you how to use these few commands at a basic level. You'll probably want to learn more about DOS, however.

Once you get it ready, GW-BASIC works the same no matter where it is located. In the examples, we'll assume you have a hard disk and use C: as the default drive. If you don't have a hard disk, substitute the drive name of the diskette that contains your GW-BASIC programs.

Hard Disk Setup

If your computer has a hard disk, all your DOS files are probably together in one directory. Figure out where the GWBASIC.EXE file is located and determine its path. The full specification for the GW-BASIC program is probably something like C:\DOS\GWBASIC.EXE. Follow these steps to create a new directory named GWBASIC and copy the program to it:

1. Get to the DOS prompt.
2. Type CD \ to get to the root directory.
3. Type MD GWBASIC to create a new directory.
4. Type CD GWBASIC to change to the new directory.
5. Type COPY C:\DOS\GWBASIC.EXE to copy the GWBASIC program to the new directory.
6. Type DIR to make sure it's there.

Diskette Setup

One of the diskettes on which DOS was supplied contains the program GWBASIC.EXE. Once you determine which one it is, place that diskette in drive A: and a clean formatted diskette in drive B:. Then follow these steps to copy the programs you'll need as you study this book:

1. Get to the DOS prompt.
2. Type COPY A:GWBASIC.EXE B: to copy the file.
3. Type B: to change to the B: drive.
4. Type DIR to make sure the files are there.

The GW-BASIC Programs

GW-BASIC is an interpretive language. That means when it reads a Basic command or statement, GWBASIC.EXE interprets it and immediately performs the action. Other computer languages, including some other versions of Basic, are compiled languages. A program written in a compiled language needs two steps before it can be run. First the program must be compiled, or translated into a machine readable form. Then the resulting compiled output is executed. It needn't be translated again unless you make changes to the program. The GW-BASIC interpreter (GWBASIC.EXE) requires only a single step to run it, but the program is interpreted every time, even if no changes were made.

There are advantages to using both interpreters and compilers, of course. The interpreter runs the program more quickly the first time and is easier for the learning process since you see the effects quicker and more directly. A compiled program runs faster, since it is already in a form the computer can read directly.

The GW-BASIC Editor

GW-BASIC has its own editor. You type commands and statements and create your programs within GW-BASIC. You also run them, store them, and edit them from within GW-BASIC.

The editor works like a very primitive word processor. When you see the cursor, you type on the screen. The characters you press appear on the screen and are stored in memory. You can edit them and delete them. Eventually, you have to save the characters to disk or you will lose them when you leave the GW-BASIC program.

GW-BASIC supports two modes of operation. Commands or statements issued in direct mode take effect immediately; they are often called immediate or direct commands. Indirect mode refers to programs, where statements and commands take effect when a program is run. In many cases, the same statement can be either direct or indirect. If you type BEEP in direct mode, for example, your computer beeps. If the statement BEEP is part of a program, it causes a beep when the program is run. A command that is part of a program is often called a statement or an instruction, especially if it involves more than a single word. In this chapter, however, we'll deal only with the direct mode of operation; every command or statement you type will be processed immediately.

The editor can also handle a set of commands that let you save, load, edit, and run files. You'll learn to use them as you proceed through this book.

Starting Up

To start up GW-BASIC, change to the drive and directory that contains the GW-BASIC program (use CD \GWBASIC if it's on your hard drive) and get the DOS prompt. Then type GWBASIC. If you get a message Bad command or file name, the GWBASIC.EXE program isn't in that directory. Be sure to use the directory name and program name that are applicable in your system.

If the GWBASIC program is available, you should see a screen like the one shown in Figure 1.1. The top line shows the program name and version, while the second line shows copyright information; yours may be a bit different. The third line shows how much memory is available; this has no connection with how much memory your system has. GW-BASIC works only with 64K of memory. When you need larger amounts, you'll be ready to go on to a more advanced BASIC, perhaps a compiled version. Most of what you learn in this book will still work in the more sophisticated forms of BASIC.

The fourth and fifth lines show the GW-BASIC prompt. Ok means the interpreter is ready for a command. The cursor shows where the characters you type will appear.

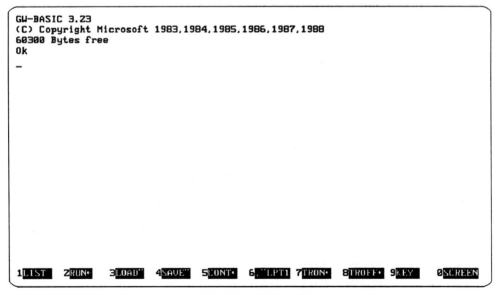

Figure 1.1. GW-BASIC Editor Start-Up Screen

The Key Line

The bottom screen line is called the key line; it shows the effect of pressing each of ten function keys. These won't mean much to you just yet. The function keys are effective whether or not the key line is displayed. We'll discuss the individual keys when we cover the commands they implement. Note that F9 in the key line is labeled KEY; function key 9 helps you turn the key line display off and on.

Typing in the Editor

GW-BASIC commands are typed at the cursor. Each line can hold up to 255 characters; the editor automatically wraps to the next line on the screen. Once you press ↵, whatever you typed is processed or added to a program being edited.

You may want to remove the key line to have more usable lines on the screen. The KEY command lets you do this. Type KEY OFF at the cursor and press ↵. The key line disappears. Type KEY ON and press ↵; the key line returns. If you press F9, the word KEY followed by a space appears. You can just type ON or OFF to complete the command and press ↵ to see the effect.

During the Self-Checks in this book, you get a chance to try out the commands and techniques covered. We tell you exactly what to do, and generally, exactly how to do it. If anything might go wrong, we tell you how to fix it. The newer you are to programming, the more important it is that you try these activities.

If you have problems in the Self-Check, don't worry about it. If you get an error message followed by Ok, try the command again. You can't do any damage here.

1. Bring up GW-BASIC.
2. Type KEY OFF and press ↵.
3. Type KEY ON and press ↵.
4. Press F9. When you see KEY on the screen, type OFF and press ↵.
5. Press F9. When you see KEY on the screen, type ON and press ↵.

If you have trouble bringing up GW-BASIC, make sure the directory that contains it is current before you type GWBASIC. If GW-BASIC is on a floppy disk, insert it into a drive, such as A, and type A: at the DOS prompt to make the drive current before you enter the GWBASIC command.

Clearing the Screen

At this point, your screen shows characters you have typed and some the computer produced. It might look like this:

```
GW-BASIC 3.23
(C) Copyright Microsoft 1983, 1984, 1985, 1986, 1987, 1988
60300 Bytes free
Ok
KEY OFF
Ok
KEY ON
Ok
KEY OFF
Ok
KEY ON
Ok
_
```

Your screen may include a few other items and messages if you made any typing errors; don't worry about them. But you may want to remove the displayed commands and messages from the screen. GW-BASIC has two ways you can clear the screen. You can type CLS and press ↵; that leaves you with Ok and the cursor on the top two lines of the screen. Or you can press Ctrl-L (hold down the control key and press L, then release both). Pressing Ctrl-L leaves the cursor in the top line of the screen; you won't see the line containing Ok. You can use the CLS command or press Ctrl-L to clear the screen whenever you want.

Using Direct Statements

You've already seen the effects of using direct GW-BASIC commands. KEY OFF and KEY ON are two forms of the KEY command. You type it, press ↵, and the command is executed immediately. CLS works the same way. Commands generally act on the GW-BASIC editor, while statements are processed by the interpreter.

The critical feature about direct mode is that the commands and statements are not preceded by a line number. Line numbers make statements part of a program, so they aren't processed immediately. In Chapter 2, you'll learn to combine various statements into a program. In the rest of this chapter, you'll learn to use several more GW-BASIC statements in direct mode.

The BEEP Statement

As you've probably noticed while using your computer with other programs, it can make noises. The BEEP statement tells the computer to produce its default sound. Type BEEP at the cursor and press ↵ to hear a beep immediately. Every time GW-BASIC executes a BEEP statement, the computer beeps. Advanced statements, not covered in this book, give more control over sound.

The PRINT Statement

Practically every program writes on the screen. You can do this in GW-BASIC with the PRINT statement. To print a specific number, just follow PRINT with the number, as in PRINT 75 or PRINT -98.6. To print a specific message, enclose the message in double quotation marks. For example, if you type PRINT "Where is the moon?" and press ↵, the message Where is the moon? appears on the next line. You can leave any number of spaces between PRINT and the value, even none. GW-BASIC knows that PRINT is the name of the statement; whatever follows it is to be printed.

String Constants. To a computer program, a string is a set of consecutive characters, such as the word "Hello"; a string enclosed in double quotation marks is often called a constant because it has a value that stays the same. The following interaction shows some examples of how character strings can be printed on the screen.

```
Ok
PRINT "Hello"
Hello
Ok
PRINT "Ruth Ashley"
Ruth Ashley
Ok

—
```

The value enclosed in double quotation marks is called a string constant; the PRINT statement displays the string starting in column 1. A string constant can be up to 255 characters long. If you omit the initial double quotation mark, GW-BASIC doesn't know you are specifying a string constant. If you omit the final one, the constant includes any additional characters on the line up to the carriage return. Often, that doesn't do any harm and saves you a keystroke. The statement PRINT "Ruth causes the word Ruth to appear on the next line.

Numeric Constants. If you want to print a number, use a numeric constant; just type the number in the statement. If you leave spaces in a number, GW-BASIC will ignore them and close up the number.

Valid numeric constants can contain any digits, a decimal point, and a leading sign; don't use commas, however. If you use two decimal points, GW-BASIC assumes you have two numbers and starts the second with the second decimal point. The number of digits in a numeric value is limited in most GW-BASIC systems, but seven digits is valid for all types. If you use too large a number, GW-BASIC will convert it to another form for display. Positive numeric constants are printed starting in column 2, since GW-BASIC always leaves space to print a plus or minus sign, even if you don't include one. Here are some examples:

```
Ok
PRINT 75.8
 75.8
Ok
PRINT -7.987
-7.987
Ok
PRINT 0
 0
Ok
PRINT 45 55 .4
 4555.4
Ok

—
```

Other Values. A printed item enclosed in quotes is a string constant, and a number not enclosed in quotes is a numeric constant. So what happens if you try to print a string without quotes? Here's an example:

```
PRINT Judi
 0
Ok

—
```

Notice what happens when you don't use quotes around a character string; a zero is printed. GW-BASIC doesn't know it is a string you want to print unless you use the quotes, so it interprets the string as a variable name. We'll cover variables a bit later in this chapter.

Since the PRINT statement is used so often, GW-BASIC lets you use a shortcut. The question mark (?) gets expanded into the word PRINT when you press ↵. Typing ? "Ruth" has the same effect as typing PRINT "Ruth"; the word Ruth is printed on the next line. Use this shortcut any time you want.

In this Self-Check, you can try out a few of these commands. Remember to press ↵ to cause each line you type to be processed.

1. Type BEEP.
2. Type PRINT 288.
3. Type CLS and press ↵.
4. Type PRINT "GW-BASIC works!"
5. Press Ctrl-L.
6. Print your age on the screen using the ? shortcut.
7. Print your name on the screen.

If the PRINT command doesn't work, make sure you are spelling it correctly and using double quotes to begin the string. Be sure and notice the difference in effect between CLS and Ctrl-L.

Printing Multiple Values

You can combine several values in one statement, using both numeric and string values. Separate constants with a semicolon or a comma. If you use a semicolon, the printed values will be adjacent on the screen. If you use a comma, they'll be separated. Here are a few examples:

```
Ok
PRINT "John";"Mary"
JohnMary
Ok
PRINT "My age is";34
My age is 34
Ok
PRINT 26;"miles across the sea"
 26 miles across the sea
Ok
PRINT 5;10;15
 5   10   15
Ok
```

```
PRINT 5,10,15
 5            10            15
Ok
```

When you use the semicolon (;) to separate items, string values are printed immediately adjacent, as you can see in the first example above, with no space between them. Numeric values always have a leading space if no sign is printed, plus a trailing space to separate adjacent numbers. The second example above shows how the automatic numeric sign position space can be used to insert a space before the preceding string. The third example shows how the automatic numeric trailing space can be used to separate a string following the number. The last two examples show the effect of semicolons and commas in separating numeric values. The semicolon causes them to be printed as nearly adjacent as possible, with only the sign position before each positive value and a separation space following the value. The comma causes them to be printed left justified in 14-character zones.

For string constants, you can omit the semicolon to cause adjacent printing. Just leaving one or more spaces, or even no space, has the same effect, as in the following examples.

```
Ok
PRINT "John"    "Mary"
JohnMary
Ok
PRINT "John""Mary"
JohnMary
Ok
PRINT "John"" ""Mary"
John Mary
Ok
PRINT "John";" ";"Mary"
John Mary
Ok
```

When you use the comma (,) to separate string or numeric items, GW-BASIC places each value in its own 14-character wide zone. String values, like numbers, are aligned on the left; if a value takes up more than 14 characters, the next item is bumped over to the next zone. The last two examples above have identical effects; both insert a string constant containing a single space between two other string constants. You can see that omitting the semicolon has the same effect as including it. Using a comma instead, however, causes the 14-character zones to be used for spacing the output. Here are a few more examples:

```
PRINT 1492; "Year of Discovery"
```

```
   1492 Year of Discovery
Ok
PRINT 1492, "Year of Discovery"
   1492          Year of Discovery
Ok
PRINT "George Bush",66
George Bush      66
Ok
PRINT "John Fitzgerald",43
John Fitzgerald                  43
Ok
```

Since the string constant in the third example is longer than 14 characters, the next value is bumped over to the third zone.

You can omit the final double quotation mark of a string constant only when it is the very last character of the statement. For example, the statement PRINT 1492; " Year of Discovery has the same effect as the second statement in the example. If you use PRINT "John Fitzgerald, 43 as a complete statement, the characters John Fitzgerald, 43 are printed, rather than the line shown above.

Using the Printer

You've seen how to display numbers and strings on the screen. It's almost as easy to print them on the printer. Of course, first you have to make sure your printer is connected properly and turned on; if it works with DOS commands, it will work under GW-BASIC.

To send lines to the printer, use LPRINT instead of PRINT. Aside from that, the command is the same. You can't use L? for LPRINT, however; you'll see the message "Syntax error" if you try. You can use a varying number of spaces following the word. Here are some examples:

```
Ok
LPRINT "This is a test print line"
Ok
LPRINT "The temperature is"; 72; "degrees"
Ok
```

The screen itself doesn't tell you what happened. But if you have a dot matrix or daisy wheel printer, you'll see (and hear) the effect.

Some laser printers do not eject the paper right away. If yours doesn't, type this statement in direct mode to eject a page: LPRINT CHR$ (12). The value of the expression CHR$(12) is a form-feed signal; the LPRINT statement sends the signal to the printer and that causes it to eject a page. It works on just about every printer.

1. Print three string constants on the screen. Use commas to put them in separate print zones.
2. Print three adjacent numeric values on the screen.
3. Type LPRINT "This is a printed message".
4. Print "This is a second message" on the printer.
5. Type LPRINT 75; "Seventy five".
6. Type LPRINT CHR$ (12) to form feed. (Try this even if you don't have a laser printer.)
7. Display some more values and print some more lines on your printer if you like.

Make sure you use PRINT for screen display and LPRINT for printer output. Be sure you use semicolons for adjacent output or commas for zoned output. You can omit semicolons for adjacent strings.

If your printer doesn't seem to respond, make sure it is turned on and on line. If it works with DOS (or virtually any DOS program), it should work fine under GW-BASIC.

If the form-feed command doesn't work, don't worry about it unless there is no other way to get paper from your printer. Read the printer documentation, check with your printer dealer, or call the manufacturer if necessary.

Using Variables

You have seen how to use numeric constants as they are in PRINT and LPRINT statements. You have also seen how to use string constants (called strings) by enclosing them in double quotation marks. While programming frequently requires constant values, it uses variables even more.

You can think of a variable as a name for a box in memory. The box can hold any value that can fit in the variable. You can also think of a variable as a name that has a value; the name remains the same but the value can vary, just as the box can hold different values. A variable in a program can hold many different values at different times. A program that processes a mailing list may have variables to hold the name, parts of the address, the city, the state, the zip code, even telephone numbers. A program that works with sales orders will have variables for the item, the price, the quantity, the tax, and even the total. If you don't give a value to a variable, GW-BASIC uses a default value. Numeric variables have default value 0. String variables have null as the default value, which is an empty string represented by "" (two adjacent double quotation marks).

You can give a value to a variable in any of several ways, then manipulate the variable in program statements. For example, suppose the variable RATE has the value 7.5. The statement PRINT RATE prints 7.5 on the screen. If you type PRINT JUDI in the GW-BASIC editor, the value 0 appears if no value has been assigned to a variable named JUDI.

Variable Names

Variable names can be any length, but most GW-BASIC interpreters recognize only the first 40. You probably won't use names this long, since you have to type variable names often in a program. Variable names must start with a letter, and they can include any letters, digits, or the period. TAXRATE, SALES, S88, MIGHTY.MAX, and BBBBBB are all valid variable names. GW-BASIC doesn't see the difference between uppercase and lowercase letters, so you can type the TAXRATE variable name as taxrate, TaxRate, or even TaXrAtE, and they are all the same variable. In fact, GW-BASIC will convert them all to TAXRATE, unless you type them as part of a string constant. A variable cannot have the same name as a word that GW-BASIC has a special use for, so you can't use PRINT, BEEP, CLS, or LPRINT as a variable name. (Appendix A includes a list of words that GW-BASIC has reserved for its own purposes.) It's a good idea to use meaningful variable names, of course, but names like X and W78 are perfectly valid.

Each variable name you use in a single program must be unique. Some GW-BASIC interpreters recognize fewer than 40 significant characters. You'll have to know what your system's limitations are, but every system recognizes at least 16 characters. The two variable names NEWLY.ORDERED.1 and NEWLY.ORDERED.2 represent two different variables.

Like constants, variables can be of various types. If you don't do something special, a variable name is assumed to be numeric; there are different types of numeric variables, which we'll cover in Chapter 3. If you want a variable to hold a string value, add a dollar sign ($) to the end of the variable name. For example, the variable SALES is a numeric variable, while SALES$ is a string variable. SALES and SALES$ are unique variable names and can be used in the same program.

System Variables

GW-BASIC has several system variables that are already defined and have values. You can use the DATE$ and TIME$ string variables to print the current date and time, according to your computer. The system keeps track of the date and time; it may not be correct, but it has values for both these items. Here's how to use them:

```
Ok
PRINT DATE$
06-11-1991
Ok
PRINT TIME$
07:22:56
Ok
```

The DATE$ value is always a ten-character value in the form *mm-dd-yyyy*. The *mm* portion is the month number from 01 through 12. The *dd* portion is the day number from 01 through 31, depending on the value of *mm*. The *yyyy* portion gives the four-digit year.

The TIME$ value is always an eight-character value in the form *hh:mm:ss*, giving the hours, minutes, and seconds based on a 24-hour clock. The hours range from 00 to 23, minutes from 00 through 59, and seconds from 00 through 59. The time 23:59:59 is one second before midnight.

Numeric Variables

You can create variables to hold values as well. For example, suppose you want a numeric variable to hold the value 3.1416; you might name this PI. Any statement that assigns a value to a variable also defines the variable. Many variables are defined in the assignment statement, in which the variable being defined appears on the left side of the equal sign and the value appears on the right. It can have either of two forms, as shown below.

```
Ok
LET PI=3.1416
Ok
PIE=3.1416
Ok
RADIUS=5
Ok
LET DIAMETER=10
Ok
```

At this point, you have four different numeric variables, two of which (PI and PIE) have the same value. The value is always assigned to the variable named on the left. While you can use variables on both sides of the equal sign, numeric constants can appear only on the right.

The word LET is always optional. Most people skip the LET (as we will most of the time). The statement that assigns a value in this way is called a LET statement or an assignment statement.

When you start GW-BASIC, all numeric variables have the value 0. Any defined variables are eliminated from memory when you leave GW-BASIC or start to run a program.

The value assigned to a variable must be the same type as the variable name indicates or you'll get an error message. A numeric variable must be given a numeric value. If you try to assign a string value, you'll get an error message. If a program is running, it is terminated. Here's an example:

```
RADIUS="six"
Type mismatch
Ok
RADIUS=six
Ok
```

Since RADIUS is a numeric variable, the value must be a valid numeric value. You can't use a quoted string or a value containing a comma. GW-BASIC lets you use an unquoted string, however, since it treats the unquoted string as a variable name. In the example above, GW-BASIC sees SIX as the name of another numeric variable. Since SIX hasn't yet been given a value, the value assigned to RADIUS is zero.

String Variables

A string variable name ends with $. You can also assign values to string variables. Just use the variable type indicator at the end of the name, like this:

```
Ok
LET LASTNAME$="Ashley"
Ok
FIRSTNAME$="Ruth"
Ok
FULLNAME$="Judi N. Fernandez"
Ok
```

One way to change a variable value is by repeating the assignment statement with a different value, as in FULLNAME$="George Bush". You can

cancel a variable and restore the default null value by typing "" and pressing
⌡ after the equals sign, as in FULLNAME$="".

If you assign a value that is not a quoted string or another string variable
name to a string variable, you'll get a Type mismatch message. At the end of
the previous series of statements, the statement NEWNAME$=FIRSTNAME$
assigns the current value of the FIRSTNAME$ variable ("Ruth") to the variable
NEWNAME$.

When you start GW-BASIC, all string variables have the default null value.
Any defined string variables are eliminated from memory when you leave
GW-BASIC or run a GW-BASIC program.

Printing Variable Values

Once a variable has a value, you can display it with PRINT or print it with
LPRINT. The comma (,) and semicolon (;) separators have the same effects as
with constants. Here are some examples, using the values similar to those set
in previous sections:

```
Ok
PRINT FULLNAME$
Judi N. Fernandez
Ok
PRINT PI, RADIUS
 3.1416          5
Ok
PRINT DIAMETER; LASTNAME$
 10 Ashley
Ok
```

Notice that the extra spaces for numeric values appear just as with constants. GW-BASIC also lets you combine constants and variables in a single
statement:

```
Ok
PRINT "The diameter is";DIAMETER
The diameter is 10
Ok
PRINT FIRSTNAME$; " "; LASTNAME$
Ruth Ashley
Ok
PRINT DIAMETER "indicates " LASTNAME$
 10 indicates Ashley
Ok
```

An extra space is included at the end of the string constant in the last example. That causes the string variable value that follows it to be separated from the first by a space in the printed line. You can include spacing in strings or use separate strings that include only spaces. The same effects can be achieved using LPRINT, but the output appears on paper instead of the screen.

1. Clear the screen in preparation for this Self- Check.
2. Type LET STATE=50
3. Type LET STATE$="Michigan"
4. Type HEIGHT=59
5. Type PERSON$="John"
6. Type a statement to show the value of STATE$ on the screen.
6. Type PRINT STATE$;" is one of"; STATE; "states."
7. Type PRINT PERSON$; " has this height: "; HEIGHT
8. Display the date and time on the screen.
9. Print some more combinations of values on your screen and printer if you like.

If you get an error message, look carefully at the line you just typed. The Type mismatch message means you assigned a value of the wrong type to the variable name. A Syntax error message means that there is something wrong with the statement itself. You probably omitted a double quote or typed an incorrect key in the statement name.

Getting Keyboard Input

Another way of assigning a value to a variable is to get it from the user at the keyboard. The INPUT statement lets you name a variable and expects some-one to enter a value for it when the statement is executed. The interpreter then assigns the entered value to the variable. When the INPUT statement is executed, it displays a prompt on the screen and waits for the user to type something and press ↵. Here are several examples:

```
Ok
INPUT HEIGHT
? _
```

```
INPUT "Please type your height "; HEIGHT
Please type your height ? _

INPUT "Please type your height ", HEIGHT
Please type your height _
```

In all three examples, when the user types a numeric value and presses ↵, GW-BASIC assigns it to the variable HEIGHT. What the computer displays is different for each example, however.

In the first example, we didn't include a message in the INPUT statement, just the variable name. The computer displays a question mark and the cursor; there is no hint for the user. Such a statement should be preceded by a PRINT statement that lets the user know what kind of value is expected.

The second example includes a message in double quotation marks. After a separating semicolon (;) is the variable name. The message is displayed on the screen, followed by the question mark and the cursor. The message is usually a prompt for the user. If it is in the form of a question, the question mark is appropriate.

The third example uses a comma (,) instead of a semicolon (;) to separate the message and the variable. This suppresses the question mark in the computer's prompt.

If you omit the variable name in the INPUT statement, you'll get the message Syntax error, since GW-BASIC requires that you supply a variable name. Just type the statement correctly and try again.

If the typed input doesn't match the variable type, GW-BASIC displays the message ?Redo from start and executes the INPUT statement again. In the example above, typing anything nonnumeric, such as Ruth, gets the ?Redo message when ↵ is pressed.

The following keyboard interaction includes most of the features of the INPUT and PRINT statements we've covered. Characters typed in response to the INPUT statement prompt are shown in bold type.

```
Ok
INPUT "What is your first name "; FIRST$
What is your first name ? Ruth
Ok
INPUT "Type your last name ", LAST$
Type your last name Ashley
Ok
INPUT "What is your age"
Syntax error
Ok
INPUT "What is your age"; AGE
What is your age? Six
?Redo from start
```

```
What is your age? 34
Ok
PRINT FIRST$; " is"; AGE ; "on "; DATE$
Ruth is 34 on 06-28-1991
Ok
PRINT "My last name is "; LAST$
My last name is Ashley
Ok
```

Input Multiple Values

Suppose you want to get both the first and last names from the keyboard, but you want to use a single command. You can name several variables, separated by commas. The user then has to enter the correct number of values in the same order as in the INPUT statement, each of the correct type, separated by commas. Here's an example:

```
INPUT "Type your name as in first,last:",FIRST$,LAST$
Type your name as in first,last:Ruth,Ashley
Ok
INPUT "What are the length and width";LONG,WIDE
What are the length and width? 47.5,18
Ok
```

The entered values must be separated by commas. If you type a single value or don't use commas, GW-BASIC won't accept any input. Similarly, GW-BASIC won't accept a value of the wrong type. In all cases, you'll get the ?Redo from start message along with the message or prompt from the INPUT statement again.

1. Clear the screen, then use the INPUT statement to give the value "Michael" to PERSON$.
2. Use a single INPUT statement to assign the value 5 to FEET and 11 to INCHES from the keyboard.
3. Use the variables to display the message "Michael is 5 feet 11 inches tall".
4. Assign a long value (at least 30 characters) to the variable LONGONE$ at the keyboard. Use your full name or anything that doesn't contain a comma.
5. Use an INPUT statement to assign three letters to three different variables.

6. Display the variables from items 4 and 5 on the screen.

If you get the ? Redo from start message, check the data you entered. If you get the Syntax error message, check the statement being processed. Multiple variable names must be separated by commas.

Your statements might look like these:

```
INPUT "What is your name"; PERSON$
INPUT "Type number of feet, then inches: ",FEET, INCHES
PRINT PERSON$; " is"; FEET; "feet"; INCHES; "inches tall"
INPUT "Type a long value ", LONGONE$
INPUT "Type three letters, separated by commas: ",ITEM1$,
   ITEM2$, ITEM3$
PRINT LONGONE$
PRINT "Item1 ";ITEM1$, "Item2 ";ITEM2$, "Item3 ";ITEM3$
```

Your statements may be different and still be correct. Remember to use a comma to separate multiple data values on input.

Terminating GW-BASIC

When you are finished using GW-BASIC, you have to exit the editor. You do this with the SYSTEM command. Just type SYSTEM at the Ok prompt and press ↲, and you will immediately return to the DOS prompt.

Summary

This chapter has introduced you to the GW-BASIC editor and the use of direct mode.

GW-BASIC Editor. You've learned to type data into the editor and control the screen appearance using three commands.

The KEY command lets you turn the function key reminder line display off and on.

The CLS command clears the screen, leaving Ok and the cursor on the top two lines of the screen.

The Ctrl-L command clears the screen, leaving the cursor on the top line.

GW-BASIC Data. You've learned the two major types of data in GW-BASIC programs.

Constants can be numeric or string; string constants must be enclosed in double quotation marks.

Variables can have numeric or character string values.

String variable names must end with $.

DATE$ and TIME$ are system variables that contain the current date and time.

GW-BASIC Statements. You've learned to use five GW-BASIC statements to cause sound and manage variables and constants in a program.

The BEEP statement causes the computer system to make a sound.

The PRINT statement causes the specified variables and constants to be displayed on the screen, using the format indicated by statement elements.

The LPRINT statement causes the specified variables and constants to be printed on the printer, using the format indicated by statement elements. LPRINT CHR$(12) causes a form feed (page eject) on most printers.

The LET or assignment statement lets you assign a value to a variable.

The INPUT statement displays a prompt on the screen and accepts keyboard input to assign values to variables.

Exercise

Each chapter in this Self-Teaching Guide ends with an exercise that lets you practice the commands and techniques covered in the chapter. In this exercise, you will be able to use all the direct commands you have learned.

What You Should Do	How the Computer Responds
1. Start up GW-BASIC.	1. Displays the editor screen, as in Figure 1.1.
2. Use KEY OFF to remove the key line. Then turn it back on.	2. Removes the key line. Restores it when you type KEY ON.
3. Assign the value GW-BASIC to a variable named LANGUAGE$ and the value 59.98 to a variable named COST.	3. Shows Ok.
4. Display the value of each variable on the screen in a separate command, then in one command.	4. Shows the values of the variables twice.

5. Display "The cost of this item is " followed by the value of COST.
6. Get the value of ITEM$ from the keyboard; use MOUSE as the value.
7. Print "The cost of the "; ITEM$; " is "; COST on the printer.
8. Show the current time and date on the console.
9. Exit the GW-BASIC editor.

5. Shows the values of the constant and variable in one line.
6. Shows your prompt, then accepts the value you type.
7. Prints "The cost of the MOUSE is 59.98" on your printer.
8. Displays its response to PRINT TIME$ and PRINT DATE$.
9. Returns to the DOS prompt after you type SYSTEM.

What If It Doesn't Work?

1. Make sure your computer is turned on and ready to go before you start the exercises. If you can't get into GW-BASIC, check the directory. Use CD \ followed by the directory path if necessary.
2. If you have trouble displaying the values, try the basic commands with single values until you can do them fine, then try the exercise again.
3. If your printer doesn't work at all, make sure it is plugged in, turned on, and on line. If a page doesn't eject, try LPRINT CHR$(12).

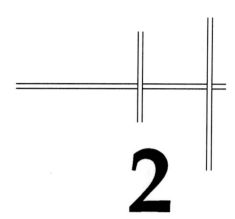

2

Your First Program

In this chapter, you'll learn to write GW-BASIC programs, using all the statements introduced in Chapter 1 as well as a few new ones. In the process, you will learn to use editor commands to create and manage programs and comments to explain programs to human readers. Specifically, you'll learn to:

- Distinguish between direct statements and program lines
- Use the NEW command to clear the program memory
- Use line numbers to identify program lines
- Use the END statement to mark the end of a program
- Use the LIST and LLIST commands to display or print a program listing
- Use the EDIT command to change program lines
- Use the DELETE command to remove program lines
- Use the SAVE command to store a program on disk
- Use the SHELL command to let you enter DOS commands from within GW-BASIC
- Use the FILES command to see what files are on disk
- Use the LOAD command to bring a program on disk into memory
- Use the RUN command to execute a program
- Add comments to a program
- Use automatic line numbering with the AUTO command
- Renumber lines in a program with the RENUM command

GW-BASIC Programs

In Chapter 1, you learned to use several statements in direct mode under GW-BASIC. You typed them in and they were executed immediately, as soon as you pressed ↵. You have to retype a direct statement to execute it again.

If you put a statement in a program, GW-BASIC saves it in memory, so it is more useful than a direct statement. It can be executed repeatedly without retyping. You can change a statement if it isn't quite right without having to type it over from scratch. In this section, you'll learn the essential features of a GW-BASIC program.

Why Use Programs?

The immediate advantages of programs are threefold. First, you can build up a series of commands and execute them all in sequence by typing RUN at the Ok prompt. Second, you can execute the same program several times without retyping it; as long as it is in memory, it will repeat every time you enter the RUN command. Third, you can save it on disk so you can recall and execute it many times in the future.

You will also discover some long-range advantages of programs. To mention a few: They can make decisions and repeat themselves. You can try them out and debug (correct) them until they do exactly what you want. And then you can sell them to other computer users. In addition, you can apply the knowledge of programming to writing batch DOS programs or macros to support such programs as spreadsheets and database managers.

A Sample Program

A GW-BASIC program can contain a single statement or many. It can be as long as 65,000 lines if necessary. A program performs a task, and it can do it repeatedly.

When you want to save commands in a program for later execution, you must precede each line with a number. Instead of typing PRINT "Hello, World", you would type 10 PRINT "Hello, World" at the keyboard. The resulting statement is line 10, and it isn't executed immediately. Instead the cursor moves to the next line and waits for you to type the next program line. It doesn't even give you the Ok prompt.

```
Ok
10 PRINT "THIS PROGRAM IS ABOUT TO SELF-DESTRUCT"
20 BEEP
30 BEEP
40 BEEP
50 CLS
60 END
```

Figure 2.1. Sample Program

As long as you start each line with a new line number, GW-BASIC adds the lines to a program in memory. When you are ready to stop entering lines, just enter a direct command starting in column 1 at the cursor.

Program Format

The sample program in Figure 2.1 demonstrates the format of a program. This program first displays the message THIS PROGRAM IS ABOUT TO SELF-DESTRUCT. Then it beeps three times (it sounds like one long beep) and clears the screen. The last line, END, merely ends the program; it doesn't really self-destruct anything.

In this program, the line numbers start with 10 and increment by 10. This is not a requirement, but it is common practice. It leaves room to insert lines later on, if necessary. For example, suppose you wanted to insert a line to display the message Goodbye, Cruel World after the three beeps. You could type this line:

```
55 ? "Goodbye, Cruel World"
```

The editor would then automatically insert the new line between lines 50 and 60 because of its line number. The next time you list or run the program, the lines are placed in numerical sequence. Programs are always processed in line number sequence. If you listed the whole program now, the screen would look like this:

```
10 PRINT "THIS PROGRAM IS ABOUT TO SELF-DESTRUCT"
20 BEEP
30 BEEP
40 BEEP
50 CLS
55 PRINT "Goodbye, Cruel World"
60 END
```

Typing the Lines

As you type program lines, you can make corrections just as you did when entering direct statements. You can also make changes to any program line that is displayed on the screen. Just use the arrow keys to move the cursor into the line you want to fix, make the correction, and press ↵. Then move the cursor back to the line you were in before and continue typing.

Table 2.1 shows many of the keys you can use while editing lines on the screen. Note that the arrow keys move one character at a time in the indicated direction. You can use Ctrl- → or Ctrl- ← to move the cursor right or left one word at a time. (Don't use Ctrl-Backspace; it doesn't have any effect.)

You can delete characters using either the Del (or Delete) key or the Backspace key, depending on whether you want to delete characters to the left of the cursor (use Backspace) or at the cursor (use Delete). When you type over characters, the new ones normally replace the old ones. Press the insert key (Ins) to turn on insert mode; then the cursor changes from an underscore to a rectangle and existing characters are pushed to the right instead of overtyped as you type new ones.

The key item in editing lines is to be sure to press ↵ after changes are made to each line. When you press ↵ , the line that contains the cursor is updated. If you make changes to several lines, and move the cursor between them instead of pressing ↵ after each line change, changes to all lines except the one containing the cursor when you finally press it are lost. How to edit lines is covered in more detail later in this chapter.

Multiple Statements Per Line

GW-BASIC lets you place multiple statements on a line, up to 255 total characters. Just use the colon (:) to separate them. Use spaces on both sides of the colon if you like. For example, the program in Figure 2.1 is valid when written like this:

```
10 PRINT "THIS PROGRAM IS ABOUT TO SELF-DESTRUCT"
20 BEEP : BEEP : BEEP
30 CLS : PRINT "Goodbye, Cruel World" : END
```

While it is valid and saves storage, saving space is not generally more important than clarity in your programs. It's more awkward to insert new statements in the program, for example. And when you run programs, any error causes the program to stop running, and the interpreter shows you the line in which the error occurred. A line with multiple statements makes it

══════════ Table 2.1. Program Editing Keys

Moving the Cursor

Arrow key   One character or line in indicated direction
Ctrl-Rt   One word right (use arrow)
Ctrl-Lf   One word left (use arrow)
Ctrl-N   To end of line
Ctrl-J   To beginning of next line
Home   To upper-left corner of screen

Deleting Characters

Del   Delete character at cursor
Backspace   Delete character to left of cursor
Ctrl-End   Delete characters from cursor to end of line
Esc   Delete entire line containing cursor

Inserting Characters

Ins   Turns insert mode on or off

---

much harder to figure out the problem. This is even more true as you learn to use more complex statements.

If you want to use multiple statements on a line, try to restrict them to statements that are extremely unlikely to cause a problem or that are related to each other in some way other than proximity. For example, no one would fault you for placing three BEEP commands on the same line.

Running a Program

When a program is in memory, you can execute it by typing RUN on a new line; you don't have to get back to the Ok prompt first. The RUN must be the only item on the line, however. When you type RUN, GW-BASIC finds the lowest numbered program line in memory and starts up the program. If it doesn't encounter any errors, the lines are all executed. When the program is complete, you'll see the Ok prompt again. You can press F2 to run the program if you prefer; you won't have to press ⏎ if you use the function key.

The RUN command has a few other options that you can use if you type the command. If you name a line number, it starts running the current program at that line number. Other options are covered later in this book.

1. Start up GW-BASIC.
2. Type the sample program from Figure 2.1; include the line 55 we showed as well. Be sure to use line numbers.
3. On the line following line 60, type RUN and press ⏎.
4. Run the program several more times to see that it acts the same way every time you run it.

If the program didn't display a message, beep, clear the screen, and display another message, your computer or the program has a problem. If you saw the message but didn't hear the beep, the problem is probably in the speaker. If you didn't see the message, you probably typed the program lines incorrectly. You'll learn to fix it later.

Ending the Program

You don't have to include an END statement to end the program. When the interpreter finishes the last line in the program, it ends automatically. In a simple program such as the one in Figure 2.1, the END statement is superfluous. But more complex programs that make decisions have multiple paths from the beginning to the end; then the END statement might be necessary to end a path that doesn't reach the last program line. END is also useful in other situations, as you will learn as you progress through this book.

It is a good idea to include the END statement in all programs, even short, simple ones. It gets you into a good habit you'll need in more complex programs, and it keeps you from flowing into leftover lines from a previous program if you forget to clear memory before you type a new program.

Saving a Program

If you want to keep a program so you can use it again, you must save it on disk. The program in memory is lost when memory is cleared in any way, such as the power going off, rebooting, or exiting to the system. It is a good idea to save what you are working on if you have spent any significant amount of time or thought on it. Programs on disk last as long as the disk lasts and can always be reloaded into memory and reused. Saving a program in a file does not clear memory, so you can save a file many times and continue working with it. Each save replaces the previous file of that name on the disk. You can provide a different file name to prevent this.

To save the current program on disk, use the SAVE command. To save the current program as a file named BLASTOFF.BAS, you would enter:

```
Ok
SAVE "BLASTOFF"
Ok
```

When you save a program, you must give it a file name of up to eight characters, following the normal DOS rules for file name formation. If you omit the extension, GW-BASIC automatically assigns the extension BAS. If you want your file stored with a different extension, just include the full file name within the double quotes. If a file of the specified name already exists in the target directory, it will be replaced without warning.

You can speed up the saving process by pressing function key 4. As you'll notice on the function key line, F4 results in the characters SAVE" appearing on the screen. You can just type the filename and press ↵. You can omit the final double quote when it is the last character on the line.

Saving to a Different Directory

You can include a drivename and path if you don't want the file stored in the default directory (that is, whatever drivename and path were current when you started GW-BASIC). The drivename and path must be included within the double quotes. The command SAVE "A:BLASTOFF" puts a file named BLASTOFF.BAS on drive A. The command SAVE "C:\ACCOUNTS\RUTH" stores the file named RUTH.BAS in the ACCOUNTS directory on drive C.

Saving in Compressed Format

By default, GW-BASIC stores files in a compressed format, which no program except the GW-BASIC editor can read. GW-BASIC has no trouble reloading the program from the compressed file, so the compressed format is usually an advantage. However, other programs usually require ASCII format. For example, you could not list the program at the DOS prompt using the DOS TYPE command; you have to restart GW-BASIC, load the program, and then list it. You could not examine or edit the program under a word processor such as WordStar, WordPerfect, or Microsoft Word, all of which can read ASCII format.

Saving in ASCII Format

Suppose you want a file saved in ASCII format so you can use TYPE or your word processor to see it or change it. To save a program in ASCII format, add an A parameter following the file name, as in this example:

```
Ok
SAVE "BLASTOFF",A
Ok
```

The closing quotation mark is required here, since it isn't the last character in the line. The comma is required as well. After this command is processed, BLASTOFF.BAS is an ASCII file that can be accessed by DOS commands, a word processor, and so on. (Any earlier version of BLASTOFF.BAS in the same directory, no matter what its format was, was replaced by this ASCII version.)

To prevent overwriting an earlier version, you can include an extension in your SAVE command. The command SAVE "BLASTOFF.ASC",A saves an ASCII version as BLASTOFF.ASC. If the disk already contained a file named BLASTOFF.BAS, it is left unchanged.

Using DOS Commands

You'll frequently find that you want to use a DOS command while in GW-BASIC. Of course, you could save your file, use SYSTEM to exit to DOS, perform whatever action you need, then start up GW-BASIC again. This is a great deal of effort. There is an easier way. The SHELL command gives you a DOS prompt within GW-BASIC. You enter the commands you need. For example, you might want to use DIR, or to TYPE a file. You can use as many DOS commands as you wish, then type EXIT (uppercase or lowercase) at the DOS prompt to get back into GW-BASIC.

Figure 2.2 shows the screen after entering SHELL and TYPEing an ASCII file. Notice that it shows the DOS copyright information, just as when you start up the system. The key line disappears while you are in the shell; the function key commands have different effects under DOS. The computer will act like it is in DOS until you type EXIT to cancel the shell.

When you return to GW-BASIC, the cursor position will be in the same location as when you entered the shell. You can use CLS to clear the screen and start over.

The SHELL command can also be used to run a single DOS command, in quotes. Suppose you want to see the contents of BLASTOFF.ASC, which you stored as an ASCII file. The command SHELL "TYPE BLASTOFF.ASC" lists the file on the screen. The cursor remains near the top of the listing, as with the straight SHELL command. This process does not affect what programs are stored in memory.

Protecting Saved Files

There is also a protected format available, which you can request with the P parameter in place of A. The resulting file is in the default compressed form with additional protection. A file saved in protected format cannot be accessed outside of GW-BASIC. It also cannot be listed or edited from within GW-BASIC. Here's how to request it:

```
Ok
SAVE "BLASTOFF.PRO",P
Ok
```

The protected format not only cannot be accessed outside of GW-BASIC, it also cannot be listed or edited inside GW-BASIC. Once you have saved a program in protected format, the only thing you can do with it under GW-BASIC is run it. You might want to distribute programs to others in protected format, especially if you don't want them to be able to list or change them. But you will probably want to be able to make future changes to your own

```
Goodbye, Cruel World
Ok
shell

Microsoft(R) MS-DOS(R) Version 4.00
          (C)Copyright Microsoft Corp 1981-1988

D:\GWBASIC>type blastoff.asc
10 PRINT "THIS PROGRAM IS ABOUT TO SELF-DESTRUCT"
20 BEEP
30 BEEP
40 BEEP
50 CLS
55 PRINT "Goodbye, Cruel World"
60 END

D:\GWBASIC>_
```

Figure 2.2. Working in the Shell

programs, so even if you save a protected version, don't forget to keep an unprotected version for yourself. The example above uses a file extension so as not to overwrite BLASTOFF.BAS. Another technique would be to copy BLASTOFF.BAS to another directory before saving it again to ensure that you can still access the file.

Loading a Program

Once a program file is saved, you can load it again at any time for further work or for execution. Just use the LOAD command, specifying the name as you did when you saved it. Remember that GW-BASIC doesn't care if you use uppercase or lowercase letters, so type either. You can omit the extension if the default BAS was used. You don't have to add any parameters. The command LOAD "BLASTOFF loads the file BLASTOFF.BAS whether it is in compressed form, ASCII form, or protected. If you used a different extension than BAS, a different drive, or a different directory name when you saved the file, you have to use it again to load the file. Files stored in the compressed default format are accessed faster, but you won't notice the difference with very short programs. A file must be in GW-BASIC default (compressed) format or in ASCII format to be loaded and run as a program.

You can use function key 3 as a shortcut if you wish; it displays LOAD" at the cursor, so you can just type the file name at the cursor and press ↵.

Loading a program overlays whatever is in memory; if you load a program before saving the previous one, you won't be able to get the previous one back. Be sure and save your work before you lose it.

Locating a File

Suppose you saved a program but you have forgotten the name. You know you could use the SHELL command and check the directory with the DOS DIR command. Alternatively, you can use a special GW-BASIC command in much the same way as DIR. The FILES command lists all the files on the current directory on the screen, then shows the Ok prompt. If you spot the file you want, you can use the LOAD command and type the name.

If you want to limit the files listed to a particular subset, such as those with extension BAS, you can add the qualifiers to the command, as in FILES "*.BAS". Notice that quotes are required around the string, although the last one can be omitted. Figure 2.3 shows how the screen might look if your disk contains many files with the BAS extension.

You can specify any path within the quotes to get file listings from other directories. For example, you might use FILES "C:\GWBASIC*.ASC" to get a listing of all the files in the GWBASIC directory of drive C that have extension ASC.

Clearing the Program Area

Once you have saved a program, you are probably ready to do other work. You can load another program if you wish. If you need to work in GW-BASIC, you want to clear memory so you can use it for another program. The editor saves all numbered lines in memory until you type SYSTEM to exit back to DOS or until you clear memory with a NEW command. You will also lose whatever is in memory in case of a power failure or reboot.

Whenever you are ready to start a new program, enter NEW to clear any previous program out of memory. Otherwise, the new program might get mixed in with lines from the previous one, causing it to malfunction. Use NEW as a direct command only; if you put it in a program, it will wipe the program out of memory.

```
GW-BASIC 3.23
(C) Copyright Microsoft 1983,1984,1985,1986,1987,1988
60300 Bytes free
Ok
files"*.bas"
D:\GWBASIC
VER1     .BAS      FIRST    .BAS      SECOND   .BAS      BLAST    .BAS
COLORS   .BAS      NOTES    .BAS      F2-2     .BAS      FIG2-2   .BAS
EX2-2    .BAS      BLASTOFF.BAS       TRYPRINT.BAS       TRYINPUT.BAS
 1282048 Bytes free

Ok
-
```

```
1LIST  2RUN+  3LOAD"  4SAVE"  5CONT+  6."LPT1 7TRON+  8TROFF+ 9KEY   0SCREEN
```

Figure 2.3. Result of FILES "*.BAS" Command

1. Press function key 4 and type BLASTOFF to save the current program in default (compressed) format as BLASTOFF.BAS.
2. Add a line 5 to display "This is the ASCII form", then save it again in ASCII format, giving it the name BLASTOFF.ASC.
3. Change ASCII in line 5 to PROTECTED, then save it again in protected format as BLASTOFF.PRO.
4. Type NEW to clear memory, then type RUN or press F2 to make sure no program is stored.
5. Type SHELL to get a DOS prompt.
6. Try to list all three files by entering these commands:

```
TYPE BLASTOFF.BAS
TYPE BLASTOFF.ASC
TYPE BLASTOFF.PRO
```

7. Type EXIT to return to GW-BASIC.
8. Type a new program that asks for two items of input in separate lines, then displays them in a single line. Use widely spaced line numbers.
9. Run the new program, then save it as MYOWN.
10. Check the list of all files stored on the default directory. Then check the list of only those with the BAS extension.
11. Reload BLASTOFF.BAS, then execute it to make sure it is loaded.

If you have trouble saving the file in different formats, be sure you used the double quotes to enclose the entire file name. The A or P parameter is not included within the quotes. Extension BAS is used if you don't include another within the quotes.

When you try to TYPE them, only BLASTOFF.ASC should be readable. The other two files should display nonsense. FILES lists all the files, while FILES "*.BAS" lists only the ones with extension BAS.

The program you save as MYOWN should have, as a minimum, two INPUT statements, a PRINT statement, and an END statement. It might look something like this:

```
10 INPUT "Type your name ", NAMEIN$
20 INPUT "Type your age", AGE
30 PRINT NAMEIN$; " is"; AGE; "years old"
40 END
```

These statements look and work just like the ones from Chapter 1 except that they have line numbers.

Listing the Program

After you load a program, GW-BASIC doesn't list the lines automatically. Any time you want to see what's currently in program memory, you can list all or part of it using the LIST command. Function key 1 produces the LIST command for you, but you still have to press ⏎.

LIST Command Parameters

To see the entire current program, press function key 1 or type the word LIST with no parameters. Suppose BLASTOFF.BAS is in memory. Here's the effect of the LIST command:

```
Ok
LIST
10 PRINT "THIS PROGRAM IS ABOUT TO SELF-DESTRUCT"
20 BEEP
30 BEEP
40 BEEP
50 CLS
55 PRINT "Goodbye, Cruel World"
60 END
```

To see a specific line, include that line number as a parameter, like this:

```
Ok
LIST 50
50 CLS
Ok
```

To see a range of lines, enter the first line number, a hyphen, and the last line number. Spacing doesn't matter, as shown here:

```
Ok
LIST 30-55
30 BEEP
40 BEEP
50 CLS
55 PRINT "Goodbye, Cruel World"
Ok
```

You can omit one end of the range to list the rest of the program in that direction. This sequence shows the lines from line 30 to the end:

```
Ok
LIST 30-
```

```
30 BEEP
40 BEEP
50 CLS
55 PRINT "Goodbye, Cruel World"
60 END
Ok
```

The next sequence lists the program from the beginning through line 30:

```
Ok
LIST -30
10 PRINT "THIS PROGRAM IS ABOUT TO SELF-DESTRUCT"
20 BEEP
30 BEEP
Ok
```

You can use a period to refer to the current line number, that is, the line that was most recently worked on or executed. To see the current line, you could enter this command:

```
Ok
LIST .
30 BEEP
Ok
```

You can also use the period to mark the beginning or end of a range, as in these examples when line 30 is current:

```
Ok
LIST .-55
30 BEEP
40 BEEP
50 BEEP
55 PRINT "Goodbye, Cruel World"
Ok
list 30
30 BEEP
Ok
LIST -.
10 PRINT "THIS PROGRAM IS ABOUT TO SELF-DESTRUCT"
20 BEEP
30 BEEP
Ok
```

If you use a number that doesn't exist, nothing is printed, as shown here:

```
LIST 25
Ok
```

Using LLIST to Print the Program

As you know, the PRINT statement displays values on the screen, while the LPRINT statement produces output on the printer. Similarly, the LIST statement displays lines on the screen while the LLIST statement produces corresponding output on the printer. To list the program on the printer, use LLIST instead of LIST. It has the same parameters and effects as does LIST, but produces output on the printer.

1. List the entire program.
2. List the current line.
3. List lines 20 through 55.
4. List from line 50 through the end.
5. List from the beginning through line 40.
6. Try listing line 48. Try listing lines 10 through 48.
7. Make sure your printer is ready, then print the entire program.
8. Print lines 20 through 40.
9. Print from the current line to the end of the program.

If you have trouble listing lines on the screen, check the examples in the text. You'll use commands like these:

```
LIST 20-55
LIST 50-
LIST -40
LLIST
LLIST 20-40
LLIST .-
```

If you have trouble printing lines, remember to use the LLIST command.

Documenting Programs

Figure 2.4 shows another GW-BASIC program. This program contains more statements, but it still has the same format and structure. Each line begins with a line number in column 1. The statements are executed one after the other. In addition to the statements you learned to use in Chapter 1, this program includes remarks and comments to document it.

```
10 REM This is a demonstration program
20 REM First it gets input from the keyboard
30 INPUT "Please type your first name: ",FIRST$
40 INPUT "Now type your last name:     ",LAST$
50 INPUT "Now type your age ",AGE
60 ' Next it displays data on the screen
70 PRINT                      '  Displays a blank line
80 PRINT "Thank you, ";FIRST$;" ";LAST$;"."
90 PRINT "You are";AGE;"years old."
100 END
```

Figure 2.4. A Documented Program

REM Statements

The first two lines (10 and 20) in Figure 2.4 are REM statements; these are remarks that tell the purpose of the program. Anyone listing the program can read these lines and tell what the program is supposed to do. A REM statement can contain up to 255 characters; you can use as many separate REM statements as you need. They have no effect when the program is run.

If you prefer, you can use the single quotation mark (apostrophe) to mark a comment statement, as on line 60. Any characters on a line that follow a single quote are ignored by GW-BASIC.

Comments on Program Lines

In Figure 2.4 you can also see a comment included on program line 70. Comments on statements can also help to explain the program. Just type the statement, then use a single quote and type your comment. It's a good idea to leave several spaces so that you can read the statements more easily, but it makes no difference to the interpreter. You can use comments on any program line, since anything following the single quote is ignored.

Changing the Program

In the entire history of programming (which goes back 100 years if you count Hollerith's original system for tabulating the 1890 census on punch cards), very few useful programs haven't been changed at least once. Even if it works perfectly the first time and needs no debugging—an unlikely event for any really useful program—people will want to upgrade and improve it. The better the program, the more useful it is, the more people will want to adapt it to their needs.To change your GW-BASIC program, you can insert, replace, edit, and delete lines.

Inserting Lines

You have already learned how to insert a line. Simply enter a new line using a line number that will position the new line correctly. For example, to insert a line between lines 10 and 20, you could use line 15 (leaving room for more insertions later).

Replacing Lines

To replace a line, enter a new line with the same line number. For example, suppose you want to replace line 10. You could use the following set of statements:

```
Ok
LIST 10
10 PRINT "THIS PROGRAM IS ABOUT TO SELF-DESTRUCT"
Ok
10 LPRINT "THIS PROGRAM TURNS ITSELF OFF"
LIST -20
10 LPRINT "THIS PROGRAM TURNS ITSELF OFF"
20 BEEP
Ok
```

Because we entered a new line 10, the old one was replaced.

Editing Lines

You've already seen how to edit lines while typing in a program. You can do the same things whenever a program line is on the screen. And by now you can use LIST to get whatever lines on the screen that you want. Then move the cursor into the desired line (see Table 2.1) and make whatever changes you want. When each line is ready, press ↵ to replace the original line with the edited one.

If you edit several lines on the screen, don't forget to press ↵ for each one. The changed version is not recorded in memory until you press ↵ while the cursor is in the line. The cursor can be anywhere in the line; the whole line will be recorded regardless of the cursor position. If you make changes in several lines before pressing ↵, only the line that contained the cursor when you pressed ↵ is changed.

If you change your mind after making revisions but before pressing Enter, you can move the cursor to an unchanged line and press ↵ or just press Ctrl+C to undo the changes. You won't see the line change on the screen, but your changes are no longer saved in memory. List the program lines again to confirm it.

You can also use the EDIT command to bring up a single line and leave the cursor in it for immediate editing. Here's how it looks:

```
Ok
EDIT 10
10 LPRINT "THIS PROGRAM TURNS ITSELF OFF"
```

Notice that the cursor is under the first character on the line. You can make whatever changes you need, then press ↵ to cause the changes to take effect.

Deleting Lines

To delete lines from your program, enter the direct command DELETE followed by the line number or range (just as in the LIST command). For example, the following command deletes lines 30 through 50:

```
Ok
DELETE 30-50
Ok
LIST
10 PRINT "THIS PROGRAM IS ABOUT TO SELF-DESTRUCT"
20 BEEP
55 PRINT "Goodbye, Cruel World"
60 END
Ok
```

All the following commands are valid:

```
DELETE 15     ' deletes one line
DELETE .      ' deletes current line
DELETE -25    ' deletes from the beginning through 25
DELETE 100-   ' deletes from 100 through end
DELETE .-     ' deletes from current line through end
DELETE -.     ' deletes from first through current line
```

You can also delete single lines by typing just the line number and pressing ↵. The existing line is replaced by a blank line. Blank lines aren't listed and have no effect on execution.

Syntax Errors

You may already have seen the Syntax error message; it usually indicates a mistake in the grammar of a command or statement. It can be caused by a misspelled word, as in this example:

```
Ok
RUM
Syntax error
Ok
```

Here we typed RUM instead of RUN. The interpreter displayed the message Syntax error, then displayed the Ok prompt. Nothing was executed. The direct statement BEEEP would also generate a Syntax error message.

Syntax errors might be caused by incorrect punctuation, as in this example:

```
Ok
RUN.
Syntax error
Ok
```

A syntax error might also mean that you've misused a word that has special meaning to GW-BASIC, such as one of the commands. For example:

```
Ok
PRINT RUN
Syntax error
Ok
```

Syntax Errors during Program Execution

When GW-BASIC encounters a syntax error while running a program, it stops executing the program, displays a syntax error message that includes the line number, and displays the line for editing so that you can correct it. The cursor is placed at the position where GW-BASIC identified an error. For example:

```
Ok
10 RUN = 5
20 PRINT RUN
RUN
```

```
Syntax error in 10
Ok
10 RUN = 5
```

The syntax error in line 10 occurs because the word RUN is reserved by GW-BASIC and can't be used as the name of a variable in an assignment statement.

The example shows both the editor and the interpreter at work. The interpreter displayed the Syntax error message. Then it returned control to the editor, which displayed the message Ok. Since a syntax error had occurred, the editor then displayed the line containing the error for editing. The cursor is in the line, waiting for you to type the correction. (It's positioned under the equal sign because that's the first character that seems incorrect. GW-BASIC sees the statement as a RUN statement with extra characters attached.)

Here's an example of another error:

```
RUN
Syntax error in 30
Ok
30 INPUT "Please type your name"YOURNAME$
```

In this case, the punctuation is missing; you must have either a comma (,) or semicolon (;) following the prompt in an INPUT statement.

Here's a similar error with a problem that's not quite so obvious:

```
RUN
Please type your name Ruth Ashley
Syntax error in 30
Ok
30 INPUT "Please type your name", NAME$
```

In this case, the statement includes the necessary punctuation. When the statement is executed, the prompt is displayed on the screen. But when GW-BASIC tries to assign the entered value to the variable, the error message appears. In this case, the variable name used is not valid; GW-BASIC uses the word NAME for its own purposes, so you can't use NAME$ as a variable.

---

1. Bring the program MYOWN.BAS (see page 34) into memory again and list it.
2. If it didn't work right the first time, fix it by editing the lines.
3. Add two comment lines at the beginning to document the program; use either REM or the single quote.

4. Add a note to the end of your END statement to show that you are the author of the program.
5. Test your revised program.
6. If you haven't gotten any errors, change the word INPUT to INPT in one line. Then run the program again.
7. Correct the program so that it runs as it should.
8. Delete the second comment line at the beginning.
9. Make sure the program still runs, then save it again as MYOWN.BAS.

Use any intervening numbers to add lines. You can start a comment with a single quote at any point on the line.

If you have trouble editing the program, list the whole thing after each change so you can see what is going on and reach any line to edit it. Use LIST, DELETE, and EDIT commands as needed.

Renumbering Lines

After you have made a number of revisions, your lines will no longer be numbered in even 10s. In fact, you might have trouble finding room to make an insertion. You can renumber the entire program with the RENUM direct command. For example:

```
Ok
LIST
2 CLS
3 BEEP
5 INPUT "WHAT IS YOUR FIRST NAME?",FNAME$
10 PRINT "HELLO, ";FNAME$
20 END
Ok
RENUM
Ok
LIST
10 CLS
20 BEEP
30 INPUT "WHAT IS YOUR FIRST NAME?",FNAME$
40 PRINT "HELLO, ";FNAME$
50 END
Ok
```

GW-BASIC assumes that you want to renumber the lines in increments of 10. You can specify another starting number and another increment if you wish. For example, to start at 20 and increment by 50, you would enter RENUM 20,,50. In this case the resulting list would look like this:

```
20 CLS
70 BEEP
120 INPUT "WHAT IS YOUR FIRST NAME?",FNAME$
170 PRINT "HELLO, ";FNAME$
220 END
```

Once GW-BASIC starts renumbering lines, it continues through to the end of the program. You can start after the beginning, however. If you have a long program, you might want to start renumbering at the current line 3000 so that it becomes 5000. To do that, you could use RENUM 5000,3000,20. The first number specifies the starting line number, as before. The second number tells where to start renumbering; it is the first line by default, which causes the entire program to be renumbered. The third number specifies the increment—how much to increase each line number from the preceding number.

Automatic Line Numbering

If you are going to enter a long program, you have to use a lot of line numbers; this adds up to a great many extra keystrokes. You can type the line numbers yourself, of course, as you type in each line. Or you can ask GW-BASIC to enter line numbers for you. Then you only have to type the statements themselves. After you have cleared memory and are ready to start typing program lines, you can ask the editor to generate line numbers by entering the AUTO command.

By default, AUTO generates line numbers starting with 10 and incremented by 10, as in this example:

```
Ok
NEW
Ok
AUTO
10 _
```

You type the line and press ↵. At this point, the last few lines on the screen look like this:

```
AUTO
10 REM This program gets mailing information
20 _
```

As you press ↵ at the end of each line, GW-BASIC generates the next line number for you. When you have finished typing the program, you can terminate automatic line numbering by pressing Ctrl-C.

If an automatic line number is followed by an asterisk (*), that line already contains a statement in memory. Usually, this means that you forgot to enter NEW first. You can check it by pressing Ctrl-C and listing the line to decide what to do. If you don't want to enter NEW and start over, the best solution is to list the entire program and delete the lines you don't want.

Starting After the Beginning

You can ask GW-BASIC to use other line number beginnings and increments. Suppose you interrupted automatic line numbering to check out an existing line. Or suppose you have typed several lines before you remember about automatic line numbering. Suppose the last few lines on the screen look like this:

```
10 REM This program gets personal information
20 REM    prepared by Ruth Ashley
30 INPUT "Type your first name: ",FIRSTNAME$

 _
```

At this point, you want to start automatic numbering, but with 40 rather than 10. Just type AUTO 40 and the screen looks like this:

```
10 REM This program gets personal information
20 REM    prepared by Ruth Ashley
30 INPUT "Type your first name: ",FIRSTNAME$
AUTO 40
40 _
```

Now you can continue typing your program as the editor generates your line numbers.

Changing the Increment

You can specify a different increment for automatically generated line numbers if you prefer. If you want to start at the beginning of the program, just use a comma and a new increment. The command AUTO , 20 starts with the line 10 and increments by 20, so the second line is numbered 30, the next 50, and so forth. AUTO 200, 30 says to start generating new line numbers at line 200 and use an increment of 30. If you want to start at the beginning, you can omit the start parameter or use the default of 10; either AUTO 10, 50 or AUTO , 50 has the same effect.

1. List the current program on the screen.
2. Use RENUM to renumber all the lines, then save it as MYOWN again.
3. Load the BLASTOFF program again. Delete line 60.
4. You are going to add several lines starting at 60, so type AUTO 60 to start there.
5. Add these lines:

```
INPUT "Do you want another beep";ANSWER$
PRINT "Here are some anyway!"
BEEP
BEEP
END
```

6. Terminate automatic numbering (Ctrl-C).
7. Run the program and correct any errors.
8. Renumber the entire program to start with 100 and increment by 20. List it to see the effect.
9. Exit GW-BASIC.

The MYOWN program lines should be renumbered to start with 10 and increase by 10.

If you have trouble with the automatic numbering, be sure to type AUTO 60 to start.

To renumber the BLASTOFF program, use RENUM 100,,20

Summary

This chapter has covered the basics of entering, editing, documenting, and running programs. You've learned several new statements, editor commands, and programming techniques.

GW-BASIC Statements. The REM and ' statements let you add comments to document a program.
The REM statement can include any comment.

The ' statement can include any comment. It can also follow another statement following a space on the same line.

GW-BASIC Editor Commands. The editor commands let you edit, control, and manipulate your programs.

The AUTO command causes GW-BASIC to provide line numbers for you automatically.

The DELETE command lets you remove one or more program lines from memory with a single command.

The EDIT command lets you edit a line.

The FILES command lets you list the files in a directory on screen. You can specify a different directory or limit the display to a subset of the files.

The SHELL command lets you use any DOS commands while you are still within GW-BASIC. Use the EXIT command at the DOS prompt to return to the GW-BASIC editor.

The LIST command lets you display an entire program on the screen or a selected portion of it.

The LLIST command lets you print an entire program on the printer or a selected portion of it.

The LOAD command lets you bring a file that contains a GW-BASIC program into memory from a disk.

The NEW command lets you clear memory of any current program lines in preparation for starting a new program.

The RENUM command lets you renumber the lines of a program when necessary.

The RUN command lets you execute a GW-BASIC program once it is in memory.

The SAVE command lets you save a file in compressed, ASCII, or protected mode.

Programming Techniques. The programming techniques covered include a few ways even short simple programs can be made more useful.

Use widely spaced line numbers to allow for later modifications.

Use only one statement per line unless they are closely related or combined for a specific reason.

Document your programs with comments using either REM or ' statements as needed.

Use automatic numbering and renumbering when necessary to keep your numbering consistent.

Exercise

In this exercise you will create a new program, run it, modify it, and play with it online. You should be able to practice most of the features covered in this chapter. Bring up GW-BASIC or clear memory with NEW before starting.

What You Should Do	What the Computer Will Do
1. Use automatic line numbering to enter program lines 10 through 50 to get values for the fullname, the street address, the city, the state, and the zip code.	1. Automatic line numbers appear as you type statements.
2. Continue with automatic numbering to enter lines 60 through 90 to print the address in three lines. Include the city, state, and zip code on the last line.	2. Your statements appear on the screen.
3. Add an END statement at 100, then cancel line numbering.	3. After you cancel line numbering, the Ok prompt appears.
4. Run your program. Fix any errors until it runs correctly.	4. For each INPUT statement, you'll see the prompt and enter data. For each PRINT statement, the value(s) you entered should print.
5. To document the program, add two comment lines before line 10. Add a documented PRINT statement to insert a blank line before the address is printed. Run the program again and fix it if there are any problems.	5. The only difference in the running should be a blank line between RUN and the first line of the address.
6. Renumber the lines starting with 100 and incrementing by 10. List the program on the screen to see the result.	6. The lines are all renumbered, and now start with 100, 110, and so forth.
7. Modify the last PRINT statement so that it displays the last line of the address in this format: "San Diego, CA 92117". Edit it until you are satisfied with the result.	7. The only change in the print should be the format of the last printed line.

8. Save the program as CHAP2-X.
9. Clear memory, then display your list of files to see this one listed, and reload it.
10. Modify the PRINT statements so the output goes to the printer. Then run the program again.
11. Don't save the program with the changes. Just exit GW-BASIC and go on with the next chapter when you are ready.

8. The Ok prompt appears.
9. The file list is displayed. After you load the file, you'll see the Ok prompt.
10. The name and address lines now appear on the printer.
11. You'll see the DOS prompt.

What If It Doesn't Work?

1. If you have trouble getting into or out of GW-BASIC, refer back to Chapter 1.
2. If your INPUT statements give you problems, make sure you used double quotes around each prompt, a comma or semicolon before the variable name, and an unreserved word for the name.
3. If your PRINT statements give you problems, make sure you used the exact same variable names as in the INPUT statements. The formatting can include connecting the variable names and constant strings with semicolons.
4. Your program should look something like the one below. Yours may be very different and still be correct.

```
10 ' This is an exercise program
20 ' Get the input data
30 INPUT "What is your full name";FULLNAME$
40 INPUT "Type your street address: ",STREET$
50 INPUT "Type your city: ",CITY$
60 INPUT "Type your state: ",STATE$
70 INPUT "Type your zip code: ",ZIP$
80 ' Now do the display lines
90 PRINT    ' blank line
100 PRINT FULLNAME$
110 PRINT STREET$
120 PRINT CITY$;", ";STATE$;"  ";ZIP$
130 END
```

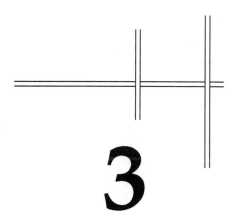

3

Arithmetic in GW-BASIC

This chapter deals with GW-BASIC commands that perform common arithmetic operations, either in immediate mode or as part of a BASIC program. The arithmetic can range from simple addition or subtraction to the use of functions such as square roots and random numbers. Printing and display of values are also covered. Since virtually all useful programs use arithmetic to some extent, you will use what you learn in this chapter in just about every GW-BASIC program you write, both as you continue in this book and when you are writing your own. You will learn to:

- Perform addition, subtraction, multiplication, and division
- Perform negation and exponentiation
- Perform complex expressions with parentheses
- Include operations in assignment (LET) statements
- Use the SQR function to determine square root
- Use the ABS function to determine the absolute value
- Use the SGN function to determine the sign
- Use the CINT, INT, and FIX functions to remove fractional parts of numbers
- Use the RND function to generate a random number
- Use the RANDOMIZE statement to reset the effect of RND
- Use the TAB and SPC functions to place spacing in output lines
- Format numbers for good-looking display and print

Arithmetic in Programs

Most programs use at least some arithmetic; many use it extensively. A program that handles payroll calculates regular and overtime pay. It may calculate deductions and keep track of earned vacation hours. A program that manages inventory might use arithmetic to count the items, to check how long a certain item has been in stock, to decide how many to order, and to determine the total value of the stock. A program that prepares reports will keep track of page numbers.

GW-BASIC Numbers

The numbers 45, 565.78, and 12345.678901 look similar to us, but GW-BASIC treats them differently internally. A number in the range –32768 to 32767 without a decimal point is an integer. A number with one to seven significant digits, which may include a decimal point, is referred to as a single-precision number. (A significant digit is any digit to the left of the decimal point except a leading zero or any digit to the right of the decimal point except a trailing zero.)

A number with eight to fifteen significant digits, which may include a decimal point, is referred to as a double-precision number. Integers are stored in the least amount of space, single-precision next, and double-precision numbers require the most storage. Similarly, integer arithmetic is much quicker than single-precision arithmetic, and double-precision arithmetic takes the longest. The needs of the program and the values of the numbers determine which type you should use in a particular situation.

By default, GW-BASIC treats all numbers with seven or fewer significant digits as single-precision and larger ones as double-precision numbers. You can force a number to be treated as one of the three types by including a special character at the end of the number. To cause 45 to be handled internally as an integer instead of a single-precision number, use 45% as the value. To cause it to be treated as a double-precision number, use 45# as the number. You can use 45 or 45! to indicate single precision.

You can force a variable to use the appropriate type of number by attaching the character to the end of the variable name. The variable COUNT% holds only an integer value. The variable PRICE or PRICE! holds a single-precision number. The variable TOTAL# holds a double-precision number.

If a number is too large to handle, GW-BASIC may convert it internally to floating point, a form of scientific notation, which lets it handle larger numbers at the expense of precision. Printed values may also appear in floating-point form, so you'll have to be able to interpret them. The value 4456.678 in floating-point format appears as 4.456678E+03; the value 0.00000123456789 in floating-point format appears as 1.234568E–6. The decimal value is called the *mantissa*; the value following E is called the *exponent*. The exponent value indicates how many places to move the decimal point to find the fixed point value. The sign of the exponent indicates whether to move the decimal point to the left (–) or right (+). If the floating-point number contains D instead of E, it is a double-precision value.

Numeric Constants

As you've seen earlier, numbers can be used as constant values in statements. GW-BASIC provides several different types of numeric constants. In this chapter, we'll deal with whole numbers and fixed-point numbers, which have decimal points. Each constant value can have up to seven significant digits for single precision.

You can use a plus or minus sign before the number if appropriate. If no sign is provided, the value is treated as positive. The number can include a decimal point as well. But commas, dollar signs, and other punctuation are not allowed.

If you don't use a special character to type your numeric constant, any number with seven or fewer significant digits is treated as single precision, while larger numbers are treated as double precision. Numbers with more than 15 significant digits may be converted internally and lose precision or they may bring up the Overflow error message.

If you use the characters % and # to specify integers or double-precision numbers, try not to mix number types in a statement. The conversions may not be exact, which causes a loss of precision. Later in this chapter, you'll learn to use functions for conversion from one type to another.

Numeric Variables

As you've already seen, variables have names of any length; the number of significant characters may be limited by your version of GW-BASIC, but 40 is common. Once you use a variable name that doesn't end in $, it is a numeric variable. If a variable hasn't been given a value, it will be given a default value of zero if it appears in a statement.

Table 3.1. Arithmetic Operators

Operator	Effect	Constant	Result	Variable
^	Exponentiation	3^2	9	PRICE^2
–	Negation	–3	–3	–PRICE
*	Multiplication	2*3	6	PRICE*COUNT
/	Division	8/2	4	COUNT/QUANTITY
–	Subtraction	8–2	6	PRICE–DISCOUNT
+	Addition	8+2	10	PRICE+TAX

As with the constants, you can attach the character %, !, and # to a numeric variable name to force the contents to be integer, single precision, or double precision. If a noninteger value is assigned to an integer variable, you get a Type mismatch error. If too large a value is assigned to a single-precision variable, it will be converted internally and digits will be lost, or you'll get the Overflow message.

Simple Arithmetic

Simple arithmetic involves only a single operation. In GW-BASIC, you can add, subtract, multiply, or divide combining numeric constants and/or variables into expressions using simple arithmetic operators. You can also use exponentiation. The operators and examples are listed in Table 3.1. You can include spaces before and after most operators, but the negation symbol must not be separated from its target with a space.

In this section, you'll see how to use each operator separately in immediate mode to act on numbers you already know or variables that have valid values. If you use a string variable in an arithmetic statement, you'll get a Type mismatch error message.

Decimal Points and Signs

GW-BASIC keeps track of the decimal point, placing it in the correct position in the result of any arithmetic operation. Adding 5.5 and 4.234 results in 9.734. Multiplying 7.1 by 2.5 results in 17.75. Subtracting 5.75 from 7 results in 1.25.

Since standard numbers in GW-BASIC cannot exceed 15 digits, they will be converted to floating-point notation.

GW-BASIC also keeps track of the sign and uses the correct one. If no sign is included in a number, it is treated as positive. If a minus sign precedes it, a number is treated as negative. Later in this chapter, you'll learn other ways of handling negative numbers.

Negation

Notice that the minus sign appears twice in the operator list in Table 3.1. It can be used before a constant or variable to negate its current value. That is, it reverses the sign. If a minus sign appears directly before a number or variable, without an immediately preceding number, it acts as a negation. To use the value –7, just type it that way. To use the negative or opposite sign with a variable named PRICE, use –PRICE. Whatever sign the value formerly had is reversed.

Don't leave a space between the negation sign and the number or variable. You can use a space on each side of other operators if you wish, but it isn't necessary. You can even use multiple spaces. You can't have two operators adjacent to each other; they must be separated by a number, a variable, or a parenthesis. This really becomes a problem only with negation. To add the value 6 to the negation of a variable called ITEMB, you could use 6 + (–ITEMB) or –ITEMB + 6, but not 6 + –ITEMB.

Addition

To add two numbers in GW-BASIC, just join the numbers to be added with a plus sign and include the expression in a statement. To add 8.97 and 65.344 you could use one of these interactions:

```
Ok
PRINT 8.97+65.344
 74.314
Ok
TOTAL = 8.97+65.344
Ok
PRINT TOTAL
 74.314
Ok
```

As you recall, in direct or immediate mode the operation is performed immediately and you see the result on the screen. You could use statements such as PRINT PRICE + 74.50 or PRINT PRICE + SURCHARGE to get valid results.

You can also add a series of values, as in the following statements:

```
PRINT PRICE1+PRICE2+PRICE3+1.5
PRINT 1+2+3+4+5+6+7+8+9+10
```

Subtraction

To subtract two numbers in GW-BASIC, just type the expression in the statement just as you would write it in a single line. To subtract 89.75 from 329.67, you would use this interaction:

```
Ok
PRINT 329.67-89.75
 239.92
Ok
```

The order of the values is more important in subtraction than in addition; $5 - 1$ gives a different result than $1 - 5$. You could use a statement like PRINT PRICE - 10.98 to get a discounted price. You can also subtract a series of numbers, as in the following statements:

```
PRINT PRICE.DISCOUNT-.50
PRINT 100-5.6-2.3
```

Multiplication

To multiply two numbers, use an asterisk (*) as the operator. In paper-and-pencil arithmetic you might use 2×28 or 2(28) to represent a multiplication operation. In GW-BASIC, however, you must use 2 * 28 or 28 * 2 to specify the same operation. To multiply two numbers, you would use this interaction:

```
Ok
PRINT 32.67*9.75
 318.5325
Ok
```

If the variable PRICE has a valid value, you could use PRINT PRICE * .065 to calculate the sales tax. You can also multiply a series of numbers, as in these statements:

```
PRINT LONG*WIDE*HIGH
PRINT LONG*WIDE*2
PRINT 1*2*3*4*5*6*7*8*9
```

Division

To divide two numbers, use a slash (that's a forward slash, found on the same key as the question mark) to indicate the operation. As in subtraction, the order of the values is important; the result of 8/2 is very different from the result of 2/8. To divide two numbers, you would use this interaction:

```
Ok
PRINT 329.67/4
 82.41751
Ok
```

If the variable PRICE has a valid value, you could use PRINT PRICE / 6 to find one-sixth of the price. You can also divide a series of values, as in the following statements:

```
PRINT AREA/TILES/2
PRINT 800/7/9/3
```

You may encounter a special problem in using operations. It is illegal to divide by zero. If you use a variable that happens to have value zero or one that hasn't been assigned a value on the right of the division operator (/), you'll get a message (Division by zero) when the statement is executed, but the program continues running. You'll also get a result that reflects machine infinity; on our computer, that's 1.701412E+38.

For example, if you forget to assign a value to the variable TWO, then use PRINT PRICE / TWO, you will get the Division by zero message. The value assigned to the expression reflects infinity. Later on, you'll learn to check for division by zero when a program is running. For now, just be aware that it's a problem. If you get the Division by zero message, modify the expression so it doesn't divide by zero.

Exponentiation

Exponentiation is multiplying numbers by themselves or raising numbers to a power. When you square a number, you multiply it by itself; this is exponent 2, since the number is used twice. The value 6^2 is 6*6 or 36. The value of 6^3 is

6 * 6 * 6 or 216. The caret (^, found on the 6 key) is the exponentiation symbol. To find the result of exponentiation, you might use this interaction:

```
Ok
PRINT 18.6^2
 345.96
Ok
```

You can use variables for either the number or the exponent. Both PRICE^2 and 278.2^EXPO are valid expressions; each will calculate a result. You can also use exponentiation in series, as in the following statements:

```
PRINT 4^4^2
PRINT LENGTH^2^3
```

Before continuing in this chapter, bring up the GW-BASIC editor and do the following Self-Check in direct mode.

1. Show the result of multiplying the current year by 25.6, as in 1991*25.6.
2. Show the result of dividing the current year by your age, as in 1991/31.
3. Show the result of adding your age to the day of the month and the current page number.
4. Show the result of subtracting your age from your height in inches, as in 70 – 31.
5. Assign your age to the variable AGE and the current year to the variable YEAR. Then try items 1 through 4 using variables where possible.
6. Show the value of the year squared, as in YEAR^2. Then try raising it to the sixth power. Notice that the very large number is displayed in floating-point format.
7. Assign your first name to the variable MYNAME$. Then try adding your age to it and displaying the result. Notice the error message that results when you use a string variable in arithmetic.
8. Try printing the result of dividing the year by a variable called EMPTY. Notice the message and value that result.

If the answers you expect don't appear, make sure you used PRINT (or ?) before each expression.

```
10 REM Sample Arithmetic Program
20 '
30 ' Set up input values
40 LENGTH = 15
50 WIDTH = 12
60 HEIGHT = 8
70 ' Do the calculation
80 VOLUME = LENGTH*WIDTH*HEIGHT
90 ' Show the result
100 PRINT "The volume is"; VOLUME
110 END
```

Figure 3.1. Sample Program

Arithmetic in Assignment Statements

You can use the assignment statement to provide a variable name to hold the result of an arithmetic operation. Most arithmetic in programs occurs in assignment statements. You've already seen how to assign a value to a variable with a statement such as one of the following:

```
LET PRICE=59.80
LENGTH=45
```

You can also use any arithmetic expression on the right of the equal sign. If you use VOLUME = 15*12*8, the result of the multiplication becomes the value of the variable VOLUME. You can then use VOLUME in later expressions or print it as needed. The value of the variable on the left side of the equal sign is replaced with the value of the expression on the right. Any variable named in an arithmetic assignment statement must be numeric or you'll get the Type mismatch error. If you use the statement VOLUME = LONG * WIDE * HIGH, and HIGH hasn't been specifically given a value, GW-BASIC uses the default value 0, so the value zero is assigned to VOLUME as a result of the multiplication. If a string variable is included, you'll see the error message Type mismatch and program execution stops.

Arithmetic in Programs

In programs, of course, you use numbered lines. You might use a program like the one in Figure 3.1 to assign values and calculate the result. To calculate the perimeter of the room, you might add these lines to the program:

```
85 PERIMETER=LONG+WIDE+LONG+WIDE
105 PRINT "The perimeter is";PERIMETER
```

Arithmetic operations are the heart of many programs. The structure is often as shown in Figure 3.1; first get any input values, then do any needed calculations, then prepare the output.

Combining Operations

To combine arithmetic operations in a single expression, you have to know a little bit about how GW-BASIC processes them. In Figure 3.1, the operators are listed in order of precedence, that is, in the order that GW-BASIC performs operations. If the same operator appears several times in the same expression, they are handled from left to right. You can use parentheses (as in paper-and-pencil arithmetic) to modify the sequence, since expressions in parentheses are handled first.

If there aren't any parentheses, GW-BASIC first does all the exponentiation, working from left to right. Then it does any negation. If you want a number negated before exponentiation, put parentheses around it. You'll get a different result from –NUMBER^2 than from (–NUMBER)^2. In the first case, GW-BASIC first squares the value of NUMBER, then reverses the sign. In the second case, GW-BASIC first reverses the sign of NUMBER, then squares the result. The final sign is different in the two results.

Then GW-BASIC does all the multiplication, then the division, then the addition, and finally the subtraction. When you use parentheses, GW-BASIC works from the inside out. When several sets of parentheses are at the same level, as in the statement RESULT=(A–B) * (C–D) * (E–F), GW-BASIC evaluates them from left to right, then the operations outside the parentheses are done. In the above example, first GW-BASIC calculates a value for A–B, then for C–D, then for E–F. Then it multiplies the three together. If there are three nested parentheses, the inner operation is performed, then the middle one, then the outer one. In the expression (((C–D) * (A–B)) + PRICE) / 6, GW-BASIC first calculates a value for C – D, then for A– B. These two values are multiplied next; this result is added to the value of the variable PRICE. The resulting value is divided by 6 to get the result. You would get a very different result with the expression C – D * A – B + PRICE / 6. GW-BASIC first multiplies D and A, then divides PRICE by 6. The temporary product is subtracted from C, B is subtracted from the result, and finally the temporary quotient is added.

The statement PRINT 5 – 3 * 4 results in –7, since GW-BASIC first multiplies 3*4. Then it subtracts the result from 5. If you use the expression

```
300 ' Get the input values
310 PRINT "Use the same units in both values."
320 INPUT "Enter the radius "; RADIUS
330 INPUT "Enter the height "; HEIGHT
340 ' Calculate the values
350 VOLUME = 3.1416*(RADIUS^2)*HEIGHT
360 ' Prepare the output
370 PRINT "The volume of this tank is"; VOLUME
380 END
```

Figure 3.2. Calculating Volume

(5–3)*4, the result is 8, since the operation in parentheses is performed first. To calculate a discount and subtract it from the price, then add tax, you could use a series of separate statements like these in a program:

```
210 DISCOUNT=PRICE*.1
220 DISCPRICE=PRICE-DISCOUNT
230 TAX=DISCPRICE*.065
240 SELLPRICE=DISCPRICE+TAX
```

In this case, the variable SELLPRICE holds the final result. But you can also perform the entire operation in a single statement, as in this one:

```
210 SELLPRICE=(PRICE-(PRICE*0.1))*1.065
```

In this case, GW-BASIC first performs the operation in the inner set of parentheses, PRICE*0.1; it saves the result in a temporary location. Then it performs the operation in the enclosing set of parentheses, subtracting the amount in the temporary location from PRICE. Finally, it multiplies that result by the value 1.065 to get a value to assign to SELLPRICE.

If you are comfortable with complex arithmetic expressions, use them in your programs. If not, you can use as many separate operations as you wish. Remember to use variables to hold any intermediate results that will be needed in later statements.

Program Examples

Suppose a program has to calculate the volume of a cylindrical tank (the formula is $\pi R^2 H$). Figure 3.2 shows part of a program that gets the values of the radius and the height, then calculates and displays the result.

In this case, the parentheses aren't absolutely necessary, since GW-BASIC would do the exponentiation first anyway. Including them just makes the statement easier to understand.

Another program has to calculate the gross pay for an employee. Any hours over 40 are paid at one-and-one-half wages; each employee works at least 40 hours. This program uses TOTHOURS to contain the total number of hours worked and BASEPAY to contain the basic hourly wage. The program might contain these lines:

```
420 OVRHOURS=TOTHOURS-40
430 GROSSPAY=(40*BASEPAY)+(OVRHOURS*(BASEPAY*1.5))
```

While the arithmetic could be done in a single statement, it is clearer to use at least two. In most programming, there's a lot to be said for statements you can understand with a single reading. It's all the same to the computer.

In this case, statement 420 calculates the number of overtime hours. Statement 430 calculates the pay for the overtime hours and saves that amount temporarily, then calculates the regular pay, then the overtime pay (using the temporary value), then adds the two together to get a value for GROSSPAY.

1. Type in the program from Figure 3.2.
2. Run the program using several different sets of values; try very large ones as well as ones with decimal components.
3. Save your program as TANKVOL.BAS, then clear memory.
4. Create a complex expression to subtract 30 from the result of multiplying your age times 6 and then divide it by 2 and add the number of the month to the result. Write a program to ask for your age, do the calculation, and display both the number you entered and the result.
5. Try out the program with several different "ages." When it works well, save it as AGECALC.BAS if you like, then remove it from memory.
6. Write a short program to ask the user to enter values for height (in inches) and weight (in pounds). Then print the average weight in pounds per inch (divide the weight by the inches). Finally, the program should convert the inches to centimeters (multiply by 2.54) and the weight to kilograms (multiply by 2.2) and print the the average weight in kg per cm.
7. Test the program with several different sets of values, then save it as CONVERT. BAS.

If you had trouble with item 4, compare your program with this one:

```
10  INPUT "What is your age";AGE
20  INPUT "What is the number of the month";MONTH
30  RESULT = (((AGE*6)-30)/2)+MONTH.
40  PRINT  "Age";AGE,  "Result"; RESULT
50  END
```

If you had trouble with item 6, compare your program with this one:

```
10  'INPUT "What is your height (in inches)";INCHES
20    INPUT "What is your weight (in pounds)";POUNDS
30  AVEWEIGHT = POUNDS / INCHES
40  PRINT "Average Weight per inch:" ; AVEWEIGHT
50  CONVWEIGHT = POUNDS * 2.2
60  CONVHEIGHT = INCHES *  2.54
70  AVECONV = CONVWEIGHT / CONVHEIGHT
80  PRINT "Average Weight per centimeter:"; AVECONV
90  END
```

Your programs may be quite different and still be correct.

Using Functions

GW-BASIC provides arithmetic functions that you can use to perform fairly complex operations. For example, you may remember trying to calculate square roots in high school. GW-BASIC provides a function you can use to do it for you. Other functions, which aren't covered in this book, let you perform common trigonometric and logarithmic operations.

A function is composed of a keyword followed (generally) by a value of some sort in parentheses. These values are called arguments. While some functions allow or require multiple arguments, the ones we'll cover in this book all use a single numeric argument; it must be numeric, but it can be a constant, a variable, or an expression.

GW-BASIC always evaluates functions as the first step in performing operations. A function enclosed in parentheses is evaluated before other functions. The resulting value of the function is used in the operation.

The Square Root

Finding a square root by hand is a fairly complex operation. The SQR function lets you do it easily. To find the square root of 87.4, use SQR(87.4). To display the square root of the value of the variable AREA, use PRINT SQR(AREA).

You can use the SQR function in an expression as well. You might use the statement RESULT=INTERIOR*SQR(X2); in this case GW-BASIC evaluates the function before its value is multiplied by the value of INTERIOR. You can also use an expression as the argument. In SQR(INTERIOR*3) the value in the parentheses is calculated, then its square root is found.

The argument must be numeric and greater than or equal to zero. If you use a negative value, you'll get the message Illegal function call when the statement is executed.

The Absolute Value

When you have a constant, you can tell at a glance if it is positive or negative. It's not obvious, however, with an expression or a variable. The absolute value ignores the sign and treats a value as positive. The result of PRINT ABS (-5) is 5; the result of PRINT ABS (5) is also 5.

When you multiply one variable by another, the result will be negative if just one of the two values is negative. If you want to ensure the result is positive, you can use the ABS function to use the absolute value of each. Suppose the quantity of items is negative when more have been ordered than are on hand. A statement such as TOTALVALUE=ABS (QUANTITY) *COST figures the total value and avoids an error message that might appear if the value of QUANTITY is negative.

The ABS function can use an expression as the argument. You could use a statement such as TOTALVALUE=ABS (QUANTITY * COST). The ABS function can also be used as the argument to another function. For example, the statement ROOT = SQR (ABS (VALUE1)) is perfectly valid.

The Sign

As noted earlier, you can easily tell if a constant value is positive or negative. It's not clear, however, whether the result of an expression or a variable is positive or negative. In some mathematical operations, you don't want to treat it as positive; you actually want to know what the sign is. The SGN function can find out.

When you use SGN, the result gives you the sign. SGN(TOTAL) returns the value 1 if the sign is positive, -1 if it is negative, and 0 if the value is zero. As with the ABS function, you can use a constant, a variable, or an expression as the argument of the SGN function.

	CINT	FIX	INT
87.4	87	87	87
–87.4	–87	–87	–88
88.9	89	88	88
–88.9	–89	–88	–89

Figure 3.3. Using Functions to Truncate Values

Truncating Values

You may want to use the whole number (or integer) portion of a value, either dropping the digits following the decimal point or rounding up to the next higher integer. GW-BASIC provides three functions that do this. Figure 3.3 shows the three functions and their effects with four different values.

The differences between the three are small but significant. Suppose a value has been assigned to variable WHAT. The function CINT(WHAT) always rounds the value of the argument to the nearest whole number. The function FIX(WHAT) always just drops the decimal point and whatever comes after it; it always truncates, giving the whole number closer to zero. The function INT(WHAT) works much like FIX, but for negative values it returns the next lower number; it always rounds down. When the variable WHAT has the value –24.47, CINT(WHAT) has the value –25, FIX(WHAT) has the value –24, and INT(WHAT) has the value –25.

If you want to round a number in a nonstandard way, you have to modify the value first. Suppose you want rounding to take place only if the first digit following the decimal place is 7 or greater; in that case, just subtract .2 from the value. CINT(WHAT–.2) will cause the whole number portion to increase by 1 if the digit following the decimal point in the original value was 7 or greater.

Data Type Conversion

When GW-BASIC works with numeric data, it uses the same precision as the values. If an expression includes more than one type, all the values are converted to the most precise during the evaluation, then converted to the type of the result variable. The result may not be as accurate as you hope. You can convert a numeric value to single precision with the CSNG(*n*) function, or to double precision with the CDBL(n) function. These functions are parallel to the CINT(n) function and work in much the same way.

1. Clear memory, then write a program that assigns the value 2.6 to PLUSTWO, 0 to ZERO, and –2.6 to NEGTWO.
2. Add a program line to show the absolute value of each variable. Test the program.
3. Add a program line to show the number returned by the sign function for each variable. Test the program.
4. Add a program line to show the square root of PLUSTWO.
5. Add a program line to show the value returned by each of the truncating functions for PLUSTWO and NEGTWO. Test the program.
6. Save your program if you like, then clear memory.
7. Load your CONVERT program (if you didn't save it, see the second Self-Check program on page 63) and modify it to round the average weight/height values to the next whole number if the decimal portion begins with 0.5 or greater.

To check your statement for item 3, it should return 1 for PLUSTWO, 0 for ZERO, and -1 for NEGTWO. Your statement for item 4 should display 1.612452.

If you have trouble with item 7, use expressions such as CINT(AVGWEIGHT) and CINT (AVGCONV) to get rounded values before printing.

Random Numbers

It is often convenient to use your computer to generate a random number, or even a set of random numbers. Many statistical and other problems require random numbers. Games and simulations often depend on random numbers for many of their features.

The RND Function

GW-BASIC generates a random number between 0 and 1 whenever it executes the RND function. RND has no arguments. Unless you do some manipulation, however, GW-BASIC generates the same sequence of "random" numbers each time you use RND in a fresh session. GW-BASIC uses a built-in seed value to start, which always produces the same set of values. It performs various internal operations on the seed value, which always produces the same result. The result of the first PRINT RND statement you use in a session is .1213501, the second is .651861, and so forth.

The RANDOMIZE Statement

You can cause the system to generate different "random" numbers by supplying a different seed value through the RANDOMIZE statement. This statement has several different formats:

```
RANDOMIZE
RANDOMIZE expression
RANDOMIZE TIMER
```

If you use RANDOMIZE by itself, you'll be prompted to enter a seed value. Here's how it looks:

```
Ok
RANDOMIZE
Random number seed (-32768 to 32767)? _
```

After you type a number and press ↵, GW-BASIC uses it to reseed the random number generator. The next time you use RND in the same program, you will not get the "standard" random number.

If you prefer, you can supply a value or expression following the RANDOMIZE word. The value will be used, and you won't be prompted. If you use the same value each time you run a program, the random numbers generated by RND will be the same each time. Some programs ask the user to enter a value, then use that value in an expression to calculate a new seed for use in a RANDOMIZE statement.

GW-BASIC has a system variable called TIMER that keeps track of the number of seconds since midnight, according to your computer's internal clock. The statement PRINT TIMER results in a value such as 45678.985. The RANDOMIZE statement can use the value of the TIMER variable as a seed, which is a special starting point for the function calculation. The statement RANDOMIZE TIMER causes it to pick up the whole number portion of the value of TIMER and use it as the seed number. Using the RANDOMIZE TIMER statement gives a more random result, since it's unlikely that the same seed number will occur twice.

Using RANDOMIZE

You generally use RANDOMIZE early in a program, before the first RND function. Here's how you might use it:

```
100 RANDOMIZE 800
110 NEWNUM=RND
120 PRINT NEWNUM
RUN
 .113302
Ok
```

You can use a numeric variable from a program that frequently has different values as the seed expression, as in RANDOMIZE QUANTITY. Or you can use the RANDOMIZE TIMER statement to give you a reasonably random seed automatically.

Random Integers

Much of the time, you don't really want a random number to be between 0 and 1; instead, you want a random integer. In fact, you often want it limited, say between 1 and 10 or between 1 and 200. To get this, you can use a more complex expression. To get a random number between 1 and 100, you could use PRINT INT (RND*100+1). The expression gets a random number, then multiplies it by 100 to turn it into a value between 0 and 99. Adding 1 causes the whole number portion to be between 1 and 100. The INT function then drops the fractional portion. If you want a number in the range of 0 to an upper limit, don't add 1 to the result. The result of INT(RND*100+1) is just as random as the number that results from the simple RND statement; the extra arithmetic doesn't affect the randomness.

Figure 3.4 shows a short program that will generate a random number between 1 and a specific integer. At the keyboard, you supply the upper limit, such as 20. The program assigns this to the variable LIMIT, then generates the random number. The statement RANDOMIZE TIMER is used to ensure that the program doesn't generate the same value each time.

To get a number in a range that doesn't begin with 0 or 1, you modify the numbers a bit. If you want to generate numbers between 100 and 199, for example, subtract the beginning number from the ending one; in this case, the result is 99. Find a random number between 0 and 99, then add 100 to the result.

```
10 ' This program generates random numbers
20 RANDOMIZE TIMER
30 PRINT "This program generates a random number "
40 PRINT "between 1 and the number you enter."
50 INPUT "Type the upper limit: ", LIMIT
60 PRINT INT(RND*LIMIT+1)
70 END
```

Figure 3.4. Random Number Generation Program

1. Try PRINT RND in direct mode.
2. Try PRINT RND again. Did you get a different number?
3. Try PRINT INT(RND*100+1) to get a random integer between 1 and 100.
4. Write a program that prints the result of the RND functions you tried in direct mode. Then have the program perform a basic RND and print the result two more times.
5. Test the program and note the results of the RND functions. Then run it again. Are the results different?
6. Modify the program to add the RANDOMIZE TIMER statement before the first RND function. Add a final statement to show an integer between 1 and 6.
7. Test the program twice. Are the values different each time?
8. Save your program as RANDNUM.

Your final program will look something like this:

```
10 RANDOMIZE TIMER
20 PRINT RND
30 PRINT RND
40 PRINT INT(RND*100+1)
50 PRINT RND
60 PRINT RND
70 PRINT INT(RND*6 + 1)
80 END
```

Your program may be different and still be correct.

Formatting Output

So far, you have had only a little control over how numbers are printed. You can use a semicolon (;) in the PRINT or LPRINT statement to cause values to be adjacent or a comma (,) to cause them to be separated and treated in 14-character zones. In addition, you have had no control over the number of decimal places that are printed or the exact placement of characters on a line. In this section, you'll see how you can tab to specific points and specify the exact format of numeric variable values.

Starting a New Line

Normally, each PRINT or LPRINT statement in a program starts a new line on the screen or printer. You can modify this effect by ending the statement with a semicolon (;). The next printed or displayed line then continues right after the current one. Suppose your program includes these lines:

```
200 PRINT "This is the";
210 PRINT COUNTER; "th time."
```

It will be printed like this when COUNTER has the value 11:

```
This is the 11 th time.
```

Skipping Across a Line

You already know how to insert a string of blank spaces into an output line by including them in a character string. In addition, GW-BASIC provides two functions to position variables on a line in either the PRINT or LPRINT statement. You can use the SPC function to skip a particular number of spaces or TAB to skip to a particular column. They have similar formats:

SPC(n)
TAB(n)

In both cases, the argument n must have a value between 1 and 255, since the line length is limited to 255. In practice, the line length is limited to what your printer or screen can handle. You can use either function before or between items in the statement. GW-BASIC assumes that either TAB or SPC is followed by a semicolon, so if you use it at the end of the line, the next similar

statement will continue with output on the same line. The statement PRINT
"Name:" SPC(5) FULLNAME$ has a result like this:

```
Name:       Ruth Ashley
```

The SPC function inserts the specified number of spaces immediately
following the preceding item, whether it is a constant or a variable. If the items
you want to print have variable lengths, the result can look odd. The statement
LPRINT FULLNAME$ SPC(5) AGE produces this output for three different
executions:

```
Ruth Ashley       42
Davida Fernandez       21
Dave Case       32
```

In this situation, you might want to use TAB instead. The statement
LPRINT FULLNAME$ TAB(25) AGE run with three different values produces
this output:

```
Ruth Ashley             42
Davida Fernandez        21
Dave Case               32
```

The TAB function skips over to the specified position on the line. You can
use the TAB and SPC functions to format lines sent to the screen with the
PRINT statement as well.

Formatting Numbers

You can use a special form of a PRINT or LPRINT statement to specify the
output format for numeric variables. The formatted output statements are
called PRINT USING and LPRINT USING statements. In addition to the word
USING, you must specify a format with a special character for each character
to be printed. Since the formatting is built in, GW-BASIC won't let you use the
TAB and SPC functions in these statements. These are the basic formats:

PRINT USING *format-string; variable-list*

LPRINT USING *format-string; variable-list*

The format string can be a constant, in which case it must be enclosed in
double quotes, or a previously defined string variable. The semicolon must
follow the format string.

Digit Positions. In a USING format string, the pound sign (#) represents a digit position and a period represents the decimal point position. If you don't include a decimal point, it is assumed at the right of your string. Since you can't include string constants in a PRINT USING statement, you must use separate PRINT statements to print constant values. Remember that the semicolon at the end causes the next PRINT or PRINT USING statement to continue on the same line. Here's an example:

```
200 PRINT "Current price:";
210 PRINT USING "######.##"; PRICE
```

The format string above describes a printed item that occupies nine character positions. It can print a value with up to five digits to the left of the decimal point; you must include an extra # to allow space for a sign even if there isn't one. You must also allow space for the decimal point. Two digits will be printed to the right of the decimal point. Here's how the result would print for several different values of PRICE:

PRICE	Printed output
12340	Current price: 12340.00
14.5	Current price: 14.50
1.876	Current price: 1.88
.9876	Current price: 0.99
987654.2222	Current price: 987654.20

Each position represented by # appears in the output. The value is aligned at the decimal point. If the value doesn't fill all the positions to the left, leading spaces are supplied. If it doesn't fill all the positions to the right of the decimal point, trailing zeros are supplied. If there are too many digits to the left of the decimal point, the format will be changed. In the last example, notice that only seven significant digits appear. The last printed digit is rounded if it is 5 or greater.

If a decimal point is included in the USING string, and digit positions appear to the left of it, a 0 is printed if the value is less than 1.

Printing Commas. If you want commas to appear in printed output, include at least one in the string, as in ######,.## or ###,###.##. If you place a comma in the format string to the left of the decimal point, the value will have commas inserted every three positions; the two examples are equivalent. Commas are printed only if a digit appears to the left. If not, a space replaces the comma position. Both strings above represent an output value that requires ten positions to print. Here are a few examples for different values of PRICE with this USING string:

PRICE	Printed output
12340	`Current price: 12,340.00`
314.5	`Current price:    314.50`
2001.876	`Current price:  2,001.88`
.9876	`Current price:      0.99`
987654.2222	`Current price: 987654.20`

Printing Dollar Signs If you include a double dollar sign at the beginning of a string, as in $$###,###.##, a dollar sign will be printed just to the left of the first printed digit. The string represents an output item that is 11 positions long; it allows for a dollar sign in front of the longest possible value and a space (for a sign) in front of that. Here are some examples using this string:

PRICE	Printed output
12340	`Current price: $12,340.00`
314.5	`Current price:    $314.50`
2001.876	`Current price:  $2,001.88`
.9876	`Current price:      $0.99`
987654.2222	`Current price:    overflow`

The last example above results in overflow because it doesn't account for all the positions to the left of the decimal point as well as a sign. To make it print correctly, you would have to insert another # in the string.

Additional USING Variations. You can include several variables in a PRINT USING statement; a single format string applies to all of them. The statement PRINT USING "$$####,###.###"; COST; TAXES; TOTAL causes three variables to use the same format. Spacing in the line is achieved by including extra digit positions at the beginning of the format string; you can't include TAB or SPC functions in a PRINT USING statement. And it makes no difference whether you use a comma or semicolon to separate the items. The format string above requires 14 character positions for each value.

If you want to include constants or to use different USING strings in one line, you can use several PRINT and PRINT USING statements, ending all but the last with a semicolon (;). It helps to plan your layout on paper first.

You can simplify your PRINT USING statements by defining the line you want printed as a string variable, then including the variable name instead of the format string in the PRINT USING statement. For example, suppose you want each line to appear in this format:

```
Item No: ####,##   Price: $$####.##   On hand: #####
```

Just define the entire output string as a variable, like this:

```
FORM$="  Item No: ####,##   Price: $$####.##   On hand: #####"
```

Then use it like this:

```
PRINT USING FORM$; ITEMNUMBER; PRICE; ONHAND
```

The PRINT USING statement uses the string variable as the format definition, including the constants and the spacing along with the formats. GW-BASIC uses each format string in turn as it encounters numeric variables. You can use this technique to print several variables in different formats with a single statement.

You can even simplify a single value to be printed with a constant by defining a variable. Any regular letter characters you include in a format string are treated as constants; they have no effect on digit positions in the values. For example, you could use these statements to replace the ones shown earlier in this section:

```
CURRENT$= "  Current price:   $$###,###.##"
PRINT USING CURRENT$; PRICE
```

GW-BASIC provides still more symbols you can use to format numeric and even string items for printing. As you use GW-BASIC, you may want to check these out in your documentation.

---

1. Clear memory, then reload your original working CONVERT program (if you haven't saved this program, see the second Self-Check answer on page 63).
2. Modify the program to display the average values in a format using three decimal places. Use two PRINT statements for each line of output, one to show the plain value and the other to show the formatted value.
3. Define a variable to hold the format as FORMAT1$, then change the PRINT USING statements to reference the string variable instead of the constant.

4. Add a PRINT statement to display labels and the rounded entered values just after the data is entered. In the display, the POUNDS should be shown on the left side of the screen and the INCHES on the right.
5. Change the spacing function you used in item 4 to use the other PRINT spacing function.
6. Save this program as CONUSING.

If you have problems with PRINT USING, remember to put a semicolon after the format string or format variable as well as after each variable listed.

Make sure you don't leave a space after a function name and before the parenthesis.

Your modified program may look something like this:

```
10 ' conversion program
20 INPUT "What is your height (in inches)";INCHES
30 INPUT "What is your weight (in pounds)";POUNDS
40 PRINT
50 PRINT "POUNDS";CINT(POUNDS);SPC(55);"INCHES" CINT(INCHES)
60 PRINT
70 AVWEIGHT=POUNDS/INCHES
80 CONVWEIGHT = POUNDS * 2.2
90 CONVHEIGHT = INCHES * 2.54
100 AVECONV = CONVWEIGHT/CONVHEIGHT
110   FORMAT1$="####.###"
120 PRINT "Your average weight per inch is ";
130 PRINT USING FORMAT1$; AVWEIGHT
140 PRINT "Average Weight per centimeter:";
150 PRINT USING FORMAT1$;AVECONV
160 PRINT "Thank you"
170 END
```

Your program may be quite different and still be correct.

Programming Techniques

Figure 3.5 shows a program that uses arithmetic and formats it for output. This program demonstrates several programming techniques that you may find useful. You have already learned to use all the statements included in this program. The techniques covered in this section are useful even in short programs; you'll find them more valuable in longer programs.

```
 10 ' Calculating and preparing a bill
 20 ' Get the input values
 30 INPUT "Type the item ordered:  ", A$
 40 INPUT "How many items"; COUNT
 50 INPUT "What is the price"; PRICE
 60 INPUT "What is the sales tax"; TAX
 70 INPUT "Is the discount $5, $10, $20, or $30";
DISCOUNT
 80 ' Do the required calculations
 90 GROSS = COUNT * PRICE
100 TAXDUE = GROSS * TAX
110 PLUSTAX = GROSS + TAXDUE
120 TOTALDUE = PLUSTAX - DISCOUNT
130 CLS
140 ' Format and display the output
150 PRINT "Item ordered:"; A$
160 PRINT
170 PRINT " Unit Price";SPC(3);"Quantity";SPC(10);
"Tax"; SPC(3); "Discount"
180 PRINT USING "$$##,###.##"; PRICE;
190 PRINT USING "########.##"; COUNT;
200 PRINT USING "$$#######,.##"; TAXDUE;
210 PRINT USING "$$#####,.##"; DISCOUNT
220 PRINT
230 PRINT "Amount due:  ";
240 PRINT USING "$$#####,.##"; TOTALDUE
250 END
```

Figure 3.5. Taxation Program

The program gets input for the item purchased, the quantity, the price, the tax rate, and the discount rate. Based on these values, it calculates how much the customer owes. Then it formats and displays the itemized information.

Program Structure

The program structure in Figure 3.5 is a typical one. The program has three major functional components, which are handled in clearly separate parts of the program. Comments help to explain the program structure.

First the program gathers all the input it needs in lines 20 through 70. In this example, the input comes from the keyboard. Next the program does all the calculations in lines 80 through 120. Finally, it formats and displays the output in lines 140 through 240. The output has a header (line 170) to help make it easier to read. The calculated values appear below the header line.

Preparing to Program

Before you start entering lines into your GW-BASIC editor, take a moment to plan your program on paper. Make sure you know what the program is going to do. Know what the output you will produce should look like. Know what calculations must take place. While it is relatively easy to modify lines in a GW-BASIC program, structural changes are awkward once the program has been entered and tested.

As you work with longer programs in later chapters, you'll find that a few minutes spent planning the program on paper saves much time at the keyboard. It is also likely to save time in debugging your program.

Effectiveness

Every program, to be any use at all, must be effective; that is, it must do what it sets out to do. If a program calculates sales tax, it must do so correctly, using the correct rate. If a program figures out the monthly payment for a particular mortgage loan at a given interest rate, it must use the correct formula.

Once you are sure you have the right details in a program, test it. Try it with values for which you know the answer. Use very large and very small values to see if you still get the right answer. If there are input limitations, display them on the screen. In Chapter 4 you'll learn to test for input that doesn't match what the program needs.

Clarity

You can make a program easier to keep up to date by keeping it simple. Make sure you and your colleagues can read it, not just the GW-BASIC interpreter. This involves placing only one statement per line and using indentation to set apart groups of statements.

Document the program well, explaining what it does. Document complex expressions. But don't bother to explain lines that are perfectly clear; if a statement multiplies two values, that doesn't call for documentation. If you used sensible variable names, the line is probably perfectly clear. Then again, if you use X1 and X2 as variable names, you might want to document that a particular line calculates the area of a rectangle.

Summary

To perform arithmetic in a program, use the operators +, −, *, /, and ^; use parentheses to modify the order in which they are evaluated. Arithmetic expressions can be used anywhere a numeric variable or constant can be used.

The CINT, INT, and FIX functions let you truncate a decimal value; CINT rounds the result, FIX truncates, and INT uses the next lower integer for negative values.

The CSNG and CDBL functions convert numeric values to single or double precision.

The SQR function calculates the square root of a nonnegative number.

The SGN function returns a value that indicates the sign of a variable value.

The ABS function gives the absolute value of a variable or expression.

The RND function generates a random number between 0 and 1; use INT(RND * n) to find a random whole number between 0 and $n - 1$.

The RANDOMIZE statement provides a new seed number for random number generation.

The TAB and SPC functions let you insert tabs and spacing into printed or displayed lines.

The PRINT USING statement lets you format values for output, specifying the number of digits to print, as well as dollar sign and comma placement if desired.

Exercise

In this exercise, you'll write three short programs that use many of the commands and techniques covered in this chapter. Arithmetic at some level becomes a part of virtually every GW-BASIC program.

1. Write a program to get six values from the keyboard, then calculate and display the average to two decimal places.
2. Test the program and modify it until it works correctly. Then save it as 3AVG.BAS and clear memory.

3. Write a program to calculate an auto repair bill. It will have to get the cost of parts and labor from the keyboard, along with a tax rate. Then it must calculate the total cost, using tax only on the parts. Display the complete statement for the customer.

4. Test the program and modify it until it works correctly. Then save it as 3BILL.BAS.

5. Write a program to generate numbers for you to use in your city lottery. Write a segment to produce 6 random numbers between 6 and 49. (You can find a value between 0 and 43, then add 6 to the result before displaying it.)

6. Test the program until it works correctly. Then save it as 3LOT.BAS.

Your programs use many of the features covered in this chapter. Here's a sample program for item 1:

```
10 ' Calculate average
20 PRINT "This program averages 6 items."
30 PRINT
40 INPUT "Enter item 1: ",ITEM1
50 INPUT "Enter item 2: ",ITEM2
60 INPUT "Enter item 3: ",ITEM3
70 INPUT "enter item 4: ",ITEM4
80 INPUT "Enter item 5: ",ITEM5
90 INPUT "Enter item 6: ",ITEM6
100 TOTAL = ITEM1+ITEM2+ITEM3+ITEM4+ITEM5+ITEM6
110 ' Print the output
120 PRINT
130 AVERAGE = TOTAL / 6
140 PRINT USING "The average is ######.##"; AVERAGE
150 END
```

Here's a sample program for item 3:

```
10 ' calculate repair bill
20 INPUT "Enter the cost of parts: ", PARTS
30 INPUT "Enter the cost of labor: ", LABOR
40 INPUT "Enter the tax rate: ", TAXRATE
50 ' calculate the total
60 TAXES - PARTS * TAXRATE
70 TOTAL = PARTS + LABOR + TAXES
80 CLS
90 PRINT USING "Total parts:   $$###.##";PARTS
100 PRINT USING "Total labor:   $$###.##";LABOR
110 PRINT USING "Tax on parts:   $$##.##";TAXES
120 PRINT
130 PRINT USING "Total due:    $$####.##"; TOTAL
140 END
```

Here's a sample program for item 5:

```
10 RANDOMIZE TIMER
20 PRINT "This program generates six random numbers between 6
and 49."
30 PRINT INT(RND*44) + 6
40 PRINT INT(RND*44) + 6
50 PRINT INT(RND*44) + 6
60 PRINT INT(RND*44) + 6
70 PRINT INT(RND*44) + 6
80 PRINT INT(RND*44) + 6
90 END
```

Your programs may be different and still be correct.

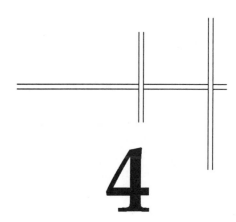

4

Branching and Decisions

So far, all the statements in your programs have been executed in sequence, one line after another. No branching or decision making has taken place. Most programs, of course, involve a lot more than just a sequential execution of statements. This chapter deals with GW-BASIC statements that let you create and manage branching. You'll learn to code conditions to make the program select the next statement to be executed depending on what is happening. These conditions can be used in several different statements to control branching in your programs. You'll also learn some programming techniques that help you write clear programs. You will learn to:

- Determine the structure of needed branching
- Define a condition
- Use the IF statement to test a condition and execute the appropriate statements
- Define a subroutine using the RETURN statement and execute it with the GOSUB statement
- Use the GOTO statement to transfer control unconditionally
- Define and use case structures with ON...GOSUB and ON...GOTO statements
- Read a single keypress with the INKEY$ variable
- Consider good programming style in branching programs

Branching in Programs

Any useful program requires a great deal of branching. It may repeat itself or a major portion of itself. It may send a special message if a certain thing happens. It may make many decisions in achieving its object. In this section we will look at branching in general. You'll see how the logic of what you want the program to do controls the sort of branching you need. GW-BASIC allows for many different logical structures in programs.

The Unconditional Branch

The easiest type of program branch to imagine is the unconditional branch. No matter what happens, you want the program to execute next a statement that isn't in sequence. GW-BASIC provides two statements that produce an unconditional branch. One (GOTO) branches to the specified statement and continues execution from that point, forgetting where it came from. The other (GOSUB) branches to the named statement and continues execution from there; but when it encounters a RETURN statement, control returns to the point where the GOSUB was executed.

Figure 4.1 shows diagrams of both types of branch. Each rectangle in these diagrams represents a single program statement.

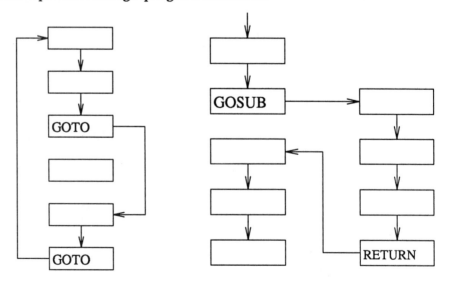

Figure 4.1. Structure of Unconditional Branches

The GOTO Statement

GW-BASIC provides the GOTO statement to jump to a different line number in the program. It lets you name a line number; whatever you name is executed next. GOTO 1000 transfers control to line 1000 and leaves it there; execution continues in sequence until some other statement transfers it again or the program ends. The diagram on the left in Figure 4.1 shows two uses of GOTO. One branch skips over several statements to a point later in the program. The other causes a branch back toward the beginning. Here's an example of branching:

```
10 PRINT "One"
20 PRINT "Two"
30 PRINT "Three"
40 GOTO 70
50 PRINT "Four"
60 PRINT "Five"
70 PRINT "Six"
80 PRINT "Seven"
90 END
```

When this program is run, the output looks like this:

```
One
Two
Three
Six
Seven
```

The statement on line 40 causes execution control to jump to line 70 and continue from there.

Using GOTO

If you use many GOTO statements in a program, it gets very difficult to read the program. It's a good idea to make the target of a GOTO statement a comment that indicates where the GOTO statement is located. The last several lines in the program segment above could be modified to look like this:

```
70 ' Target of line 40 GOTO
80 PRINT "Six"
90 PRINT "Seven"
100 END
```

```
10 'This program shows how to create a loop with GOTO
20 PRINT "You can use this program to calculate volumes."
30 PRINT "To end the program, press Ctrl-Break."
300 'Beginning of loop from 370
310 PRINT "Use the same units in both values."
320 INPUT "Enter the radius: "; RADIUS
330 INPUT "Enter the height: "; HEIGHT
340 VOLUME = 3.1416*(RADIUS^2)*HEIGHT
350 PRINT "The volume of this tank is"; VOLUME
360 PRINT
370 GOTO 300
380 END
```

Figure 4.2. Creating a Loop with GOTO

The GOTO statement provides an easy way to create a loop in a program; at the end of a series of statements, you use a GOTO statement to branch back to the beginning. Figure 4.2 shows an example. When execution of this program begins, lines 20 and 30 produce messages on the screen. Lines 310 through 360 display messages, get input, calculate, and produce output. Line 370 then branches back to line 300 and the loop repeats. Line 300 contains a comment that marks the target of the GOTO statement.

If you use RENUM to renumber the lines in this program using the default values, they will be numbered from 10 through 120. The current line 370 will look like this: 110 GOTO 40. The line number reference is automatically changed to match the new number of the target line. But line 40 (the former line 300) still has the same comment. The renumber function doesn't affect comments, but it does change references if a referenced line is renumbered.

A loop like the one in Figure 4.2 has no exit; it is a closed, endless, or infinite loop. At the keyboard, you can interrupt an endless loop by pressing Ctrl-ScrollLock or Ctrl-Break. Later in this chapter you'll learn to include conditions to let the user (or the program) end the loop.

You can use an unconditional branch command to transfer control to the beginning of a set of statements to be executed, then at the end use another GOTO statement to return control. The more you use GOTO in a program, however, the harder it is to track the logic of your program.

When to Use GOTO

A program that uses this technique for branching can accumulate many GOTO statements. It can be very difficult to read such a program and figure out what is happening, especially when it isn't running correctly.

```
10 ' Calculating and preparing a bill
20 PRINT "Press Ctrl-ScrollLock when you are ready to
stop"
30 ' Start the program processing
40 ' Get the input values
50     INPUT "What is the item ordered";A$
60     INPUT "How many items"; COUNT
70     INPUT "What is the price"; PRICE
80     INPUT "What is the sales tax"; TAX
90     INPUT "Is the discount $5, $10, $20, or $30";
DISCOUNT
100 ' Do the required calculations
110     GROSS = COUNT * PRICE
120     TAXDUE = GROSS * TAX
130     PLUSTAX = GROSS + TAXDUE
140     TOTALDUE = PLUSTAX - DISCOUNT
150     CLS
160    ' Format and display the output
170     PRINT "Item ordered: "; A$
180     PRINT
190     PRINT " Unit Price"; "    "; "Quantity";
SPC(10); "Tax    ";" Discount"
200     PRINT USING "$$##,###.##"; PRICE;
210     PRINT USING "########.##"; COUNT;
220     PRINT USING "$$#######,.##"; TAXDUE;
230     PRINT USING "$$#####,.##"; DISCOUNT
240     PRINT
250     PRINT "Amount due:   ";
260     PRINT USING "$$#####,.##"; TOTALDUE
270 GOTO 30
280 END
```

Figure 4.3. Using GOTO for Branching

In short simple programs, GOTO is a convenient way to set up a loop and repeat a series of lines. The GOTO statement is also useful in error situations, when you want to get out of the program easily. Later in this chapter you'll learn to test for conditions that might call for use of a GOTO statement. The program in Figure 4.3 shows how you might use GOTO to set up a repeated set of lines. This program is based on the one in Figure 3.5. We added a message about how to break the loop on line 20, a comment to mark the beginning of the loop on line 30, and a GOTO statement on line 270.

Given that you don't want to use GOTO for all your branching, there are some appropriate times to use it. In most cases, if you use GOTO, branch to a higher line number, toward the end of the program. Or use it to create a loop within a closed set of statements as in Figure 4.3. Documenting the target of

GOTO statements helps you keep your program clear. Using too many GOTO statements, especially without documenting the branch points, can make it difficult or impossible to track the program logic.

1. Enter the program from Figure 3.4 and test it. Then list it on the screen.
2. Modify the program so that it repeats itself until the user presses Ctrl-ScrollLock or Ctrl-Break.
3. Test the program. Use Ctrl-ScrollLock or Ctrl-Break to stop it. Modify it if it isn't working correctly.
4. Renumber the lines, then save it as MORENUMS.

The bold lines in the program below are added to the program from Figure 3.4:

```
10 ' This program generates random numbers
20 ' Beginning of program loop
30 RANDOMIZE TIMER
40 PRINT  "This program generates a random integer between"
50 PRINT "   1 and the number you enter."
60 INPUT  "Type the upper limit: ", LIMIT
70 PRINT INT(RND*LIMIT+1)
80 GOTO 20
90 END
```

Your program may be different and still be correct.

The GOSUB Statement

You can use GOSUB much as you do GOTO, but the effect is quite different. Execution jumps to the line number you supply, but when GW-BASIC encounters a RETURN statement, control returns to the statement following GOSUB, as shown in the diagram on the right in Figure 4.1.

The set of lines called by a GOSUB statement is called a subroutine, and it generally performs a single task. It can be executed from anywhere in the program. Subroutines aren't normally executed in the regular program sequence, so they aren't numbered in with the main line of your program. They generally start with a higher round number, such as 500 for a short program or 4000 for a long one. Here's a sample subroutine:

```
2000  REM THIS SUBROUTINE CALCULATES VARIOUS VALUES
2010  REM BASED ON TWO FIELDS NAMED LENGTH AND WIDTH
2020  AREA=LENGTH*WIDTH
2030  PERIMETER=(LENGTH+WIDTH)*2
```

```
10 REM PROGRAM TO DEMONSTRATE SUBROUTINE USAGE
20 PRINT "This program asks for length and width
values."
30 GOSUB 1000      ' get the input
40 GOSUB 2000      ' do the processing
50 GOSUB 3000      ' prepare the output
60 PRINT "To check another set of values, type RUN."
70 END
1000 ' This subroutine gets the input values
1010 PRINT "Use the same unit of measurement for
each."
1020 PRINT "Use decimal points if appropriate."
1030 INPUT "Length: ", LENGTH
1040 INPUT "Width:  ", BREADTH
1050 RETURN
2000 ' This subroutine calculates the results
2010 ' based on two variables named LENGTH and BREADTH
2020 AREA = LENGTH * BREADTH
2030 PERIMETER = (LENGTH+BREADTH) * 2
2040 AVESIDE = ((LENGTH*2)+(BREADTH*2)) / 4
2050 RETURN
3000 ' This subroutine prepares and sends the output
3010 PRINT "Area:         "; AREA
3020 PRINT "Perimeter:    "; PERIMETER
3030 PRINT "Average side: "; AVESIDE
3040 PRINT
3050 RETURN
```

═══════════ Figure 4.4. Program with Subroutines

```
2040 AVESIDE=LENGTH+WIDTH/2
2050 RETURN
```

Every subroutine ends with RETURN; that's all there is to the statement. When a subroutine is executed, RETURN sends control back to where the program called the subroutine. If a RETURN statement is executed without a subroutine having been called, GW-BASIC ignores it.

To execute the above subroutine, a program would use the statement GOSUB 2000. The GOSUB statement includes the line number of the first line in the subroutine. Figure 4.4 shows a program that uses GOSUB statements to execute subroutines. The program first displays a message. Line 30, GOSUB 1000, branches to the subroutine starting at line 1000 to get input values; when GW-BASIC encounters RETURN (line 1050) it branches back to the end of the GOSUB 1000 statement. Then line 40 executes the subroutine starting at line

2000. Line 50 executes the subroutine starting at line 3000. Notice that each subroutine ends with a RETURN statement. After control returns from the last subroutine, the message on line 60 is printed and the program ends. If the END statement were omitted, all three subroutines would be executed once more when control reached them normally.

To cause the program to repeat, line 60 could be replaced with these lines:

```
60 PRINT "Press Ctrl-Break to end the program"
65 GOTO 30
```

When execution reaches line 65, control branches back to line 30 and the three subroutines are executed again.

Advantages of Subroutines

The major advantage of subroutines is that they can be executed many times from many locations in a program. They can even be copied into other programs and used there. A subroutine must be included as part of the program that calls it, since GOSUB refers to a line in the same program.

Subroutines also make the structure of the program clear to both the programmer and any later readers. The programmer can decide what subroutines are needed and code them separately; this makes finding program errors much easier. Notice in Figure 4.4 that lines 30, 40, and 50 execute the subroutines and briefly explain their functions.

In addition, subroutines make it easier to modify the program later. You might replace an entire subroutine, for example. At the very least, you have to make changes in only one place that can have effects in all parts of the program.

Techniques with Subroutines

In general, put all your subroutines at the end of the program; use an END statement before the first subroutine. Number your subroutines with round numbers, starting with a number larger than the highest program line. It's a good idea to use a remark as the first line to document the purpose of the subroutine. As your programs get longer, you'll find you forget the purpose of some of them. Since each subroutine ends with RETURN, you'll be able to see them easily. Some programmers like to indent the lines between the first and last in a subroutine to make them more obvious in a program listing.

It really doesn't matter what sequence you code subroutines in. It is convenient to number them in the logical sequence in which they are used, but that isn't necessary. If you find you need another subroutine, just give it an entry line number higher than the end of the last one in the program. Or use a group of sequential line numbers that haven't yet been used. Remember that GW-BASIC puts all lines in their numbered order internally.

You can use subroutines for many actions, even if they are performed only once as shown in Figure 4.4. They are most useful, however, when they are performed several times. Use the main sequential line of the program to call subroutines. For example, typical programs like the one just examined get input, do some processing, and produce some output. Here's a general structure for coding programs using subroutines:

```
10 REMarks about program
30 'Set up whatever looping is needed
40 'Subroutine 700 gets the input
50 GOSUB 700
60 'Subroutine 800 does the processing
70 GOSUB 800
80 'Subroutine 900 does the output
90 GOSUB 900
100 REM Final statements
110 END
700 'LINES TO GATHER THE INPUT
...
780 RETURN
800 'LINES TO DO THE CALCULATIONS
...
880 RETURN
900 'LINES TO PREPARE THE OUTPUT
...
980 RETURN
```

A similar structure can be used in most programs, as you'll discover as you continue learning GW-BASIC through this self-teaching guide.

1. Write a subroutine beginning at line 1000 to ask the user to enter the first and last names.
2. Write a subroutine beginning at line 2000 to print the message "Hello, firstname lastname".
3. Write the main line of the program, from a comment through END, to execute both subroutines one time.
4. Test the program, then save it as SUBS1.

5. Modify the program so that it repeatedly executes the printing sub-routine itself. Each time the Hello message is printed, it should be preceded with a number indicating whether it the first, second, and so forth time it is being printed.
6. Test the program, then save it as SUBS2.

Your final program will look something like this:

```
10 ' Program to prepare and number messages
20 GOSUB 1000
30 ' Target of repeating loop
40 COUNTER = 1
50 GOSUB 2000
60 GOTO 30
70 END
1000 ' Subroutine to get input values
1010 INPUT "Type your first name: ",FIRSTNAME$
1020 INPUT "Type your last name:  ",LASTNAME$
1030 RETURN
2000 ' Subroutine to print output
2010 PRINT USING "###" ; COUNTER;
2020 PRINT "Hello, "; FIRSTNAME$; " "; LASTNAME$
2030 RETURN
```

Your program may be quite different and still be correct.

Conditions

A branch is often based on some condition. You may want the program to execute several statements if the value of a variable is over 21. You may want it to branch somewhere if the value of a variable is negative. You may want it to do something if two variables have the same value. You might use statements such as the following to handle these situations:

```
100 IF AGE>21 THEN PRINT "This person is over twenty
one.":BEEP:BEEP

200 IF SGN(TOTAL)=(-1) THEN PRINT "The value of
TOTAL is negative."

300 IF NAME <> BINGO THEN GOSUB 1000 ELSE GOSUB 2000
```

The condition in each appears in bold. You'll learn to handle all these types of conditions in this chapter.

Operator	Relationship	Expression
=	Equal to	AGE=OFAGE
<>	Not equal to	NAME<>OLDNAME
<	Less than	AGE<21
>	Greater than	AGE>21
<=	Less than or equal to	AGE<=MINOR
>=	Greater than or equal to	AGE>=65

Figure 4.5. Relational Operators

Writing Simple Conditions

A condition is specified in the form of a relational expression, which expresses how two objects are related. AGE = 30 is a relational expression, as is AGE < 65 (AGE less than 65). In both cases, the objects on both sides of the relational operator are related. You can use constants, variables, and arithmetic expressions on either side. The condition in a relational expression is always part of a larger statement. GW-BASIC evaluates the expression and gets a result, which it uses in determining the step in executing the program. If the condition is false, the result is 0. If the condition is true, the result is 1. You can consider a true result to be true, yes, or –1; a false result is false, no, or 0.

Figure 4.5 shows the relational operators, their meanings, and an example of each. Unlike arithmetic expressions, no variable values are changed in the relational expression. The value of –1 or 0 is generated internally and is available automatically to the statement that includes the condition. The program never uses these values.

In a relational expression, you use variable names and constants much as for arithmetic expressions. You can use variables, constants, or a combination on both sides if necessary. Variable names are treated as having value zero if they haven't been given a different value. Type numeric constants in valid format. And use double quotes to enclose string constants, as in NAME$ = "JANE". Both sides of the expression must be either numeric or string; you'll get an error message if you mix them.

The relational operators work just as they do in mathematics for numeric values. As in arithmetic expressions, you can include spaces around the operators if you wish. And as in arithmetic expressions, you can't have two operators adjacent. If you want to compare a variable to a negated one, you could use –PRICE < NEGVAL or NEGVAL >= (–PRICE).

Evaluating Simple Conditions

When AGE has the value 21, both AGE < 21 and AGE > 21 are false; in this case, AGE = 21 is true. Suppose the value of the variable AGE is 64 and JOB has the value 6. The expression JOB < 6 is false, since JOB has the value 6. The expression JOB < AGE is true, since 6 is less than 64. The expression AGE+10 < 75 is true, since AGE+10 equals 74 which is less than 75. Whenever an arithmetic expression is included in a relational expression, the arithmetic is performed first. You can use parentheses to make this clear if you like. The expression (AGE+10) < 75 has the same result as the expression AGE+10<75; the parentheses have no effect here.

Reversing Conditions

Some of the relational operators can be reversed and have the same effect; when they are reversed, you can transfer the objects to the opposite side of the operator. For example, AGE = 21 and 21 = AGE are both true. AGE = HOLDER and HOLDER = AGE will have the same value, no matter what the current values of the two variables. The same is true for the not equal condition; if AGE doesn't equal HOLDER, then HOLDER doesn't equal AGE so AGE <> HOLDER has the same result as HOLDER <> AGE. The opposite of the equal operator (=) is the not equal operator (<>); with the same objects it will have the opposite result.

It's not the same for the other relational operators. Clearly, AGE > 21 is not the same as 21 > AGE. And using AGE < 21 is not the opposite either, since when AGE has the value 21 both conditions are false. The opposite of the less-than operator (<) is the greater-than-or-equal-to (>=) operator. Similarly, the opposite of the greater-than operator (>) is the less-than-or-equal-to (<=) operator. A good way to test this is to try a known value on one side of the operator.

String Operations

String conditions are handled in much the same way as numeric ones. You use the same operators. For string values, GW-BASIC uses the ASCII collating sequence, which is basic alphabetical order with the numbers first, then lowercase letters, followed by uppercase letters. Symbols appear at various locations before and after these characters.

Strings are compared one character at a time. If the values are "Michael" and "Monica", GW-BASIC starts by comparing the first character in each string. They are identical, so it continues to the second character in each string. The letter "i" is higher than "o," so "Michael" is greater than "Monica." You can find the complete ASCII collating sequence in Appendix B. The important thing to remember is that lowercase letters are always higher than uppercase letters, so "michael" is greater than "Michael."

Complex Conditions

You can create more complex conditions by using arithmetic expressions on both sides of the relational operator. For example, suppose your program has to check to see if the balance on a purchase exceeds the remaining credit limit by at least $10. The condition (assuming all variables have valid values) looks like this: (CLIMIT–OUTSTANDING) > (BILLBALANCE+10). GW-BASIC will do the arithmetic, but it won't change the values of any of the variables involved. It will then compare the temporary values as specified in the expression.

Even though you can develop complex and compound conditions, your program will be easier to debug if you keep the conditions simple and straightforward. Use a series of separate conditions rather than one very complex one whenever you can.

Program Logic

Once you have a condition, you can have the program decide what to do. How the program makes these decisions, what it compares, and how it handles decision and branching are some of the factors that make programming the complex and useful skill it is. Logic can have several structures; we'll cover just a few in this section.

Simple Logic Structures

The simplest logic structure evaluates a condition and performs some operation if it is true. Then program execution then continues as before. A slightly less simple logic structure evaluates a condition, then performs a particular operation if it is true and a different one if it is false. Then, in either case, it

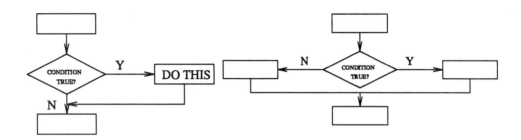

Figure 4.6. Simple Logic Structures

proceeds with the same operation. Figure 4.6 shows diagrams of these two structures. In English, the structure on the left could be written out like this:

```
if the condition is true
  then do this
continue with other statements
```

The structure on the right could be written out like this:

```
if the condition is true
  then do A
  else do B
continue with other statements
```

The simple logic structures let you specify a single statement or a set of statements to be executed if the condition is true and, if you like, another set to be executed if the condition is false. You can use a GOTO statement to branch out of the sequence. And you can use a GOSUB to execute a subroutine then return control.

The IF Statement

Now that you have some idea of what conditions are, you are ready to try to use them in programs. One major use of conditions is in the IF statement, which lets your program make decisions and take alternative actions. The IF statement can create either of the logic structures shown in Figure 4.6. It can specify something to be done when the condition is true or a specific action for each case.

IF Statement Format

The IF statement format is more complex than any you've seen so far, including both optional and required elements. Here it is:

IF *condition*[,]THEN *statement(s)*[,][ELSE *statement(s)*]

Any item in square brackets is optional, so you can omit the commas or include them. The entire ELSE part is optional; use it if you need a false action. The words in uppercase letters are required if you use the part of the statement that includes them. So you must use the words IF and THEN in each IF statement that uses this format, but you need ELSE only if you provide a false action. Here are some examples of valid IF statements:

```
IF JOB=0000 THEN PRINT "No job number entered"
IF JOB>40 THEN GOSUB 4000 ELSE GOSUB 8000
```

You can include one or more statements following THEN and ELSE. If more than one statement is to be executed, use a colon (:) to separate them. The statements following THEN, up to ELSE or the carriage return at the end of the line, are executed when the condition is true. If the ELSE portion is included, the statements following ELSE, up to the carriage return at the end of the line, are executed when the condition is false. The entire IF statement must be included on one line; that limits it to 255 characters in length.

Suppose the value of AGE is 71 when the program encounters this statement: IF AGE > 65 THEN PRINT "Possibly retired". The condition is true, so the message is printed. The statement IF AGE > 65 THEN PRINT "Possibly retired" : BEEP ELSE PRINT "Most likely not retired" causes the appropriate message to be printed. If the condition is true, the computer beeps as well. If you omit the colon when you use multiple statements, you'll get a syntax error when running the program.

Using GOSUB is generally easier than using multiple statements for either the true or false action. You can then code the appropriate subroutine at the end of the program and it will be executed when needed.

Using GOTO in an IF statement lets you branch out very easily depending on a condition. In fact, GW-BASIC lets you omit the word THEN or GOTO if you use GOTO; IF AGE > 21 GOTO 1000 and IF AGE > 21 THEN 1000 are both valid statements. Since the word THEN is always valid and often required, we'll continue to use it. As indicated earlier, use GOTO only when GOSUB won't do the job.

The statements included in an IF statement can be any valid GW-BASIC statements, even one that sends control to another part of the program. If you use GOTO following either THEN or ELSE, make it the last statement of the action; you can't transfer control back to the middle of an IF statement, only to a specific line number. Using GOSUB gives you more control; you could use ... THEN GOSUB 8000 : BEEP ELSE ... in a program. The system will beep on returning from executing the subroutine and before continuing to the next statement.

You can even use an IF statement if you need nested decision making. Using nested IF statements is covered later in this chapter.

Structuring IF Statements

The general format of an IF statement lets you easily use a THEN (true) branch or both THEN (true) and ELSE (false) branches. Sometimes you may want to use only a false branch. In that case, you can omit the statement to be executed for a true condition, but you must include the word THEN; you can change the condition around and omit the ELSE portion if you prefer. For example, suppose you want a program to check the age to see if it is over 21. If so, there is no problem, but if not, you want to print a message. You could use either of these logical structures:

```
if age greater than 21
    then do nothing
    else print message
continue
```

or

```
if age less than or equal to 21
    then print message
continue
```

The first logical structure could be written as IF AGE > 21 THEN ; ELSE PRINT "Age wrong". The second could be written as IF AGE <= 21 PRINT "Age wrong". The effects are the same.

Programs Containing IF Statements

The program shown in Figure 4.7 uses an IF statement to send a message based on the user input. If the user enters a value larger than 10, a message is displayed. If not, the system beeps.

```
10 ' Beginning of program
20 PRINT "Enter 10 or lower to hear the beep"
30 INPUT INVALUE
40 IF INVALUE > 10 THEN PRINT "So you don't want the
beep, right?"
50 IF INVALUE <= 10 THEN BEEP
60 GOTO 20
70 END
```

══════════════ Figure 4.7. Simple IF Statements

The program in Figure 4.7 uses two separate IF statements to accomplish the desired result with the simplest form of IF. You could combine the two in one statement with 40 IF INVALUE > 10 THEN PRINT "So you don't want the beep, right?" ELSE BEEP instead. If you delete line 50 the effect is the same when the program is run.

You have probably noticed that the program lines can get quite long if you include messages to be printed. While that doesn't bother GW-BASIC, you may like to have shorter program lines. One way to handle it is to define messages as variables and print them that way. Figure 4.8 shows an example. Using variables to store messages is a good programming technique. You can then print the same message from anywhere in the program by naming the variable in a PRINT statement. If you decide to change the message, you must fix it in only one place.

If several statements are to be executed by either action, the best technique is to use a GOSUB statement following THEN or ELSE. After the subroutine is executed, control returns to the point within the IF statement to continue execution.

You can also use IF statements to end a loop. You could modify the program in Figure 4.7 to let the user choose to continue. Here's how the last part of the program would be changed:

```
70 INPUT "Press 1 and Enter to continue"; CONTINUE$
80 IF CONTINUE$ = "1" THEN GOTO 20 ELSE END
```

Another possibility is to let the computer decide when to quit based on an internal value. For example, here's how you would modify the program to end after 10 times:

```
15 COUNTER=0
70 COUNTER=COUNTER+1
80 IF COUNTER < 10 THEN GOTO 20 ELSE END
```

```
10 ' Message demonstration
20 MESSRET$ = "Possibly retired"
30 MESSNOT$ = "Most likely not retired"
40 INPUT "Please enter your age "; AGE
50 IF AGE >= 65 THEN PRINT MESSRET$ : BEEP ELSE PRINT
MESSNOT$
60 END
```

Figure 4.8. Using Variables for Messages

Combining Conditions

GW-BASIC lets you combine conditions in an IF statement by connecting them with logical variables AND and OR. If you use AND, both (or all) the conditions must separately evaluate as true in order for the combined condition to be true. If you use OR, only one of the separate conditions need be true. Suppose you want to execute a subroutine only when the value of AGE is over 21 and the value of SEX is "M." You could use IF AGE > 21 AND SEX = "M" THEN GOSUB 4000. If either condition is not true, control won't branch to the subroutine starting at line 4000. Suppose you want to execute the subroutine if the age is under 21 or over 65. You could use IF AGE < 21 OR AGE > 65 GOSUB 4000. When they are connected by OR, only one of the conditions must be true for the combined condition to be true.

If you connect more than two conditions with AND, they must all be true for the THEN portion to be executed. If you connect more than two conditions with OR, only one must be true for the THEN portion of an IF to be executed. While you can construct much more involved condition combinations, avoid them if possible unless you are more experienced at logic. Using straightforward logic helps your programs run more efficiently and is less likely to result in logic errors in your programming.

1. Load the MORENUMS program if necessary.
2. Modify the program so it will show 10 random numbers in the range you specified, then ask the user to press the letter C to see some more. In the IF statement, use OR to connect two conditions to check for either uppercase or lowercase.
3. Test the program, then save the result as MORENUM2.
4. Modify the program again so that it asks for a new value if the requested LIMIT is 10 or 20.

5. Test the program, especially with the values 10 and 20. Save this version as MORENUM3.

Here's how MORENUM2 might look:

```
10 ' This program generates random numbers
20 ' Beginning of program loop
30 RANDOMIZE TIMER
40 PRINT  "This program generates random integers between"
50 PRINT "   1 and the number you enter."
60 INPUT  "Type the upper limit: ", LIMIT
70 COUNTER = 1
80 ' Beginning of small loop
90    PRINT INT(RND*LIMIT+1);
100   COUNTER = COUNTER + 1
110   IF COUNTER < 10 THEN GOTO 80
120   INPUT "Press C to continue", CHOICE$
130   IF CHOICE$ = "C" OR CHOICE$ = "c" THEN GOTO 20
140 END
```

Your MORENUM3 program could include a line like this:

```
65 IF LIMIT <> 10 AND LIMIT <> 20 THEN GOTO 70 ELSE PRINT "Don't
use 10 or 20" : GOTO 60
```

Your program lines could be quite different and still accomplish the desired result.

A New Input Statement

You have been using the INPUT statement to get user input. GW-BASIC has a special variable that holds a single character; if you use this variable, the user won't have to press Enter after typing a single character as input. The INKEY$ variable can be used like this:

```
320 PRINT "Type a number between 1 and 9"
330 A$=INKEY$: IF A$="" THEN GOTO 330
340 PRINT "You pressed  ";A$
```

Notice that the INKEY$ variable is always a string. As such, it has the default null value until a key is pressed. When line 330 is executed, the system just repeats it until such time as a key is pressed. The INKEY$ variable is especially useful when you don't want the user to have to press the Enter key. You might do this if the user is responding to a menu or answering a question. One problem with INKEY$ is that it always produces a string. Even if the user presses 2, it is stored as a string. A condition would have to refer to it as "2" in quotes, rather than as the numeric value 2.

```
10 ' Program segment to try out multiple branching
100 ' Display menu
110 PRINT "You have a choice of four actions:"
120 PRINT "      1. List all the files on screen"
130 PRINT "      2. Print all the files on the printer"
140 PRINT "      3. List just the BAS files on the screen"
150 PRINT "      4. Print just the BAS files on the printer"
160 PRINT "Press a number key from 1 to 4."
170 B$ = INKEY$ : IF B$ = "" THEN GOTO 170
180 IF B$ < "1" OR B$ > "4" THEN PRINT "You pressed the wrong
key. Try again." : GOTO 170
190 IF B$ = "1" THEN GOSUB 1000
200 IF B$ = "2" THEN GOSUB 2000
210 IF B$ = "3" THEN GOSUB 3000
220 IF B$ = "4" THEN GOSUB 4000
230 ' end of multiple branch
240 PRINT "End of program"
250 END
1000 ' user pressed 1
1010 PRINT "You pressed 1" : RETURN
2000 ' user pressed 2
2010 PRINT "You pressed 2" : RETURN
3000 ' user pressed 3
3010 PRINT "You pressed 3" : RETURN
4000 ' user pressed 4
4010 PRINT "You pressed 4" : RETURN
```

Figure 4.9. Menu Program Segment

Figure 4.9 shows a program segment in which the user makes a menu selection, typing a character. Notice that the program segment displays the menu and choices, then waits for the user to press a key. It then checks if the key is in the desired range. If not, another message is displayed and the user is branched back to the INKEY$ statement. When an appropriate key is pressed, a series of IF statements identify the key and execute the appropriate subroutine.

Nested IFs

You have seen how to combine several conditions into a combined condition with AND and OR. In Figure 4.9, you saw how you can use a series of IF statements to perform the appropriate action. Suppose you have four different subroutines to execute based on sex (which has the value "M" or "F") and age (above 65 or not). Figure 4.10 shows three different ways you could code statements to accomplish the same thing.

Example 1: Separate IF statements
```
IF SEX = "M" AND AGE > 65 THEN GOSUB 1000
IF SEX = "M" AND AGE <= 65 THEN GOSUB 2000
IF SEX = "F" AND AGE > 65 THEN GOSUB 3000
IF SEX = "F" AND AGE <= 65 THEN GOSUB 4000
```

Example 2: Secondary IF statements in subroutines
```
IF SEX = "M" THEN GOSUB 920 ELSE GOSUB 950
...
920 'Choices for sex = M
930 IF AGE > 65 THEN GOSUB 1000 ELSE GOSUB 2000
940 RETURN
950 'Choices for sex = F
960 IF AGE > 65 THEN GOSUB 3000 ELSE GOSUB 4000
970 RETURN
```

Example 3: Nested IF statement
```
IF SEX = "M" THEN IF AGE > 65 THEN GOSUB 1000
ELSE GOSUB 2000 ELSE IF AGE > 65 THEN GOSUB 3000 ELSE
GOSUB 4000
```

Figure 4.10. Using Multiple Decisions

As you can see, using separate IF statements or using subroutines to hold subordinate IF statements creates a more readable program. When you nest IFs in a single statement, you have to be careful to make sure the logic is what you intend. An ELSE action is paired with the most recent THEN that isn't paired yet. So in the example, the first ELSE action matches with the immediately preceding THEN action. The second ELSE action matches with the first THEN action; these check the age for value "M" and anything else. The final ELSE matches with the final THEN. If you find this confusing, try to stick with the simple constructions. Place your nested IF statements in subroutines when possible for easier reading. This will help you avoid logic errors in your programs.

1. Suppose you want the user to press any key to continue. Write a statement to stop the program until the user presses something.
2. You want to execute subroutine 1000 if the user pressed "1", 2000 if "2", and 3000 if "3". Write a nested IF to handle this.
3. Write another IF statement to follow the above and display a message for invalid values.

4. If you want, write a short program asking for input and try out your nested IF.

Your statements might look like these:

```
30 C$=INKEY$ : IF C$="" THEN GOTO 30
300 IF C$ = "1" THEN GOSUB 1000 ELSE IF C$ = "2" THEN GOSUB 2000
ELSE IF C$ = "3" THEN GOSUB 3000
310 IF C$ <> "1" AND C$ <> "2" AND C$ <> "3" THEN PRINT "Invalid
value. Try again."
```

Your statements may be different and still be correct. If you write a program to try these out, be sure to prompt the user for appropriate input.

Multiple Branching Logic

Sometimes you may want to perform operations based on several different values of a variable. For example, you might display a menu on the screen and want to execute different statements or subroutines depending on what the user enters. You saw one way of handling this in Figure 4.9. You can also use a multiple branching logic statement for this. The ON statements let you execute a set of statements for each value of a variable or expression.

The ON statements require that the variable be numeric. If you can arrange your program so the values of the variable range from 1 to the upper limit, it works easily. For example, if you start numbering menu items at 1, valid values might be 1, 2, 3, 4, and 5. If the user can enter any numeric value between 1 and another value, the same applies. Then you can use the ON...GOSUB or ON...GOTO statement. Here's how their formats look:

ON *expression* GOSUB *line-numbers*

ON *expression* GOTO *line-numbers*

The expression is an arithmetic expression or a numeric variable name. If the value isn't an integer, it is rounded up to the next whole number. You can separate the line numbers by commas if you wish, but it isn't necessary.

If you use a statement such as ON COUNTER GOSUB 2000, 3000, 4000, 5000, the program will branch to line 2000 if the value of COUNTER is 1, 3000 if the value is 2, and so forth. You can use the same number again if different values of the expression are to have the same effect. You can't omit any numbers, however.

```
10 ' Program segment to try out multiple branching
100 ' Display menu
110 PRINT "You have a choice of four actions:"
120 PRINT "     1. List all the files on screen"
130 PRINT "     2. Print all the files on the printer"
140 PRINT "     3. List just the BAS files on the screen"
150 PRINT "     4. Print just the BAS files on the printer"
160 INPUT "Type a number from 1 to 4 and press Enter: ", B
170 MESSAGE$ = "You pressed the wrong key. Try again."
180 IF B < 1 OR B > 4 THEN PRINT MESSAGE$ : GOTO 160
190 ON B GOSUB 1000, 2000, 3000, 4000
230 ' end of multiple branch
240 PRINT "End of program"
250 END
1000 ' user pressed 1
1010 PRINT "You pressed 1" : RETURN
2000 ' user pressed 2
2010 PRINT "You pressed 2" : RETURN
3000 ' user pressed 3
3010 PRINT "You pressed 3" : RETURN
4000 ' user pressed 4
4010 PRINT "You pressed 4" : RETURN
```

━━━━━━━━━━ Figure 4.11. Multiple Branching with ON...GOSUB

When GW-BASIC encounters an ON...GOTO or ON...GOSUB statement, it first evaluates the expression. In most cases, it's convenient to use a numeric variable. The result must be between 0 and 255 or an error message (Illegal function call) appears. If the value is 0 or greater than the number of line-numbers in the statement, the next statement in sequence is executed. The program can let this happen automatically, or it can include statements to check the values and perform the appropriate action. When the value is between 1 and the number of line numbers listed, control branches to the given line-number that corresponds to the value of the expression.

If your values start at 33 and range upward, you might use an expression like ON VALUE–32 in the statement. If the values are 10, 20, 30, 40, and 50, you could start the statement with ON VALUE/10.

Using ON...GOSUB. Figure 4.11 shows a variation of the program segment in Figure 4.9. This one still lists four choices and asks the user to press 1 through 4 and Enter to select one. (INKEY$ isn't appropriate here because we need a numeric value.) Line 180 checks that the value entered is valid and transfers control back to the INPUT statement if it isn't. While the ON statement does this automatically, checking here keeps the program logic clear to readers. In a practical program, you'll want the user to get a chance to correct errors. When the program knows the value is valid, the ON...GOSUB statement executes the appropriate subroutine based on the value entered.

```
10 ' Program segment to try out multiple branching
100 ' Display menu
110 PRINT "You have a choice of four actions:"
120 PRINT "      A. List all the files on screen"
130 PRINT "      B. Print all the files on the printer"
140 PRINT "      C. List just the BAS files on the screen"
150 PRINT "      D. Print just the BAS files on the printer"
160 INPUT "Type the capital letter and press Enter: ", B$
170 MESSAGE$ = "You pressed the wrong key. Try again."
180 IF B$="A" THEN GOSUB 1000 ELSE IF B$="B" THEN GOSUB 2000 ELSE
IF B$="C" THEN GOSUB 3000 ELSE IF B$="D" THEN GOSUB 4000 ELSE PRINT
MESSAGE$ : GOTO 160
230 ' end of multiple branch
240 PRINT "End of program"
250 END
1000 ' user pressed A
1010 PRINT "You pressed A" : RETURN
2000 ' user pressed B
2010 PRINT "You pressed B" : RETURN
3000 ' user pressed C
3010 PRINT "You pressed C" : RETURN
4000 ' user pressed D
4010 PRINT "You pressed D" : RETURN
```

Figure 4.12. Multiple Branching with Nested IF

If lines 180 and 190 in the program are reversed, there will be no effect in execution if the entered value is between 0 and 255. If it is outside this range, however, attempting to execute the ON...GOSUB statement would cause an Illegal function call message and terminate the program. Checking the values before executing ON...GOSUB prevents a possible program interruption.

Using ON...GOTO. Branching with GOTO works just as you might expect. The statement transfers control to the specified line numbers without keeping track of where the control came from. Although this method uses a great many more GOTO statements, it is possible to keep it contained. In most cases, ON...GOSUB produces a cleaner program and is more desirable.

Remember that control falls through or the program is terminated when a value doesn't fit into the listed range. You'll need a statement before or after ON...GOTO to handle any invalid conditions.

Using a Nested IF. You can achieve much the same effect with a nested IF, although the structure of the program isn't as obvious. You'll need to use a nested IF when the values can't be easily converted to range from 1 to whatever. Figure 4.12 shows a similar segment prepared with a nested IF, using GOSUB to handle the separate parts.

In Figure 4.12, the input is in the form of a letter instead of a number. Not only can you not use the ON statements, you have to check for uppercase or lowercase letters. Notice that we used the INKEY\$ variable here to make it easier for the user.

1. You want the user to enter a value between 1 and 4 to indicate the number of years of college completed. Write a brief program to ask for the input, then use ON...GOSUB to display a message indicating which year for each possible response. If the entry is invalid, ask for a new value. You can write short subroutines to handle the different output. TIP: Sketch it out on paper first!
2. Test your program and correct it until it works. Then save it as COLL1.
3. Now write a similar program to have the user enter F for freshman, S for Sophomore, J for Junior, or L for Senior (last year). You can use the same subroutines as in COLL1. Use a nested IF to handle the branching this time.
4. Test your program and correct it until it works. Then save it as COLL2.

Your first program should look something like this:

```
10 ' Program using ON...GOSUB
20 ' Ask for user input
30 INPUT "How many years have you completed"; YRS
40 IF YRS < 1 OR YRS > 4 THEN GOSUB 500 : GOTO 20
50 ON YRS GOSUB 1000, 2000, 3000, 4000
60 PRINT "Thank you"
70 END
500 ' Subroutine to ask for different input
510 CLS
520 PRINT "You entered"; YRS
530 PRINT "The value must be 1, 2, 3, or 4."
540 PRINT
550 RETURN
1000 ' Subroutine when user entered 1
1010 PRINT "You are a freshman."
1020 RETURN
2000 ' Subroutine when user entered 2
2010 PRINT "You are a sophomore."
2020 RETURN
3000 ' Subroutine when user entered 3
3010 PRINT "You are a junior."
3020 RETURN
4000 ' Subroutine when user entered 4
4010 PRINT "You are a senior."
4020 RETURN
```

Your program could be quite different. You can't use INKEY$ to get the input, since it must be numeric to use ON...GOSUB.

Your second program should look something like this:

```
10 ' Program using ON...GOSUB
20 ' Ask for user input
30 PRINT "Enter the letter that indicates your current standing:"
40 PRINT "    F = Freshman"
50 PRINT "    S = Sophomore"
60 PRINT "    J = Junior"
70 PRINT "    L = Senior (last year)"
80 YR$ = INKEY$ : IF YR$ = "" GOTO 80
90 IF YR$ ="f" THEN YR$="F"
100 IF YR$ ="s" THEN YR$="S"
110 IF YR$ ="j" THEN YR$="J"
120 IF YR$ ="l" THEN YR$="L"
130 IF YR$ ="F" THEN GOSUB 1000 ELSE IF YR$="S" THEN GOSUB 2000
ELSE IF YR$="J" THEN GOSUB 3000 ELSE IF YR$="L" THEN GOSUB 4000
ELSE GOSUB 500
140 PRINT "Thank you"
150 END
500 ' Subroutine to ask for different input
510 CLS
520 PRINT "You entered "; YR$
530 PRINT "The value must be F, S, J, or L."
540 PRINT "You may use lowercase letters if you like."
550 PRINT
560 RETURN
```

This program can use lines 1000 through 4020 (the subroutines) as in the previous program. Your program may be different and still be valid. The real test is whether it works.

Summary

This chapter covered the logic and commands involved in unconditional and conditional branching. Several techniques were covered that will come in handy in most programs you write in the future.

The GOTO statement transfers control to the specified line number and leaves it there.

The GOSUB statement transfers control to the specified line number, executes lines until a RETURN statement is encountered, and then returns control to the statement following GOSUB.

Subroutines executed by GOSUB statements make for clearer and less error-prone programs than those that use many GOTO statements; most programmers avoid GOTO statements unless absolutely necessary.

Conditions let a program determine the next action in a program; program logic is determined by conditions. Relational expressions form the basis of most conditions.

The AND, OR, and NOT operators can be used to create combined conditions and more complex program logic.

The IF statement includes a condition and allows selective statement execution, depending on whether the condition is true or false. IF statements can be nested or they can transfer control out of the main line of the program.

The INKEY$ statement lets the program get a single key input from the keyboard without ⏎ being pressed. It is especially useful in menu selections.

Multiple branching can be set up with ON...GOSUB or ON...GOTO statements, in which the value of a variable determines which of several line numbers is the target of the branch.

Exercise

In this exercise, you will create a complete working program using many of the commands and techniques covered in this chapter. Try writing each section on paper first. The instructions include hints for testing the program as you complete each portion.

1. The first part of the program displays a message, such as "This program will start when you press Enter", then uses INKEY$ to tell when the user is ready. Write and test this part first.
2. The next part of the program should ask if the user wants to do arithmetic (press A) or quit (press Q). It must display a message and get the input (you can use INKEY$ again). Then it must test the input (with IF) and branch based on what it is. Repeat the message and input if the user enters a key other than A or Q (or a or q).
3. If you want to test this part before going on, put in a line for each branch that prints a message if it is reached. You'll replace these lines later.
4. The next major part of the program displays a menu offering a choice between the four arithmetic operations and gets numeric input so it can use ON ... GOSUB to do the work. If you stop after coding the menu but before the ON...GOSUB, you can test it out.
5. Write the part of the program that processes the input and performs the ON...GOSUB operation. You can write "dummy" subroutines that

just print a message for testing purposes. If you'll be polishing up the subroutines at the end, you may want to get input in this part of the program.

6. When control returns from the ON...GOSUB subroutine, the program must display the calculated result and return to the arithmetic/quit choice to continue. Write this part next.

7. The next part of the program handles ending. If your program already has an ending routine (executed when the user selects Quit) you needn't code it again.

8. If your program hasn't handled the possibility of a wrong choice on the arithmetic menu, add it now.

9. If you like, polish up the subroutines so they perform arithmetic. If your IF and ON...GOSUB statements are all working as you expect, you may want to skip this last step. When the program works the way you want it to, save the program as 4CHAPEX.BAS.

Your program will look something like the following. It is broken up into parts that correspond to the questions in the exercise.

1. These lines complete the first item:

```
10 ' Chapter 4 Exercise
20 PRINT "This program will start when you press Enter"
30 A$=INKEY$ : IF A$="" THEN GOTO 30
```

2. These lines complete the second item. You need not do the same formatting we did.

```
40 ' Original choice of arithmetic or quit
50 CHOICE$=""
60 CLS
70 PRINT "Press A for arithmetic or Q to quit: ",CHOICE$
80 CHOICE$=INKEY$ : IF CHOICE$ = "" THEN GOTO 80
90 IF CHOICE$ = "A" OR CHOICE$ = "a" THEN GOTO 130
100 IF CHOICE$ = "Q" OR CHOICE$ = "q" THEN GOTO 280
110 PRINT "You typed the wrong key. Try again."
120 GOTO 70
```

Line 50 is needed after the first time through the loop. The variable that holds the user's choice must be reset to null or line 90 won't work correctly. You may have used a different technique here.

3. If you test at this point, you need temporary statements at lines 80, 130, and 280 (or whatever line numbers you used) so GW-BASIC can find the GOTO targets.

4. These lines complete the next part of the program:

```
130 ' Arithmetic section of program
140 PRINT "What type of arithmetic do you want to do?"
150 PRINT "    1. Addition"
160 PRINT "    2. Subtraction"
170 PRINT "    3. Multiplication"
180 PRINT "    4. Division"
190 INPUT "Type the number and press Enter: ",ARITH
```

5. These lines interpret the input and do the ON...GOSUB operation:

```
200 IF ARITH < 1 OR ARITH > 4 THEN GOTO 400
210 INPUT "What is the first number? ",COUNT1
220 INPUT "What is the second number? ",COUNT2
230 ON ARITH GOSUB 500, 600, 700, 800
```

6. These lines handle the result of the arithmetic subroutines:

```
240 PRINT "The result is "; RESULT
250 PRINT "Press Enter to continue"
260 B$=INKEY$ : IF B$="" THEN GOTO 260
270 GOTO 40
```

7. These lines end the program when the user selects Quit:

```
280 ' Target of QUIT choice
290 PRINT : PRINT "Program ended at your request"
300 END
```

8. These lines handle an invalid choice on the menu:

```
400 ' Wrong choice on arithmetic menu
410 PRINT "You must press a number from 1 to 4. Try again."
420 GOTO 150
```

9. These lines complete the subroutines. You can use just a PRINT statement in each if you just want to test your overall program logic.

```
500 ' Addition subroutine
510 RESULT = COUNT1 + COUNT2
520 RETURN
600 ' Subtraction subroutine
610 RESULT = COUNT1 - COUNT2
620 RETURN
700 ' Multiplication subroutine
710 RESULT = COUNT1 * COUNT2
720 RETURN
800 ' Division subroutine
810 RESULT = COUNT1 / COUNT2
820 RETURN
```

Your program may be quite different and still be correct. If you had trouble with any of the parts, examine the sample solution to help you solve the problems.

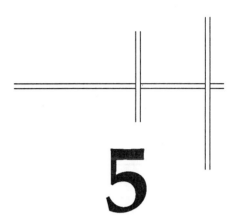

5

Loops and Debugging

This chapter deals with GW-BASIC commands that let you create program loops to be executed in programs as well as to help you debug programs to make them run correctly. Techniques that contribute to both these aims are also included. You will learn to:

- Use FOR and NEXT statements to set up numbered loops
- Use WHILE and WEND statements to set up loops and automatically end them when a condition becomes true
- Interpret error messages and make corrections
- Use TRON and TROFF commands to trace execution of a program
- Use the STOP command to halt program execution during debugging
- Use the CONT command to resume program execution
- Use the CLEAR command to reset all variables to their default status
- Use the FRE function to check the amount of free memory in your system
- Debug programs

Counting Loops

You have seen how to use the GOTO statement to set up a loop in a program. You have also seen how to use the IF statement to escape from a loop as shown in Figure 5.1. As you can tell, this loop causes the values 1 through 10 to be

```
100 I = 1
110 IF I > 10 GOTO 150
120 PRINT I
130 I = I + 1
140 GOTO 110
150 END
```

Figure 5.1. Loop with GOTO and IF Statements

printed before the IF statement causes the loop to end. Similarly, in the FOR...NEXT loop, you specify a beginning and ending value for the loop and an amount to increase the value each time. While a FOR...NEXT loop accomplishes the same thing as the loop shown in Figure 5.1, it executes much faster.

The FOR...NEXT Loop

FOR and NEXT are two separate statements, but they are always used in a pair. You use the FOR statement to start a loop and specify how many times, and what variable to use for counting. Since the FOR variable often isn't integral to the program's meaning, it is convenient to use a single letter to save typing. You'll see variables such as X and I used in FOR statements. You use the NEXT statement to mark the bottom of the loop and cause a branch back to the FOR if the final value of the variable hasn't been reached.

Here's a simple FOR...NEXT loop that executes six times.

```
50 FOR I = 1 TO 6
60    PRINT "Line"; I
70 NEXT
```

When line 50 is executed, the variable I is given the value of 1, then line 60 is executed and "Line 1" is displayed. When line 70 is executed, the value 1 is added to the variable I, making it have the value 2. Then control branches back to the FOR statement on line 50. The variable hasn't reached the value 6 yet, so line 60 is executed, displaying "Line 2" this time. The process continues until the value of I passes 6, then control passes to the statement following the NEXT statement on line 70.

You don't have to use the FOR variable within the loop, although it is often useful. If you want to display the same message 800 times, you could use the following loop:

```
800 FOR X = 1 TO 800
810   PRINT "I will not speak in class."
820 NEXT
```

GW-BASIC uses X to count the loops, but it doesn't use X for anything else. If you want to do calculations using the value of the FOR variable, you could do it as in this example:

```
890 LPRINT "VALUE","SQUARED","CUBED"
900 FOR I = 1 TO 40
910   LPRINT I, I^2, I^3
920 NEXT
```

You'll get the value of I, the squared value, and the cubed value printed for values from 1 through 40. Many of the squared and cubed values will be in scientific notation to save space.

Notice that we indent the line between FOR and NEXT to show the lines that are contained within the loop. This is not necessary to the computer; the GW-BASIC interpreter ignores extra spaces anyway. The indented lines make it a bit easier for the human reader to see the structure of the program at a glance.

While you can use the value of the FOR variable in the loop, be cautious about changing it. While you might want to increase the value to the maximum to cause the loop to end, any other changes in this variable can have unexpected effects.

The Format

You can do much more with FOR loops, making use of the complete statement format. Here's the FOR statement format:

FOR *variable* = n1 TO n2 [STEP n3]

The FOR variable gets its value when the FOR statement is executed. While we used I in these examples, you can use any numeric variable that is not being used for something else. Even if the FOR variable already has a value, it will be reset and modified automatically during execution of the FOR...NEXT loop.

The objects n1, n2, and n3 can each be a constant or variable value or an expression. The initial value of the loop is n1, the final value is n2, and the amount of increment or the step value is n3. If the initial value exceeds the final value at the start, the loop is not executed at all. Initially, the FOR variable is set to the value of n1. Each time a NEXT statement is encountered, the FOR variable is incremented by the value of *n3*; if no STEP value is included, GW-BASIC uses 1. When the FOR variable exceeds the value of *n2* at a NEXT statement, the loop ends and the following statement is executed.

If you use expressions for any of the three, the expression is calculated before the first execution of the FOR...NEXT loop. For example, look at this loop:

```
600 S = 6
610 FOR S = 1 TO S + 5
620    PRINT S;
630 NEXT
```

The semicolon at the end of the PRINT statement causes all the values to appear on the same line. Here's the displayed output:

```
 1   2   3   4   5   6   7   8   9   10   11
```

As soon as the FOR statement execution begins, the expression S + 5 is evaluated, giving the loop a final value of 11. Then S is reset to 1 as the initial value. If the program changes the value of the FOR variable in the loop, the effect can be noticed. As mentioned earlier, a statement in the loop might increase the FOR variable to the maximum to end the loop.

You can use a numeric variable for any of the three values in a FOR statement. As long as the variable is numeric, there are no restrictions. Here's an example:

```
400 INPUT "What is the loop size";FINAL
410 INPUT "What is the step size";STEPSIZE
420 FOR I = 1 TO FINAL STEP STEPSIZE
430 '   body of loop here
440 NEXT
```

Using Fractional Steps. The values of *n1*, *n2*, and *n3* need not be whole numbers and need not be positive, though they often are. If you are counting, you'll be using integers, probably starting with 1. But you may want to calculate something that changes in a different increment, such as .5 or 3.6.

Figure 5.2 shows a loop that calculates the interest on a loan amount in increments of 0.25%, along with the resulting output. This loop is executed 13 times, for interest rates of 9.00, 9.25, 9.50, and so on through 12.00. During each execution, it calculates the interest and prints the current rate and the calculated interest. Figure 5.3 shows the program output.

Using a Negative Step. A FOR...NEXT loop can also use negative numbers, although they must be consistent. FOR I = 10 TO 1 STEP –1 is consistent, since repeatedly applying the step variable to the initial value results in the final

```
200 INPUT "Enter the loan amount: ", LOAN
210 PRINT
220 PRINT "Loan amount requested:   ";LOAN
230 PRINT "        Rate     Amount"
240 FOR I = 9 TO 12 STEP .25
250    RATE = I/100
260    INTEREST = LOAN * RATE
270    PRINT USING "######,.##";I,INTEREST
280 NEXT
290 END
```

Figure 5.2. Routine to Calculate Interest

value. When the step is negative, the body of the loop is skipped if the initial value is less than the final value.

Suppose you want to do a count-down listing. The following loop accomplishes this:

```
300 FOR I = 20 TO 1 STEP -1
310    PRINT I
320 NEXT
```

The result is a listing down the screen starting with 20, 19, and 18 and so on through 3, 2, and 1.

```
260    INTEREST = LOAN * RATE
270    PRINT USING "######,.##";I,INTEREST
280 NEXT
Ok
run
Enter the loan amount 10000

Loan amount requested:    10000
       Rate     Amount
       9.00     900.00
       9.25     925.00
       9.50     950.00
       9.75     975.00
      10.00   1,000.00
      10.25   1,025.00
      10.50   1,050.00
      10.75   1,075.00
      11.00   1,100.00
      11.25   1,125.00
      11.50   1,150.00
      11.75   1,175.00
      12.00   1,200.00
Ok

1LIST   2RUN◆   3LOAD"   4SAVE"   5CONT◆   6,"LPT1 7TRON◆   8TROFF◆ 9KEY      0SCREEN
```

Figure 5.3. Output from Figure 5.2

The NEXT Statement. So far, you've always seen NEXT as a single word. It is valid that way and easiest to type. But you can follow it with the name of the FOR variable for documentation if you wish. This tells the interpreter which FOR...NEXT loop is involved. If a program includes many FOR...NEXT loops, it is often helpful to see NEXT X as a statement, especially if you used several different FOR variables in different loops.

If you do use a variable on the NEXT statement, it must be the correct one. If you use I as the FOR variable, you'll get an error message (NEXT without FOR) if you use NEXT S to mark the bottom of the loop.

FOR...NEXT Programming Techniques

When you create a loop in a program, treat it as a single entity; it should have a single entrance point—the FOR statement—and a single exit point—the NEXT statement. So don't use any point between FOR and NEXT as the target of a GOTO or GOSUB statement. No other part of the program should branch into the middle of the FOR...NEXT loop. And no statement in the loop should branch permanently out of it. If you have to escape the loop, set the FOR variable for the final value, transfer control to the NEXT statement (you can use GOTO here), and you'll be out. You can use a GOSUB statement within the loop, since control automatically returns to that point.

1. Write a loop to print your name five times, numbering the lines.
2. Enter it into GW-BASIC and test it. Correct it until it works.
3. Add a second loop to your program that also prints your name. This one should start numbering lines at 11 and end at 1. Print only the odd numbered lines.
4. Test the program. Correct it until it lists the name six times, numbered 11, 9, 7, 5, 3, and 1.
5. Delete the lines in the second loop, leaving the program with just the first loop.

Your answer to item 1 will look something like this:

```
10 MYNAME$="Ruth Ashley"
20 FOR X=1 TO 5
30   PRINT X, MYNAME$
40 NEXT
```

Your answer to item 3 will look something like this:

```
50 FOR X=11 TO 1 STEP -2
60    PRINT X, MYNAME$
70 NEXT
```

Your programs might be different and still be correct.

Nesting FOR...NEXT Loops

A FOR...NEXT loop can be completely contained within another, as shown in Figure 5.4. Notice that each loop is complete in itself. The loops do not overlap. If they do, you'll get an error message. Each FOR...NEXT loop has a different FOR variable, which is also named on the appropriate NEXT statement. GW-BASIC assumes each NEXT statement refers to the most recent FOR statement; you can omit the FOR variable in the NEXT statement if you like.

For the first value in the outer FOR...NEXT loop, all statements enclosed within it are executed; that means every statement included in the innermost FOR...NEXT loop is executed for each value of the outer loop. In the example, the outer loop is performed three times and the inner loop three times, so the PRINT statement in the inner loop is executed nine times in all.

```
list
100 ' Nested FOR ... NEXT loop
110 FOR X = 1 TO 3
120    PRINT "Outer loop"; X
130    FOR Y = 1 TO 3
140      PRINT "  Inner loop"; Y
150    NEXT
160 NEXT
Ok
run
Outer loop 1
  Inner loop 1
  Inner loop 2
  Inner loop 3
Outer loop 2
  Inner loop 1
  Inner loop 2
  Inner loop 3
Outer loop 3
  Inner loop 1
  Inner loop 2
  Inner loop 3
Ok
```

```
1LIST  2RUN+  3LOAD"  4SAVE"  5CONT+  6,"LPT1 7TRON+  8TROFF+ 9KEY    0SCREEN
```

Figure 5.4. Nested FOR...NEXT Loops with Output

If two FOR...NEXT loops end on successive lines, you can combine the NEXT statements, naming the FOR variables in the order in which the separate NEXT statements would be written. The innermost NEXT must be executed before any outer NEXT, since the inner loop must be ended before the outer loop ends. The nested loops cannot overlap, although they can end at the same place. The two NEXT statements included in the program in Figure 5.4 could be combined and rewritten as NEXT Y, X.

1. Modify the first loop you wrote in the last Self-Check to include a nested loop that runs three times and prints the values of both FOR variables in a line with the name. Use a separate program line for each NEXT statement.
2. Test it and correct the program until it works. The inner loop should execute nine times in all.
3. Modify your nested loop so that both loops are ended by the same NEXT statement.
4. Test the program and correct it until it works.

Your answer to item 1 will look something like this:

```
10 MYNAME$="Ruth Ashley"
20 FOR X=1 TO 5
30    FOR Y=1 TO 3
40       PRINT X, Y, MYNAME$
50    NEXT
60 NEXT
```

The last line after you modify the loop in item 3 should look like this:

```
NEXT Y, X
```

The variable from the inner loop must be specified first.

Conditional Loops

Another way of creating loops lets you build a condition into the loop creation statement. The WHILE...WEND loop allows you to specify a condition in the WHILE statement. If the condition is true, GW-BASIC executes the following statements until it encounters a WEND statement. Then it branches back to the WHILE statement and tests the condition again. When the condition is not true, even at the first iteration of the loop, control branches to the statement following WEND.

A WHILE...WEND loop can do the same thing as a FOR...NEXT loop, but it takes a bit longer to execute. WHILE...WEND loops do not have to be based on numbers, however, which gives you more control over the type of condition that ends the loop. No values are set or incremented automatically in a WHILE...WEND loop. Any initialization or changing needed must be done in separate GW-BASIC statements. Statements within the loop must change at least one variable included in the condition or the loop will never be interrupted.

WHILE...WEND Format

The WHILE statement takes a condition just as the IF statement does. The WEND statement has no options. Here are the formats:

WHILE *conditional-expression*

...

WEND

The *conditional-expression* can be any expression of the type you can use in IF statements (see Chapter 4). As long as the condition is true, execution proceeds in sequence to the next WEND statement. If the condition is false, control skips down to the WEND statement and continues from there.

Here are several valid WHILE statements:

```
200 WHILE TRAIL$="G"
250 WHILE CUSTNUMBER < 99999
300 WHILE AGE > 21 AND AGE <= 65
500 WHILE ENDFLAG="N"
800 WHILE CUSTNUM <> NEWNUM
```

If GW-BASIC encounters a WEND statement when it is not performing a WHILE...WEND loop, you'll get the WEND without WHILE message. If it reaches the end of a program during a WHILE loop, you'll get the WHILE without WEND message. In either case, check your program. Even if both are included in the program, in the right sequence, control may have bypassed the WHILE or WEND statement.

Figure 5.5 shows how a WHILE...WEND loop can be used to repeat a program segment until the user chooses to end the program. The program sets the variable AGAIN$ to "Y". The WHILE condition tests this variable and it is true, so the statements following are executed. Near the bottom of the loop,

```
10 ' This program calculates square roots
20 CLS
30 AGAIN$ = "Y"
40 ' Begin portion to be repeated
50 WHILE AGAIN$ = "Y" OR AGAIN$ = "y"
60    INPUT "What number"; NUMBER
70    PRINT "Square root of"; NUMBER; "is"; SQR(NUMBER)
80    PRINT
90    PRINT "Press Y to continue. Any other key quits."
100    AGAIN$=INKEY$ : IF AGAIN$ = "" THEN GOTO 100
110 WEND
120 END
```

Figure 5.5. WHILE...WEND Loop

a new value is assigned to AGAIN$ (line 100). If the user presses "Y" or "y", the loop is repeated. Any other keypress causes the WHILE condition to be false, so the control passes to the statement following WEND and the program ends.

Nested WHILE...WEND Loops

You can nest WHILE...WEND loops to any level. Each time GW-BASIC encounters a WEND statement, it is matched with the most recent unmatched WHILE statement. You can't combine WEND statements as you can NEXT statements.

Figure 5.6 shows an example of a nested WHILE...WEND loop. In this program, the outer WHILE...WEND loop (lines 50 through 230) controls program repetition. The inner loop (lines 110 through 170) calculates payments for a loan, based on interest rate, principal, and monthly payment. Notice that the statements following WEND complete the processing for the last line or two of output.

The program in Figure 5.6 gets values for loan amortization, based on a specific loan value, an interest rate, and a monthly payment. It calculates the amount of each payment that is principle and interest, prints it, then continues with the next payment. Subroutine 1000 handles the data print statement, which is needed at several different points in the program. Subroutines 1100 and 1200 handle the last payment or two, depending on the amount still owed when the balance remaining is less than the standard monthly payment.

```
10 ' This program calculates principal and interest
20 CLS
30 AGAIN$ = "Y"
40 ' Begin portion to be repeated
50 WHILE AGAIN$ = "Y" OR AGAIN$ = "y"
60    INPUT "Enter the full loan amount: ",LOAN
70    INPUT "Enter the interest rate:    ",INTEREST
80    INPUT "Enter the monthly payment:  ",PAYMENT
90    INTEREST=INTEREST/12        ' get monthly interest
100   PRINT "     Begin";"   Payment";" Principle";"
Interest";"   Balance"
110   WHILE LOAN > PAYMENT
120     PAYINT = LOAN * INTEREST
130     PAYPRIN = PAYMENT - PAYINT
140     BALANCE = LOAN - PAYPRIN
150     GOSUB 1000
160     LOAN = BALANCE
170   WEND
180   PAYINT = LOAN * INTEREST
190   IF PAYINT + LOAN <= PAYMENT THEN GOSUB 1100
ELSE GOSUB 1200
200   IF BALANCE <> 0 THEN GOTO 180
210   PRINT: PRINT "Press Y to do another. Any other
key quits."
220   AGAIN$= INKEY$ : IF AGAIN$ = "" THEN GOTO 220
230 WEND
240 PRINT "Program ended"
250 END
1000 ' Subroutine to print a line in output
1010 PRINT USING "###,###.##"; LOAN, PAYMENT,
PAYPRIN, PAYINT, BALANCE
1020 RETURN
1100 ' Subroutine to handle last payment
1110 PAYPRIN = LOAN
1120 PAYMENT = PAYINT + PAYPRIN
1130 BALANCE = 0
1140 GOSUB 1000
1150 RETURN
1200 ' Subroutine to handle next-to-last payment
1210 PAYPRIN = PAYMENT - PAYINT
1220 BALANCE = LOAN - PAYPRIN
1230 LOAN = BALANCE
1240 GOSUB 1000
1250 RETURN
```

Figure 5.6. Nested WHILE...WEND Loop

Programming Techniques

Programming techniques for using WHILE...WEND loops are similar to those for FOR...NEXT loops. Always start processing the statements at the WHILE statement; don't let another statement branch to a point between WHILE and WEND. The interpreter sends an error message if it processes a WEND statement before encountering WHILE.

Don't bypass the end of the loop. To escape the loop completely, set some variable so the condition will be false, then use GOTO with the line number of the WEND statement. You can use GOSUB from within the loop effectively, since control will return when the subroutine is finished. GW-BASIC will let you use GOTO, assuming you will then branch back into the loop, but you can get into complex problems that way.

Make sure you use the right conditional expression. If you are checking for a keyboard entry, use INKEY$ for a single character so the user won't have to press ⏎. Check for both uppercase and lowercase using an OR operator.

1. Suppose you want to generate random numbers between 1 and 100. Write a program segment that uses a WHILE...WEND loop to generate an internal seed and display one random number in the desired range. Let the user press a key to get another one. Use 0 as the key to press to stop the program.
2. Try out your program and make sure you can generate another number with the press of various keys. Pressing 0 should end the program.
3. Save the program as 5SELF.BAS.

Your program might look something like this:

```
100 PRINT "Press 0 to stop program. Any other key gets"
110 PRINT " another random number between 1 and 100."
120 RANDOMIZE TIMER
130 B$="A"
140 WHILE B$ <> "0"
150    PRINT INT(RND*100+1)
160    B$=INKEY$ : IF B$="" THEN GOTO 160
170 WEND
180 END
```

Your program could be quite different and still be correct.

Debugging Programs

Very few useful programs run correctly the first time. You may get various error messages from the interpreter, indicating syntax or other errors in individual statements. If the message indicates a type mismatch, look at the variable names and consider the type of value you try to assign. If the message indicates an illegal function call, check it carefully. You may have used an invalid value in parentheses. Errors such as these are generally easy to fix, since the interpreter gives you the statement number. Just check the statement format and any variables and try again.

Once the statements all pass the interpreter, the program may not yet be correct. You may have used the wrong operator in a relational or arithmetic expression. You may have used the wrong variable or constant. You may have statements in the wrong sequence, so a variable value is changed before you use it. Usually, you can tell from the output that there is a problem. For example, suppose in running the program in Figure 5.6 you get continuous output; the balance keeps getting bigger instead of smaller. You might suspect that the problem is in one of the arithmetic statements. On careful examination of the program, however, you might discover that you input the interest rate of 9% as 9 instead of .09. The solution here is to clarify the instructions for inputting interest or to divide the entered value by 100. Careful analysis of any output and comparison of it with what you expected can tell you what the computer actually did.

Any time you get a message when the program comes to an abnormal termination, read the message; it may tell you all you need to know about the error. If the output doesn't seem right with the input you used, try to trace the values through the program. As long as you have even partial output, you may be able to figure out what the computer did to get the result. If you don't approve, you can change the program. To do this you need a printed copy (use LLIST) of your program by your side as you write down the value of the input variables each time they change or are worked with.

One fairly easy technique is to insert PRINT (or LPRINT) statements to show the values of critical variables before and after decision points. With this technique, you may be able to spot where an error has crept in. Then you can fix the part of the program that is off track and run it again. Remember to renumber the program if you insert very many new statements.

In most cases, using your eyes, your head, and your pencil will help you find the problem. In case they don't, however, GW-BASIC provides several commands and techniques you can use to help in debugging your programs. They are covered in the remainder of this chapter.

Tracing Program Execution

Suppose you have a program that runs just fine; that is, it starts up and comes to a normal termination. But it doesn't seem to be doing what you asked it to do. This can be an especially frustrating problem in a program that makes several decisions, uses many different conditions, and includes loops. The trace commands can help you see what statements are executed in what sequence. You can include these commands in a program, if necessary, but they are often more useful in direct mode.

The Commands

The TRON command starts program tracing, while TROFF turns it off. Both of these commands are available from the GW-BASIC editor key line. Press F7 to get TRON or F8 to get TROFF; you won't even have to press ↵. The command is executed and the Ok prompt appears.

The Effect

When the trace facility is turned on—that is, when you have used the TRON command—GW-BASIC displays the number of each program line that is executed. They are displayed across the screen line until it is full or until some statement in the program starts a new line. The line numbers are interspersed with program output and requests for keyboard input. Figure 5.7 shows the effect of TRON on the program shown in Figure 5.2. The output of this program without trace was shown in Figure 5.4. Notice that each traced line number is enclosed in square brackets.

Uses of Trace

Tracing is most useful when you are not sure how a certain effect occurs. For example, suppose you have written a program that includes several loops and decisions. It doesn't seem to be making the right decisions. You put in a value that should have a known effect, and it doesn't. You could use TRON to check it out. Use F7 to start trace, then run the program again. When it ends, press F8 to turn trace off. Then examine the screen. Imagine the input value and see what it should be at each point. When the next line executed doesn't match

```
Ok
TRON
Ok
run
[200]Enter the loan amount 5000
[210]
[220]Loan amount requested:   5000
[230]      Rate     Amount
[240][250][260][270]     9.00     450.00
[280][250][260][270]     9.25     462.50
[280][250][260][270]     9.50     475.00
[280][250][260][270]     9.75     487.50
[280][250][260][270]    10.00     500.00
[280][250][260][270]    10.25     512.50
[280][250][260][270]    10.50     525.00
[280][250][260][270]    10.75     537.50
[280][250][260][270]    11.00     550.00
[280][250][260][270]    11.25     562.50
[280][250][260][270]    11.50     575.00
[280][250][260][270]    11.75     587.50
[280][250][260][270]    12.00     600.00
[280]
Ok

1LIST   2RUN←   3LOAD"   4SAVE"   5CONT←   6. "LPT1 7TRON← 8TROFF← 9KEY      0SCREEN
```

Figure 5.7. Tracing Effect

what you think it should be, examine the line before. Try to figure out what happened.

Remember to turn trace off (with TROFF) when you are finished. If you leave it on, the next program you run will be traced as well. The LOAD and NEW commands also turn off the trace facility.

If necessary, you can include TRON and TROFF in a program. For example, if you know the problem is in one loop of a program that uses several, you could include the command TRON just before the loop begins and TROFF just after the loop. Once you figure out the problem and fix it, remove the tracing commands from the program. Tracing output not only clutters up the screen, but it also makes the program take longer to run.

1. Press F7 to turn trace on.
2. Run the program from the previous Self-Check (5SELF.BAS) and notice the effect of tracing it.
3. Insert an error into the program by changing the line with the INKEY$ input to use a different variable name. Then try running the program again.

4. Turn trace off, correct the error you inserted, and run the program.

You'll see many line numbers on the screen, interspersed with normal output. After you turn trace off, the program should run as before.

Stopping and Continuing Execution

Whether or not a program is performing as you expect, you may want to stop it at different points and examine variable values in direct mode. This helps you discover what a program is doing. Once you find out what the values of variables are, you can change them if necessary with direct statements. Then you may want to start up the program again at the point where it was interrupted.

You already know how to stop a program with the END statement. When a program is stopped this way, you see the Ok prompt. While well-designed programs include a single END statement, some contain more than one. If you include multiple END statements, perhaps to exit after errors, you can't tell which END statement terminated execution.

You can also stop a program with Ctrl-Break in an emergency. If you do, you see the message Break in *nnnnn*, letting you know what line was being executed when you pressed Ctrl-Break.

The STOP Statement

If you want a program to pause temporarily at a particular point, use the STOP statement in the program; that's all there is to the format. Execution is terminated and you'll see a message like Break in line *nnnnn*, just as with Ctrl-Break. No variables are reset, so you can then check out whatever you want in direct mode. You might use PRINT commands to examine them, for example. You could even change the value of some variables while execution is stopped.

Suppose a program includes these lines:

```
40 PRINT "Type length, width, height--";
50 INPUT "separated by commas ", LONG,WIDE,HIGH
60 IF HIGH > 10 THEN STOP
70 VOLUME = LONG * WIDE * HIGH
```

It might look like this on screen:

```
Type length, width, height--separated by commas 10,20,40
Break in 60
Ok
```

Since the user entered a value greater than 10 for height, the STOP statement was executed at line 60. The message gives the line number. Typing ? HIGH at the keyboard lets you know the value. You could, if you want, follow this by typing HIGH=8.5 if you know that is the correct value.

You can include many STOP statements to identify possible errors and let you check them out at different phases of program execution. Whenever a STOP statement is executed, the line number is displayed, so you know which STOP you are working with. If you have a long program with many STOP statements, it helps to have a printed (or hard) copy of your program on hand; use LLIST to get the copy before you get into serious debugging.

The CONT Command

When program execution is interrupted, you can use the CONT command at the keyboard to continue it at the point of interruption; pressing F5 also gives the CONT command and restarts the program. This works well after STOP, since you planned the STOP for some particular reason. You may have changed or at least checked some values, for example. When you type CONT at the Ok prompt, the program starts up again, using any changes you have made.

CONT will also restart a program after END or Ctrl-Break is encountered. Following END, you can't be sure where the program was interrupted. It may have been just before the subroutines, for example. Pressing F5 or typing CONT at this point would start executing subroutines, which is seldom what you really want.

Following Ctrl-Break, you may know where the interrupt occurred from the displayed message, but if an emergency caused you to interrupt execution, you probably need more than just variable checking and changing before running the program again.

While you can use direct commands such as PRINT and change variables CONT has no effect if you made any changes to actual program lines. If you added a line, changed any value in a numbered line, or even deleted a line, CONT will have no effect. You'll have to use RUN to start program execution over from the beginning.

Continuing from a Different Line

In most cases, you'll want to continue execution at the point of interrupt. If you happen to want to start somewhere else, you can use the GOTO statement in direct mode. If you use GOTO 3400 instead of CONT, execution will continue starting at line 3400 instead of at the point of interrupt. If you use RUN 3400, you'll lose current settings and start a new execution at the specified line. While you can start at a specific line number with RUN at any time, you can start with CONT only after execution was interrupted.

1. Load the program you wrote at the end of Chapter 4 (4CHAPEX.BAS). Run it to make sure you remember how it works.
2. Insert a STOP statement just after the user enters a character from the menu (after line 220 in our version).
3. When the program stops, display the value that was just entered. In our version, you would type PRINT ARITH.
4. Press F5 or type CONT to continue with the program.
5. Run it again. When it stops, set the menu selection to a different value than was entered. Then press F5 or type CONT to continue with the new value.
6. Save the version with STOP as 5STOP.BAS.

When the program stops, you can examine any variables with PRINT in direct mode or change them with assignment statements in direct mode.

When the program continues, it uses any changes you have made.

Resetting Variables

In the process of debugging a program, you may want to set all your variables back to their default status; that's 0 for numeric variables and null (no value) for string variables. The CLEAR command does this. Here is the format:

CLEAR [,[expression1][,expression2]]

When you use just the word CLEAR, GW-BASIC resets all variables to their defaults.

If you use a CLEAR statement within a FOR...NEXT or WHILE...WEND loop, GW-BASIC forgets about the loop because any variables and automatic counters involved in controlling the loop are reset. If the program keeps executing, you'll get a NEXT without FOR or WEND without WHILE message very soon.

CLEAR has some additional effects that control features we haven't yet covered. It closes files, releases disk buffers, turns off sound, turns off a light pen or joystick trigger, and disables some error trapping. We'll cover some of these features in later chapters.

Expression1 specifies a memory location (less than 65328); if you use it, this expression limits the amount of space available for GW-BASIC, protecting any memory above that point. If a machine language program resides in upper memory, you might want to do this. The command CLEAR , 32768 resets all variables to their defaults and protects memory above 32768. You need the comma before the value or the command will not work correctly.

Expression2 sets aside stack space; you'll learn to use it later when you learn to use arrays. The command CLEAR , , 2000 sets aside 2000 bytes of stack space, while resetting all program variables to their defaults. You need two commas before the value to tell GW-BASIC what the value means.

Checking the Available Memory

Occasionally, you may get an error message that indicates there isn't enough memory. GW-BASIC can only deal with 64K, no matter how much is available. If you are really using more memory than that, you may want to move up to a compiled form of BASIC or even a different language.

But sometimes you aren't really using too much memory. Instead, something in the program is taking up more than it should. This is more likely to become a problem once you start working with files and arrays. If you see the message Out of string space, you will want to try to free some space up before you panic.

You can check the memory with the FRE function. Here's its format:

FRE(*value*)

The argument is a dummy; it doesn't have any effect. You can use 0 or A$ if you like. The statement PRINT FRE (0) results in a display of the amount of memory available to store strings. When you use FRE, it first gathers up whatever is stored in string memory and reorganizes it. If the program uses a number of long strings, especially if it assigns them to the same variable names, quite a bit of space can be occupied by old string fragments. When you use FRE, GW-BASIC discards unused portions of fragmented strings to save space. After this "garbage collection" is done, FRE displays the amount of memory available. Here's how it might look:

```
PRINT FRE(A)
 14542
Ok
```

If you use FRE frequently, it keeps the garbage collected and the maximum amount of string memory space available. If you don't use it until you have a memory problem, it may take a minute or so to collect all the garbage and dispose of it.

1. Run the program 5STOP.BAS again. Display the amount of available memory after it stops.
2. Press F5 or CONT to continue the program. Check the memory again after it ends.
3. Run the program again. This time clear all the variables after the STOP statement is executed. Press F5 or CONT to continue and notice the effect.

Use PRINT FRE(0) to check the amount of free memory. Notice that there is less while the program is stopped than when it has ended normally.

Use CLEAR to clear all the variables. You might get some error message or bad output when the program continues after CLEAR. In our program, the value 0 results in telling the user the wrong number was pressed.

Summary

This chapter covered various commands for executing loops and debugging programs. All the commands and techniques covered here are useful in most practical programs you'll write.

Loops
The FOR and NEXT statements let you set up a loop based on a counter with a variable increment.

The WHILE and WEND statements let you set up a loop based on a condition.

Both FOR...NEXT and WHILE...WEND loops can be nested as needed to handle the logic of a program.

Debugging

Use TRON and TROFF command to trace statement execution. The number of each statement executed is displayed on the screen.

Use the STOP command to force the program to stop so you can examine or change variables at any point.

Use the CONT command to continue after a program STOP is executed.

Use the CLEAR command to set all variables to the defaults.

Use the FRE function to show the amount of free memory available to GW-BASIC programs.

Use common sense and careful checking to correct errors in programs.

Exercise

1. Write a program to calculate factorials. A factorial is the product of all numbers from 1 to the given number. Assume the program gets the value TOP in an INPUT statement to serve as the end point of the loop. Use the variable TOTAL to hold a continuing factorial value.
2. Test the program using various values of TOP to make sure that it works. The factorial values get very large. Don't worry if they are displayed in a format you aren't familiar with.
3. Modify the program to repeat itself until the user enters the value 0 instead of a valid value of TOP.
4. Write the WHILE statement to set up the program repetition loop. Then write any statements needed to get data for the FOR...NEXT loop.
5. Add the loop you wrote for item 2.
6. Add lines to show the factorial calculated and let the user decide to continue or not. Then add the WEND statement and end the program.
7. Test your program. Use TRON to see what lines are executed.
8. Add a STOP statement within the FOR...NEXT loop. Each time it stops, display the values of TOP and TOTAL so you can see how large the values get.
9. While the program is STOPped, check the amount of free memory.

10. Once the program works, save it as 5CHAPEX.BAS.

Your program for item 1 should look something like this:

```
10 ' Calculate a factorial
20 PRINT "This program calculates factorials"
30 INPUT "Enter the number whose factorial you want: ",TOP
40 TOTAL = 1
50 FOR X = 1 TO TOP
60    TOTAL = TOTAL * X
70 NEXT
80 PRINT TOP; "factorial is "; TOTAL
90 END
```

Your modified program for item 3 might look something like this:

```
10 ' Chapter 5 Exercise program
20 CLS
30 ' begin major repeat section
40 WHILE C$ <> "0"
50    PRINT "This program calculates factorials."
60    INPUT "Enter the number whose factorial you want: ",TOP
70    TOTAL = 1
80    FOR X = 1 TO TOP
90       TOTAL = TOTAL * X
100    NEXT
110    PRINT TOP; "factorial is "; TOTAL
120    PRINT "Press 0 to end. Any other key continues."
130    C$=INKEY$ : IF C$="" THEN GOTO 130
140 WEND
150 PRINT "Program ended"
160 END
```

Your program can be quite different and still be correct. The value displayed for 4 factorial should be 24. The value displayed for 10 factorial should be 3628800. Factorials for any higher numbers will be shown in scientific notation.

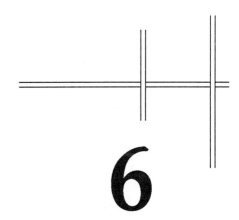

6

Console Input and Output

This chapter deals with GW-BASIC commands that give you more control over how and where data appears on the screen. You'll learn more ways a program can be set up to interact with the user. This includes ways of displaying data on the console screen as well as ways of treating any data entered by the user using the keyboard. Techniques that contribute to these aims are also included. You will learn to:

- Use the SCREEN statement to change the display characteristics
- Use the WIDTH statement to set the line width for the console or printer
- Use the COLOR statement to select screen colors
- Use the PALETTE statement to change the colors that are currently displayed
- Use the LOCATE statement to position the cursor on the screen and control its appearance
- Use the SPACE$ and STRING$ functions to return a string of spaces or other characters
- Use the CSRLIN and POS functions to find out where the cursor is on the screen
- Use the LINE INPUT command to read an entire line of data at once
- Use the INPUT$ function to read keyboard presses without requiring ⏎
- Control function key trapping with KEY and ON KEY statements
- Develop user-friendly screen displays for your programs

The Console Screen

GW-BASIC normally uses a set of default values for determining where and how to display information on the screen. It uses a particular width setting, for example, and a particular screen display mode. It uses a monochrome color scheme (usually white or green characters on a black background) for display. You can change many of these effects, as you'll learn in this section.

The WIDTH Statement

By default, GW-BASIC uses a display line width of 80 characters. You can use a width of 40 characters instead if you choose. When the smaller width is used, the characters are expanded and displayed twice as wide; there is no change in the height of the characters. To use large characters, use WIDTH 40. To restore the default width, use WIDTH 80. Figure 6.1 shows how a listed program looks after WIDTH 40 has been used.

The WIDTH statement works in direct or program mode, and it affects the entire screen. If you use the command WIDTH 40, the screen is cleared, the cursor goes to the top of the screen, and any future characters typed or

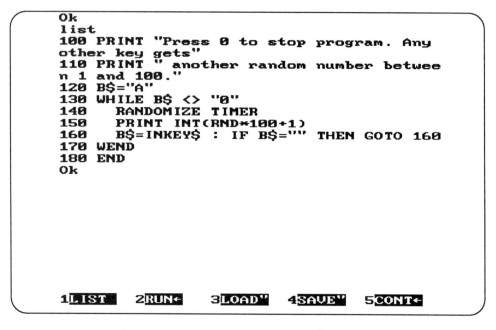

```
Ok
list
100 PRINT "Press 0 to stop program. Any
other key gets"
110 PRINT " another random number betwee
n 1 and 100."
120 B$="A"
130 WHILE B$ <> "0"
140     RANDOMIZE TIMER
150     PRINT INT(RND*100+1)
160     B$=INKEY$ : IF B$="" THEN GOTO 160
170 WEND
180 END
Ok




1LIST     2RUN←     3LOAD"     4SAVE"     5CONT←
```

Figure 6.1. Wide Characters Resulting from WIDTH 40

displayed are shown double wide. You can't have part of the screen with normal-sized characters and part with double-wide characters.

The WIDTH statement doesn't work with all screen configurations; however, it always works with the default screen display. It may also have an effect on screen colors. If you are at your computer, try it out. Load any GW-BASIC program. Then type the direct statement WIDTH 40, followed by LIST. Restore the default width with the WIDTH 80 direct statement.

The SCREEN Statement

Your screen will work in more than one mode. The default mode, mode 0, is text only; it doesn't handle any graphics. Every personal computer can handle mode 0. Additional modes are 1, 2, 7, 8, 9, and 10. Table 6.1 shows the modes you may be able to use depending on your system's display console and adapter types. GW-BASIC doesn't have any special commands for VGA adapters and display screens. Use the EGA modes for a VGA setup.

Each screen mode has special characteristics that determine how it displays text, graphics, and color. The next section of this chapter deals with color in more detail. Graphics are covered in Chapter 9.

Mode 0 is for text only; it gives high resolution, but has no graphic capability. It can handle a 40 or 80 character wide display and up to 16 colors.

Mode 1 provides medium-resolution graphics (320 by 200 pixels) and handles text characters in width 80 or width 40. (A pixel is the smallest point that can appear on the screen.) It can handle up to 16 colors.

Mode 2 provides high-resolution graphics (640 by 200 pixels) and text characters in width 40. It can handle up to 16 colors with special treatment, but only 2 at a time.

Mode 7 provides medium-resolution graphics (320 by 200 pixels) and text characters in width 40. It differs from mode 1 in that it provides more flexibility

Table 6.1. Hardware/Screen Mode

Adapter	Display	Screen Mode 0	1	2	7	8	9	10
MDPA	Monochrome	x						x
CGA	Color	x	x	x				
EGA	Color	x	x	x	x	x		
EGA	Enhanced color	x	x	x	x	x	x	
EGA	Monochrome							x

in color handling. For an EGA display screen, it also provides extra memory pages for more effective use of color displays.

Mode 8 provides high-resolution graphics (640 by 200 pixels) and text characters in width 80. Otherwise it has the same features as Mode 7.

Mode 9 provides extra-high-resolution graphics (640 by 350 pixels) and handles text characters in width 80 with much more resolution than the lower modes. Depending on the amount of EGA memory available, it lets you use up to 16 colors (less than 64K) or up to 64 colors (64K).

Mode 10 provides extra-high-resolution graphics (640 by 350) and very-high-resolution text characters, but it is only available on EGA adapters with monochrome display. It lets you use up to nine pseudocolors. If you use mode 10 in a program, it won't run on any color or EGA display screens, even if they have the required EGA display card.

1. Start GW-BASIC and load any working program you've already written and saved.
2. List the program on the screen.
3. Type WIDTH 40, then list the program again.
4. Run the program. Notice the characters on the screen.
5. Type width 80, then list the program again.
6. If you have an EGA (or VGA) monochrome display, try SCREEN 10 and list the program again.
7. If you have a color or EGA display screen:
   a. Try SCREEN 1 and list the program.
   b. Try SCREEN 2 and list the program.
8. If you have an EGA (or VGA) display screen:
   a. Try SCREEN 7 and list the program.
   b. Try SCREEN 8 and list the program.
   c. Try SCREEN 9 and list the program.
9. Type SCREEN 1 and list the program. Then type SCREEN 0 and list it again. Type WIDTH 80 to restore the default conditions.

The character width and resolution of characters should change to reflect the statements you enter. If you get an Invalid function call message, the effect you have requested is not valid for your system.

Handling Colors

If your system has a color, EGA, or VGA display, you can control the colors it displays through GW-BASIC. Colors can appear in several areas, depending on the current screen mode. Colors are specified by numbers; the numbers are called attributes. For EGA displays, you can control which color is assigned to which attribute number. The attribute numbers and colors available depend on the screen mode and the exact hardware.

A background color can have either of two effects, depending on the screen mode. In mode 0, the background color appears behind each text character but does not affect the entire screen. In higher modes, only one background color can be used at a time, because it affects the entire screen. The default background color is black.

A foreground color becomes the default color of text and graphics. You can use many different foreground colors on the screen at a time. If the foreground and background colors are the same, the text or graphics won't be visible.

A border color appears around the edge of the screen. Border colors can be used only in mode 0. The default border color is black.

A color palette determines the display color to use for a particular color number and changes colors already displayed on the screen. You must use a palette to control color in mode 1; you can use them for more control in higher numbered modes with an EGA adapter installed. Palettes are covered later in this chapter.

The COLOR Statement

The COLOR statement can be used with any screen mode except 2; it has two different formats:

COLOR *foreground[,background[,border]]*
COLOR *background[,palette]*

Each argument in a COLOR statement can be a whole number or an expression that indicates a number within the acceptable range for the statement and the equipment. Numbers 0 through 15 represent 16 different colors. Numbers 16 through 31 represent the same 16 colors, in blinking rather than solid form. Table 6.2 lists the standard color assignments for most displays. Some very early monitors may repeat the first eight for colors 8 through 15.

Table 6.2. Standard Color Assignments

0	black	8	gray
1	dark blue	9	bright blue
2	green	10	bright green
3	cyan	11	bright cyan
4	red	12	bright red
5	magenta	13	bright magenta
6	brown	14	yellow
7	white	15	bright white

Changing the screen mode with a SCREEN statement resets the color to the default. To set the color back to the default for your system without changing the screen mode, you will probably be able to use COLOR 7, 0.

With SCREEN 0. The first COLOR statement format is used with screen mode 0. The foreground color must be between 0 and 31. The statement COLOR 3 causes a mode 0 screen to use cyan (a light blue) as the foreground color; text characters will appear in this color. The statement COLOR 17 causes the text characters to appear in blinking dark blue. To use blinking text characters, add 16 to the basic color number and use the resulting value in the COLOR statement.

Border colors can be used only on a CGA monitor attached to a CGA display. The border color in mode 0 must be between 0 and 15. It cannot blink, but you can use more colors than in the background. The statement COLOR

```
10 REM This program prepares colorful displays
20 SCREEN 0
30 COLOR 1,7
40 PRINT "The text is blue on white background"
50 COLOR 2,0
60 PRINT "The text here is green on a black back-
ground"
70 COLOR 3,6
80 PRINT "The text here is cyan on a brown background"
90 COLOR 7,0         ' Reset default colors
100 END
```

Figure 6.2. Colors in Screen Mode 0

3, 6, 10 specifies a light green border surrounding cyan characters on a brown background.

The background color must be between 0 and 7 for mode 0; you can't use the blinking colors in the background. The statement COLOR 3, 6 results in cyan characters displayed on a brown background. The background characters appear only behind the foreground characters; they do not cover the entire screen background in mode 0 as they do in other modes.

In mode 0, you can use several different background colors on the same screen. For example, look at the program in Figure 6.2. A COLOR statement precedes each PRINT statement. And each message is printed in a different set of colors. Line 90 resets the default colors.

To include a larger section of color behind a block of text in mode 0, you can use extra display lines and spaces. For example, the following lines cause a block of text to be displayed in cyan in the center of a red block:

```
290 COLOR 3,4
300 PRINT "                                              "
310 PRINT "                                              "
320 PRINT "            CHAPTER ONE                        "
330 PRINT "                                              "
340 PRINT "                                              "
350 COLOR 7,0
```

Lines 300, 310, 330, and 340 set up the background rectangle; line 320 includes spaces for the background on that line. The default colors are restored in line 350.

All other screen modes use only a single background color per screen. If a COLOR statement specifies a different background color, the background of the entire screen is changed. Other modes can also use several different foreground colors on one screen, however.

---

1. Type the program from Figure 6.2 and test it.
2. Change the colors in one of the lines and try it again.
3. Now change the color to a number between 16 and 32, then try the program again. Notice the blinking effect.
4. Add another line to show a magenta message on a cyan background.

If you have a color, EGA, or VGA monitor, this program should work just fine. If you have a monochrome monitor, you may see different background patterns. If you see no effect, you might as well skip ahead to the LOCATE statement later in this chapter.

The statement COLOR 5,3 produces magenta foreground characters on a cyan background.

With SCREEN 1. Mode 1 requires the use of a color palette, so you must use the second format above. In this case, the first color argument specifies the background color rather than the foreground; as with Mode 0, the background color must be between 0 and 7. The statement COLOR 5 sets the entire screen background to magenta while leaving the foreground colors at the default.

The second argument is a palette value; it selects one of two available palettes for the foreground color based on whether it is odd or even. Use COLOR 0 , 7 to restore the default colors to a mode 1 screen.

For CGA displays, the use of an even palette value, such as 0 or 2, means that color 1 is green, 2 is red, and 3 is yellow; use COLOR , 0 to set or restore this palette. The use of an odd palette value, such as 1 or 3, means that color 1 is cyan, 2 is magenta, and 3 is high-intensity white; use COLOR , 1 to set or restore this palette.

While you can set the background freely with the first argument, text characters for many CGA setups remain in white. The other palette colors can be used only in graphics commands, which are covered later in this book.

For EGA displays, you can use the default palettes if you wish; they are almost the same as the CGA palettes. The even EGA palette, specified with the statement COLOR , 0, sets color 1 to green, 2 to red, and 3 to brown. The odd EGA palette, specified with the statement COLOR , 1, sets color 1 to cyan, 2 to magenta, and 3 to high-intensity white. As with CGA setups, you can change the background color with the first argument. If you use an odd number as the second argument, the foreground characters will be either cyan or white, depending on the background color. If you use an even number as the second argument, the foreground characters will be red or brown, again depending on the current background color.

When we discuss the PALETTE statement a bit later, we'll cover what these mean and how you can change the color palettes for EGA screens.

The statement COLOR 2 , 0 sets an EGA background to green and uses red for the text characters. You can use other colors in the palette for graphics commands, covered later in this book.

With SCREEN 2. You can't use the COLOR statement with screen mode 2. If you do, you'll see the message Illegal function call. On an EGA setup, you can use the PALETTE statement, however, to set both the background and foreground colors.

```
10 FOR F = 1 TO 15
20    FOR B=15 TO 0 STEP -1
30       COLOR F,B
40       PRINT "Foreground:";F;" Background:";B;"         "
50    NEXT
60    PRINT "Press F5 to continue"
70 STOP
80 NEXT
90 END
```

Figure 6.3. Color Display Program

With SCREEN 7, 8, or 9. Modes 7, 8, and 9 require the use of the first format of the COLOR statement, in which the first argument is the foreground. These screen modes can use foreground and background colors, but they can't use a border color. And the background color is the same for the entire screen. If you change the background color in a COLOR statement, the current screen background changes, but the foreground colors do not. Text and graphics are placed on the background color, which must be in the range supported by the equipment. All three EGA modes can use up to 16 colors. Some mode 9 systems can use up to 64 color numbers or attributes. The foreground text color is the color assigned to the highest number in the palette. This becomes the default drawing and text color; it cannot be 0, even if the background is a different color. You can use other colors in graphics statements.

The statement COLOR 3, 5 sets the foreground to cyan and the background to magenta. The statement COLOR 2, 2 sets both foreground and background to the same color, green. Anything printed won't be visible.

With SCREEN 10. Mode 10 uses patterns and hatching to simulate color on an EGA monochrome system. You can use up to 4 pseudocolors at a time. The first COLOR statement format works just as it does for other modes. You'll have to try it out to see the effects on your own system.

Using Colors

Figure 6.3 shows a short program that produces many of the valid color combinations; it is designed to work in mode 0, so it should work on most systems. When it is run, the outer FOR...NEXT loop sets one foreground color at a time, then uses the inner FOR...NEXT loop to show it with all the background colors. We omitted 0,0, so the printed characters are readable the first time, although any time the foreground and background are the same, you won't be able to read the foreground characters. The program pauses after each set of foreground color displays so that you can examine the result. It prompts you to press F5 (CONT) to continue the program following the STOP statement.

If you try this program, you'll see that the lines of color on the screen break before the edge of the screen. If you are writing programs, you'll have to worry about such effects, but they won't be a problem now.

You can try the program in other modes with a few modifications. To use it with mode 7, 8, or 9, you'll have to change the outer FOR statement to loop from 1 to 15; color 0 is invalid in these modes. And when you run it, the entire background will change each time a COLOR statement changes it. If you want to examine each combination at leisure, add the statement 45 INPUT "Press Enter to continue "; B$. This will cause the program to pause until you press ⏎ after each color change in the inner loop.

Using Palettes for Screen Mode 1

A palette is a set of colors that are available for use. You must use predefined palettes with screen mode 1. You may use them with EGA setups for the higher screen modes.

In screen mode 1, you can generate colors using the odd or even palette. You won't notice any difference while you are using only text characters. The statement COLOR 3, 1 produces a cyan background with white text characters, while COLOR 3, 0 produces the same effect. The differences occur when you use graphics statements.

On an EGA screen, the result is similar for the COLOR 3, 1 statement, but COLOR 3, 0 produces red letters on the cyan background. For all backgrounds, using the odd palette gives a cyan or white text, while the even palette gives a red or brown text.

You can also use the PALETTE statement to get other colors of text, but you are limited to four colors. PALETTE 0, 1 changes the background to blue. PALETTE 3, 5 changes the foreground characters to magenta. The other palette colors (1 and 2) can be used in graphics statements.

Using Palettes for Higher Screen Modes

If you have an EGA (or VGA) display, you can use palettes for modes 2, 7, 8, 9, and 10 to get more control, rather than less, over the colors. Where the COLOR statement determines the color of text characters to follow, the

PALETTE statement changes points on the screen from one color to another. It also determines colors used in graphic elements drawn later on the screen.

While you can't use COLOR with mode 2, you can use PALETTE to change colors. You are limited to 0 and 1. PALETTE 0, 1 sets the background to blue. PALETTE 1, 5 sets the foreground (text) to magenta.

When the COLOR statement refers to a color number, it is actually referring to an attribute or color assignment that produces that color by default. The PALETTE statement lets you change the default colors assigned to different numbers. If you have assigned color 4 (red) to number 1 (blue), for example, the statement COLOR 1 will produce red characters, not blue ones. If you then assign color 3 (green) to color 1, all characters on the screen in color 1 will be changed to green. You can use the PALETTE statement to assign different numbers to various colors. Then you use the COLOR statement to set the even or odd palette.

The palette contains a set of colors, each assigned to a number. Each number is thus paired with an actual display color. For example, if you assign color 1 to palette number 3, all points on the screen that were formerly in color blue (standard color 1) are immediately changed to cyan.

The numbers in the palette range from 0 through 16. You can assign the standard 16 colors to these palette numbers, although some EGA setups allow you to assign up to 64 colors. The color assigned to palette number 0 becomes the background color. The color assigned to the highest number in the palette (usually 15) becomes the foreground color and is used for text characters. Other colors can be used with graphics statements.

What you actually see on the screen depends on the screen mode and the actual equipment in use.

The PALETTE Statement

The PALETTE statement causes a color already displayed on the screen, in whatever location, to change to a newly specified color. It may also cause future characters to appear in the new color. Using PALETTE with no arguments resets the default palette; as such it may change colors on the screen. It doesn't cancel colors, however. Here's the format:

PALETTE *attribute,color*

The number of attributes depends on the screen mode and the equipment. Table 6.3 shows the equipment, attribute ranges, and color ranges for EGA (or VGA) adapters. If a PALETTE statement uses a value that is invalid for the

Table 6.3. Acceptable Palette Values

Mode	Monitor	Attribute	Color
0	Mono	0-15	0-2
0	EGA	0-31	0-15
1	EGA	0-3	0-15
2	EGA	0-1	0-15
7	EGA	0-15	0-15
8	EGA	0-15	0-15
9	EGA(64K)	0-3	0-15
9	EGA(>64K)	0-15	0-63
10	Mono	0-3	0-8

current screen mode, you'll get an Illegal function call error message and any program in progress will be terminated. PALETTE also raises the Illegal function call message on CGA setups.

When a PALETTE statement is executed, colors may change on screen if the color mentioned as the second argument is displayed. The color you specify will be displayed whenever the attribute you set is referenced in a statement that calls for a screen display or a color. In Chapter 9, you'll learn to use such statements as DRAW, which can use the additional color attributes. The statement PALETTE 0,3 changes the background to cyan, because palette number 0 always refers to the background. The statement PALETTE 0,2 changes the background to green; all points colored with attribute 0 change to color 2. PALETTE 1,3 assigns cyan to number 1, so all blue text changes to cyan. PALETTE 2,5 changes all magenta to green. PALETTE 1,1 restores all points currently of attribute 1 (and displayed in cyan) to the standard blue.

Using the Palette

Figure 6.4 shows a sample program that shows the effects of using the PALETTE statement on your system (if you have an EGA or VGA adapter). The screen prompts you for various values, which result in changes on the screen.

1. Type in the program shown in Figure 6.3.
2. Set the screen mode to 0, and run the program.

```
10 REM Program to show PALETTE and COLOR statements
20 CLS
30 PRINT "This is a demonstration of color"
40 PRINT
50 INPUT "Type 1 for blue, 2 for green, or 4 for red
background ",B
60 PRINT
70 INPUT "Type 3 for cyan, 5 for magenta, or 14 for
yellow text ",F
80 COLOR F,B
90 PRINT "Notice this message is in the colors you
chose"
100 INPUT "Press another of the three background
colors above ",PB
110 INPUT "Press 3, 5, or 14 to change the text to
another color ",PF
120 PALETTE 0,PB            ' Sets the backgound color
130 PALETTE F,PF            ' Changes previously set
color to new one
140 PRINT
150 PRINT "Notice that the colors changed this time"
160 PRINT "Press any key to end program and restore
color defaults"
170 A$=INKEY$ : IF A$="" THEN GOTO 170
180 COLOR 7,0 : PALETTE
190 END
```

================ Figure 6.4. PALETTE Sample Program

3. If you have a CGA setup:
   a. Change the values for the foreground colors to range from 0 to 3.
   b. Set the screen mode to 1.
   c. Run the program.
   d. Modify it until it works.
4. If you have an EGA or VGA setup:
   a. Change the values for F to range from 1 to 15.
   b. Add line 45 INPUT "Press Enter to continue ",B$
   c. Set the screen mode to 8.
   d. Run the program.
   e. Modify the program until it works.
5. Try various PALETTE and COLOR commands in direct mode for several different screen modes.
   a. In mode 0, try COLOR 1,2,3.
   b. In mode 1, try COLOR 3,1 and COLOR 3,2.

c. In mode 2, try COLOR 1, 2. Then try PALETTE 1, 2.
d. In mode 9, try COLOR 1, 2. Then try PALETTE 1, 3.
6. If you like, enter the program from Figure 6.4 and try it out.

For each mode, you should see appropriate colors on screen. When the statements don't seem to have the correct effect, restore the original colors by changing to another screen mode and back, then try again. If you don't have a color, EGA, or VGA display, you won't see colors on the screen.

Positioning Text on the Screen

So far, you have had very little control over positioning output on the screen. You can use spacing and tabbing in PRINT statements, or use comma (,) or semicolon (;) between items being printed to control where items appear horizontally. You can use CLS to cause the next displayed line to appear at the top of a cleared screen. You can use a PRINT statement to insert a blank line. By default, each PRINT statement starts on the next row, unless the prior PRINT ends with a semicolon. GW-BASIC provides even more control over placement with the LOCATE statement.

The LOCATE Statement

The LOCATE statement moves the cursor to a specified position on the screen. The next statement that displays something, whether it is PRINT or INPUT, continues from that point. You can specify the row (from 1 to 25) and the column (from 1 to 40 or 80, depending on the screen mode and current width). Here's the basic format:

LOCATE [*row*][,*col*][,*cursor*]

The statement LOCATE 1, 1 places the cursor in the upper-left corner of the screen. The display resulting from the next PRINT statement begins at that point. Later printed data follows as usual, unless another LOCATE statement occurs. The line LOCATE 10, 20 : PRINT "Message" causes the word Message to be printed on the screen starting in the tenth row, twentieth column. The next PRINT statement will start in row 11, column 1.

```
100 ' Routine to display in location
110 CLS
120 LOCATE 6,10
130 PRINT "What would you like to do next?"
140 LOCATE 8,15
150 PRINT "A.   Change the name"
160 LOCATE 9,15
170 PRINT "B.   Change the address"
180 LOCATE 10,15
190 PRINT "C.   Change the phone number"
200 LOCATE 11,15
210 PRINT "D.   Remove the customer"
220 LOCATE 12,15
230 PRINT "E.   Add a new customer"
240 LOCATE 14,10
250 PRINT "Press the letter--> ";
260 L$ = INKEY$ : IF L$ = "" THEN GOTO 260
270 IF L$ = "A" OR L$ = "a" THEN GOSUB 2000
```

Figure 6.5. Using LOCATE in a PROGRAM

If you are using LOCATE statements, you will probably want to use CLS first. This clears the screen to give you the entire area to position your text. If you use LOCATE for some of the screen output, you will probably want to use it for all the program's PRINT statements for accurate positioning. You may want to put the LOCATE and the associated PRINT statement on the same line (separated by a colon) to show that the two are related.

You can omit the first argument (row) to use the default row location but a different column. LOCATE ,20 specifies the default row and column 20. Similarly, you can omit the second argument (col) to use the default column and the nondefault line. The statement LOCATE 4 specifies the default (first) column on line 4.

The third argument of the LOCATE statement is a cursor option; it specifies if the cursor is to be visible (on) or invisible (off). The value 0 turns it off, while any other value turns it on. On is the default. The line LOCATE 4,4,1 : PRINT MESSAGE3 causes the value of MESSAGE3 to be displayed starting on line 4, in column 4, and with the cursor suppressed.

Figure 6.5 shows a program segment that uses LOCATE statements to format the screen. Notice that every PRINT statement in the program is preceded by LOCATE. When the output is to be printed on the next line, the row can be omitted.

```
100 SCREEN 0
110 ' Routine to display in location
120 CLS
130 COLOR 1,3
140 LOCATE 6,10
150 PRINT "  What would you like to do next?          "
160 COLOR 5,1
170 LOCATE 8,15
180 PRINT "  A.   Change the name            "
190 LOCATE 9,15
200 PRINT "  B.   Change the address         "
210 LOCATE 10,15
220 PRINT "  C.   Change the phone number    "
230 LOCATE 11,15
240 PRINT "  D.   Remove the customer        "
250 LOCATE 12,15
260 PRINT "  E.   Add a new customer         "
270 COLOR 3,4
280 LOCATE 14,10
290 PRINT "  Press the letter-->             "
300 L$ = INKEY$ : IF L$ = "" GOTO 300
310 IF L$ = "A" OR L$ = "a" GOSUB 2000
```

Figure 6.6. Using LOCATE and COLOR

Figure 6.6 shows the same program modified to use the COLOR statement as well. Notice that the screen mode is set to 0 here, so that the background colors can apply to individual lines.

1. Load your program CONVERT.
2. Modify the program to position the PRINT and INPUT statements for an attractive display. Then test the program.
3. Modify the program again to use at least three different colors. Then test the program.

Your program might look like this:

```
10 ' conversion program
20 CLS
30 LOCATE 5,15 : COLOR 3,4
40 INPUT "What is your height (in inches)";INCHES
```

```
50 LOCATE 7,15
60 INPUT "What is your weight (in pounds)";POUNDS
70 AVWEIGHT = POUNDS / INCHES
80 CONVWEIGHT = POUNDS * 2.2
90 CONVHEIGHT = INCHES * 2.54
100 AVECONV = CONVWEIGHT / CONVHEIGHT
110 LOCATE 11,15 : COLOR 5,1
120 PRINT"Your average weight per inch is ";AVWEIGHT
130 LOCATE 12,15
140 PRINT"Your average weight in grams per centimeter is ";
AVECONV
150 LOCATE 14,25 : COLOR 2,6
160 PRINT"Thank you"
170 PRINT : PRINT
180 COLOR 7,0
190 END
```

All the LOCATE and COLOR statements have been added. Your program may be quite different and still be correct.

The SPACE$ Function

You already know how to use the TAB and SPC functions to insert spacing in a PRINT statement. Sometimes you want a string of spaces to insert in different locations. You can define these individually, as in BLANKS$="   ", if you wish. You can also use the SPACE$ function to return a string of spaces. SPACE$(10) returns a string of ten spaces. When the value of NUM is 6, SPACE$(NUM) returns a string of 6 spaces. The screen print in Figure 6.7 shows a program that uses SPACE$ and the effect.

The SPACE$ argument is automatically rounded to a whole number; it must be within the range of 0 to 255, since that is the maximum length of a displayed or printed line.

ASCII Characters and Decimal Representation

The characters you see on the screen are ASCII characters. Each of them has an ASCII code that represents the character. You can find the ASCII code for a character with the ASC function. Conversely, you can find the ASCII character for a particular code with the CHR$ function. Appendix C includes a list of the standard ASCII codes, ranging from 0 to 255; codes above 127 are different in some systems. Notice that codes 48 through 57 are the digits 0 through 9, codes 65 through 90 are the uppercase letters, and codes 97 through 122 are the lowercase letters. Symbols (such as * and space) and special system signals (such as DEL for delete) make up the other codes. A monochrome

```
Ok
list
100 ' Sample use of SPACE$
110 FOR COUNT = 1 TO 6
120    S$ = SPACE$(COUNT)
130    PRINT "Line": S$: COUNT
140 NEXT
Ok
run
Line  1
Line   2
Line    3
Line     4
Line      5
Line       6
Ok
_
```
```
1LIST  2RUN‹  3LOAD"  4SAVE"  5CONT‹  6 "LPT1 7TRON‹  8TROFF‹ 9KEY     0SCREEN
```

Figure 6.7. The SPACE$ Function

screen with a monochrome display adapter can display only up through ASCII code 127. And some printers have the same limitation. But any color adapter or dot matrix printer will be able to handle all of these.

The STRING$ function uses the ASCII code to create a string of the represented ASCII character. The ASC, CHR$, and STRING$ functions are all covered in this section.

Finding ASCII Codes

The ASC function gives you the ASCII code; the argument must be a string. Suppose X$ has the value "T". The function ASC(X$) returns the value 84. The function ASC("+") returns the value 43, which represents the symbol + (plus). You can use a string variable or an actual string in the function. And the function can replace a string constant or variable in any statement that can use strings.

If the string specified contains more than one character, the function returns the ASCII code for the first character in the string. If LASTNAME$ has the value "ashland," ASC(LASTNAME$) returns the value 97, which represents the lowercase letter a.

```
10 ' Produce ASCII code listing
20 CLS
30 FOR X = 1 TO 22
40    FOR Y = 0 TO 7
50       IF Y = 0 THEN P = 1 ELSE P = 10*Y
60       A = X + 22 * Y
70       CHAR$ = CHR$(A)
80       LOCATE X, P
90       IF A = 12 THEN GOTO 110
100        PRINT A; CHAR$
110    NEXT Y
120 NEXT X
130 END
```

Figure 6.8. Producing an ASCII Code List

Finding ASCII Characters

The CHR$ function converts an ASCII code into its character equivalent. You've already seen that CHR$(12) produces a form feed, or ejects a printer page. PRINT CHR$(7) produces a beep on your system, just like BEEP does. CHR$(84) has the value "T." You can use either a numeric variable or an actual value in the function. If it is outside the range 0 to 255, you'll get an error message.

Figure 6.8 shows a program that produces a formatted display of ASCII codes 1 through 176 on the screen. You are already familiar with all the statements in the program. Line 30 starts a loop that will print 22 lines on the screen. Line 40 starts a loop that prints eight ASCII equivalents per line. The effect is to display 176 values on the screen at once. You'll notice that line 90 bypasses CHR$(12); a form-feed signal sent to the screen clears the screen and resets the cursor. While you may want to do that in some situations, it just messes up the display in this program.

If you want to produce a printed listing, you can use a much simpler listing of one equivalent per line, like this:

```
30 FOR X = 1 TO 255
40   PRINT X, CHR$(X)
50 NEXT
```

The effect is to print the equivalents in sequence up to 255; a form feed when X = 12 won't keep you from reading the rest of the output. If you find that your printer can't handle ASCII codes greater than 127, modify the program to go only that far.

Creating an ASCII String

Sometimes a program may need to use a string of all the same characters. GW-BASIC provides the STRING$ function for this purpose. To use the STRING$ function, you specify how long you want the string to be and the ASCII code for the character in one of these formats:

STRING$(*length,ASCII-code*)
STRING$(*length,string-variable*)

The function STRING$(15,61) requests a string of 15 equal signs. It might be used in this way:

```
200  TOP$=STRING$(15,61)
210  EDGE$=SPACE$(3)
220  PRINT EDGE$;TOP$;TITLE$;TOP$;EDGE$
```

The printed line has three spaces, followed by 15 equal signs, followed by the value of TITLE$, followed by 15 more equal signs, and three more spaces.

As with other functions, you can use variables instead of constants as arguments. If a string variable contains more than one character, only the first is used.

Using Screen Positions

Several GW-BASIC functions allow you to deal with individual positions on the screen. You've already seen how to use the LOCATE statement to position output on the screen. You can also find the contents of a particular location on the screen or determine the current cursor location.

The SCREEN Function

You can identify the contents of a particular location on screen with the SCREEN function. Notice that this is **not** the same as the statement that sets the screen mode. Here's the basic SCREEN function format:

x=SCREEN(*row,col*)

The variable x must be numeric; the function returns the ASCII code of whatever is at the location indicated by (*row,col*). The row is the line on the screen; it must be between 1 and 25. The column indicator must be between 1 and 40 or 1 and 80, depending on the screen mode and width. Here's how you might use the SCREEN function in a program after the user has been prompted to press 1 to see additional information.

```
500 ' routine to check screen contents
505 LOCATE 20,20
510 A$=INKEY$ : IF A$ = "" THEN GOTO 510
520 ITEM=SCREEN(20,20)
530 IF ITEM=49 THEN GOSUB 3000 ELSE GOSUB 4000
540 IF ITEM>49 THEN PRINT "Item pressed was ";
CHR$(ITEM)
```

You can use numeric variables in the SCREEN function if appropriate.

The POS Function

The POS function returns the column containing the cursor position, from 1 to 40 or from 1 to 80, depending on the screen mode and width. While POS has an argument, the argument has no effect; it is a dummy argument. You can use POS(0) or POS(X) and it has the same effect.

You can use the POS function to find the location of the cursor and use that location in the SCREEN function. Here's an example:

```
700 WHERE = POS(X)
710 ITEM = SCREEN(2,WHERE)
720 PRINT CHR$(ITEM)
```

Line 700 finds the position of the cursor on the line and assigns the result to the variable WHERE. Line 710 assigns the ASCII value of whatever appears on the screen on line 2 in the WHERE position to the variable ITEM. Line 720 then displays the character form of whatever was in that position.

If you use the POS value as the column number in a LOCATE statement, it must be the second value named. For example, the statement LOCATE 5, POS(0) refers to the fifth line and the column where the cursor is currently located.

The CSRLIN Variable

The CSRLIN variable holds the value of the current row, or the line that contains the cursor. Here's how to use it:

x=CSRLIN

The variable x receives the value of CSRLIN; it is always between 1 and 25. Here's a routine that uses both CSRLIN and POS:

```
1000 X=CSRLIN
1010 Y=POS(0)
1020 LOCATE 12,20
1030 PRINT "Hello, Sailor"
1040 LOCATE X,Y
```

In this routine, the numeric variables X and Y receive the current row and column values. The LOCATE statement resets the cursor and the PRINT statement prints a message at that location. Finally, the last LOCATE statement restores the original cursor location.

Suppose we add statements `1035 B=SCREEN(12,24)` and `1050 PRINT CHR$(B)` to the routine. Line 1035 captures the ASCII code of the character displayed on row 12, position 24; that's the fifth character of the message that begins at 12,20. So the character "o" would be displayed by line 1050 in the original cursor location.

1. In direct mode, find the ASCII code for "C".
2. In direct mode, display the ASCII character that has code 124.
3. Write a short program that accomplishes these steps:
   a. Uses the STRING$ and SPACE$ functions to set up strings of eight asterisks and eight spaces.
   b. Clears the screen, then displays five sets of the two strings on line 10, each in a different color.
4. Test the program, then modify it so it restores the default colors and displays the character shown on line 10, position 20.
5. Test the program, then modify it so that it saves the cursor position when the program begins (before the screen is cleared), then prints the character from item 4 in that location after printing the colored line.

The result of `PRINT ASC("C")` *is 67. The result of* `PRINT CHR$(124)` *is* |*; a vertical bar is displayed on the screen.*

Here's a complete sample program for items 3, 4, and 5:

```
10 X = CSRLIN
20 Y = POS(0)
```

```
30 CLS
40 A$ = STRING$(8,42)
50 B$ = SPACE$(8)
60 LOCATE 10
70 FOR C = 1 TO 5
80    COLOR C
90    PRINT A$;B$;
100 NEXT
110 COLOR 7,0
120 LOCATE X,Y
130 PRINT SCREEN(10,20)
140 END
```

Lines 30 through 100 make up the program as specified in item 3. The added lines accomplish items 4 and 5. Your program can be different and still solve the problem.

Inputting a Complete Line

You have learned to use the INPUT statement to let a program receive data from the keyboard. When you input a string, the ↵ ends the string. If you input several variables by specifying them in a single INPUT statement, you must separate them with commas. If you use a comma in a single variable, you get the ?Redo from start message. To include a comma in a variable value with INPUT, you must use double quotation marks to enclose the value.

If you want to allow entry of a long string of data from the keyboard, without regard to contents, you can use the LINE INPUT statement. Here's the format:

LINE INPUT [*prompt;*]*string-variable*

The statement works much like INPUT, but the variable must be a string, and there must be only one. No question mark is displayed following the prompt. The user enters data, and it is accepted until the user presses ↵. Commas and quotes can both be included in the value; everything typed before the carriage return becomes a part of the value.

You'll find that LINE INPUT is useful in many programs where the simple INPUT statement requires too many on-screen instructions to make the data acceptable. The INPUT statement might not be adequate in the following examples:

```
Type your full name: John H. Smith, Jr.
?Redo from start_
Type your full name: Ashley, Ruth
?Redo from start_
```

Suppose a program includes the command LINE INPUT "Type your full name: "; FULLNAME$. Here's how the screen might look:

```
Type your full name: Davison Smith, Sr.
Type ...
```

If the program used the basic INPUT statements, the commas would cause problems. You can use LINE INPUT instead of INPUT whenever it seems to be appropriate.

Receiving a Predetermined Number of Characters

You have seen how to use the INKEY$ function to receive a single character from the keyboard. With INKEY$, the program must create a short loop to pause the program until the keyboard entry is made. A similar function is INPUT$, which can specify a length. When the program encounters the INPUT$ function, it automatically waits for keyboard entry of the number of characters specified. Here's the format:

string-variable=INPUT$(*n*)

The value of *n* can be as small as 1 or as large as 255; in most cases you'll use 1, 2, or a similar small number. Like INKEY$, INPUT$ provides no on screen prompt. And no characters that are entered appear on the screen. A statement such as CHOOSE$=INPUT$(1) causes the program to wait until a single character is entered. CHOOSE$=INPUT$(3) causes the program to wait until three characters are entered; the three-character string is then assigned to CHOOSE$.

All characters except Ctrl-Break or Ctrl-ScrollLock are assigned to the string variable, even carriage returns and commas. Here's a short example:

```
100 PRINT "Type 1 to continue or 2 to stop."
110 CHOICE$ = INPUT$(1)
120 IF CHOICE$ = "1" THEN GOSUB 1000
130 IF CHOICE$ = "2" THEN GOSUB 9000
140 GOSUB 3000
```

Trapping Key Presses

GW-BASIC lets a program trap noncharacter key presses while a program is running and execute various subroutines. The KEY statement names the key to be turned on or off, and the ON KEY statement tells the program what to do when one is trapped. This lets you easily use the function keys, for example, to let program users make quick choices. The keys in the key line display are in effect in direct mode. While a program is running, however, you can use the keys for other purposes.

Key trapping can get very complex. For example, you can define your own key combinations (such as Ctrl-B) to trap. We won't go into all the details. In this section, you'll learn to trap function keys 1 through 10 and the four arrow keys. Table 6.4 lists the keys that can be trapped and the number assigned to each. We aren't covering the user-defined keys in this book.

Setting Keys for Trapping

You already know how to use the KEY statement to turn the key line display in the GW-BASIC editor on or off. You can also use it to turn on one or more keys for trapping. Here's the format:

KEY(*n*) ON
KEY(*n*) OFF
KEY(*n*) STOP

The numbers shown in Table 6.4 are used to refer to the various keys. Using KEY(1) ON enables trapping of F1; KEY(2) OFF turns off trapping of F2; KEY(3) STOP stops the effect of trapping F3, but saves the keypress just in case KEY(3) ON is used later.

Suppose you want to capture the last four functions keys while a program is running. You could use separate statements or one like this:

KEY(7) ON : KEY(8) ON : KEY(9) ON : KEY(10) ON

Table 6.4. KEY Variable Values

1 - 10	F1 - F10
11	Up-arrow
12	Left-arrow
13	Right-arrow
14	Down-arrow
15 - 20	User-defined

Once a key is enabled, it will be trapped until turned off or paused with STOP, except while the interpreter is waiting for INPUT or LINE INPUT entry to end. The program must be running for the capture to occur. You may have to use a loop to make the program pause; keys can be trapped while waiting for INKEY$ input. Or you could use a FOR...NEXT loop that does nothing several thousand times to pause the program briefly, then continue if nothing occurs.

Key Capture Effect

Once a key is turned on for trapping, what happens? Whenever the key is pressed, the program saves it. You tell it what to do with the ON KEY statement. Here's the format:

ON KEY(*n*) GOSUB *line-number*

You specify a subroutine to be executed for each key being trapped. Both the KEY and ON KEY statements must occur before the key is pressed. Then GW-BASIC watches constantly for all the keys turned on. Whenever one is pressed, the subroutine specified is executed. Then standard program execution resumes, at the point where the key was trapped. You might want to let the user press a function key to get help at any time while the program is running. Figure 6.9 shows how this looks in a program.

Notice that line 100 uses the INPUT$ function. Line 10 turns F1 on and specifies the effect. Line 50 tells the user to press F1 for help. The subroutine beginning at line 500 uses many features covered in this chapter. Line 510 saves the current cursor position from the screen. Lines 520 through 550 set up the color, position, and text for a help message, while line 560 restores the default colors. Line 570 restores the cursor position to what it was when the subroutine began. If the cursor position is not saved and restored, the next random number displayed after the subroutine ends will be on the line following the displayed information, rather than following the last standard output.

The catch with key capture is that the same key has the same effect until you change it. If you want pressing F1 to have a different effect later in the program, use a new statement, like this:

```
1200 ON KEY(1) GOSUB 8000
```

Alternatively, you could turn the key off, either permanently with KEY(*n*) OFF or temporarily with KEY(*n*) STOP. The key trapping is especially useful

```
10 KEY (1) ON : ON KEY (1) GOSUB 500
20 CLS
30 PRINT "Press 0 to stop program. Any other key gets"
40 PRINT " another random number between 1 and 100."
50 PRINT "Press F1 for help at any time."
60 B$="A"
70 WHILE B$ <> "0"
80    RANDOMIZE TIMER
90    PRINT INT(RND*100+1)
100    B$=INPUT$(1)
110 WEND
120 END
500 ' F1 trap subroutine
510 X=CSRLIN : Y=POS(0)    ' get cursor position
520 COLOR 1,3
530 LOCATE 20,40 : PRINT "Press any key to get
another random"
540 LOCATE 21,40 : PRINT "number. When you have seen
enough, "
550 LOCATE 22,40 : PRINT "just press 0 (zero)        "
560 COLOR 7,0            ' restore default colors
570 LOCATE X,Y           ' restore cursor position
580 RETURN
```

Figure 6.9. Key Pressing

in games and other highly interactive programs. You'll see several uses for
key trapping as you continue in this book.

1. In direct mode, use an INPUT A$ statement and type a variable that in-
   cludes a comma. Notice the result.
2. In direct mode, try the same thing with a LINE INPUT statment. Use
   PRINT A$ to see the effect.
3. Write a short program to receive two characters from the keyboard,
   then display them on line 10, column 20.
4. Write a program segment to accomplish the following:
   a. Set up key capture for F1, F2, and F3.
   b. Use LINE INPUT to receive a line of input that includes commas.
   c. Ask the user to press one of the three function keys being trapped.
   d. Display the function key pressed and the line entered.

5. Test the program.

You'll get the ?Redo from start message from the INPUT statement, while the LINE INPUT statement works fine. The PRINT A$ statement displays the message with its commas.

Here's a program that accomplishes the problem in item 3. Your program can be different and still be correct.

```
10 ' use INPUT$ function
20 CLS
30 PRINT "Type two characters; don't press Enter"
40 TYPED$ = INPUT$(2)
50 LOCATE 10,20
60 PRINT "You entered "; TYPED$
70 END
```

Here's a program segment that solves the problem in item 3:

```
100 ON KEY(1) GOSUB 1000
110 ON KEY(2) GOSUB 2000
120 ON KEY(3) GOSUB 3000
130 KEY(1) ON
140 KEY(2) ON
150 KEY(3) ON
160 COUNT = 0
170 PRINT "Type four verbs, separated by commas"
180 LINE INPUT A$
190 PRINT "Press F1, F2, or F3"
200 IF COUNT = 0 THEN GOTO 200
210 END
1000 ' pressed F1
1010 PRINT "You pressed F1, after typing "; A$
1020 COUNT = 1
1030 RETURN
2000 ' pressed F2
2010 PRINT "You pressed F2, after typing "; A$
2020 COUNT = 1
2030 RETURN
3000 ' pressed F3
3010 PRINT "You pressed F3, after typing "; A$
3020 COUNT = 1
3030 RETURN
```

Your program could be very different and still be correct.

Summary

This chapter covered several commands and techniques you can use to control console I/O as programs are running.

The SCREEN statement changes the mode of the screen, allowing different resolution and graphic capabilities.

The WIDTH statement allows the screen to use double-wide or single-wide characters.

The COLOR statement works with the SCREEN statement to determine which colors are displayed in which areas of the screen.

The PALETTE statement works in some SCREEN modes to control the effect of COLOR statements.

The LOCATE statement positions the cursor and text that follows it on the screen.

The SPACE$ and STRING$ functions create strings of spaces or ASCII characters.

The CSRLIN and POS functions capture the line or character position of the cursor on the screen.

The LINE INPUT statement receives a value that includes commas and semicolons; it puts quotes around the value.

The KEY and ON KEY statements trap key presses while a program is running and execute subroutines for any enabled keys.

Exercise

In this exercise, you'll modify the program you wrote in the Chapter 5 Exercise. Refer back to it if you didn't write that program or if you neglected to save it.

1. Load 5CHAPEX.BAS and list it. Run it so you recall what this program does and how it works.
2. Modify the program so that it uses INPUT$ instead of INKEY$ to get information from the keyboard.
3. Modify the program to use green characters on the default background. For the actual data line output, use a white background.
4. Add statements to position the displayed lines vertically on the screen, spaced as you want them. Start each at the tenth position.
5. At the end of the program, restore the original colors.
6. Take time to try out the program. Correct it until it works, then renumber the lines before continuing.
7. Now set up the program so that the user can press F1 to get an explanation of factorials. The explanation should appear in the lower-right

part of the screen. (If you don't know how factorials work, just put a few lines of anything in the message.) First set up the KEY and ON KEY commands.

8. Now write the subroutine to handle the message. Print it in a colored rectangle with characters of a different color.

The program is shown below. All added lines are shown in bold.

```
10 ' Chapter 6 Exercise Program; modified from Chapter 5
20 KEY (1) ON : ON KEY (1) GOSUB 1000
30 COLOR 2
40 C$ = "C"
50 ' begin major repeat section
60 WHILE C$ = "C" OR C$ = "c"
70 CLS
80 LOCATE 5,10
90 PRINT "This program calculates factorials"
100 LOCATE ,10
110 INPUT "Enter the number whose factorial you want: ",TOP
120 TOTAL = 1
130 FOR X = 1 TO TOP
140     TOTAL = TOTAL * X
150 NEXT
160 COLOR 2,7 : LOCATE 8,10
170 PRINT TOP "factorial is " TOTAL
180 COLOR 2,0 : LOCATE 9,10
190 PRINT "Press F1 any time to find out how factorials work."
200 LOCATE 11,10
210 PRINT "To continue press C. Any other key quits."
220 C$=INPUT$(1)
230 WEND
240 PRINT "Program ended"
250 COLOR 7,0
260 END
1000 ' What are factorials
1010 LOCATE 15,40 : COLOR  3,4
1020 PRINT "A factorial is calculated by multiplying"
1030 LOCATE ,40
1040 PRINT "1 times 2 times 3 times 4 up to the      "
1050 LOCATE ,40
1060 PRINT "number in question.                      "
1070 COLOR 2,0
1080 RETURN
```

We didn't save and restore the cursor position because each PRINT statement in the program has its own LOCATE statement. If you didn't LOCATE each or clear the screen before asking for input, you should save and restore the cursor position in the subroutine. However, your program could be very different and still be correct.

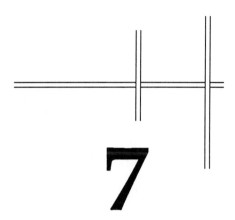

7

Sequential Files

T his chapter deals with programs that create and use sequential files. Files are stored on disk and contain data values that can be processed by computer programs. This eliminates the necessity of providing input at the keyboard while a program is running. Most GW-BASIC programs use one or more files. Once you become comfortable using files, you will be able to write GW-BASIC programs to create files of data and process them. In this chapter, you will learn to:

- Use MKDIR, CHDIR, and RMDIR commands to manipulate directories from within GW-BASIC
- Use the NAME command to rename a file from within GW-BASIC
- Use OPEN statements to prepare sequential files for use
- Use WRITE # and PRINT # statements to place records in sequential files
- Use INPUT # and LINE INPUT # statements to read records from sequential files
- Use CLOSE statements to save sequential files
- Use the EOF function to detect the end of a sequential file
- Use the LOF function to determine the length of a sequential file
- Use the LOC function to determine the position of a record in a sequential file
- Write and execute complete programs to create and access sequential files
- Debug programs

DOS Disk Structure

To use files efficiently in a GW-BASIC program, you must know a bit about the structure of the DOS disk and how it stores data.

DOS Disks

A DOS computer generally has several different disk drives. It always has at least one diskette drive named drive A:. It doesn't matter to GW-BASIC what size or density a drive is; the DOS system takes care of that. Many systems have additional disk drives, named B: and other letters. GW-BASIC programs can handle data on floppy disks on any drive, no matter what type.

Many DOS systems also have hard disks; the first one is generally named C:. Other hard disks may be named D: and other letters. Each letter refers to a specific hard disk. It doesn't matter to GW-BASIC what size, density, or speed the hard disk is. Your system may also have RAM drives (which are actually in memory), which have letter names and are treated like other drives by GW-BASIC. If you are working on a network, you may also have network drives available to you. If you provide GW-BASIC with a valid drive name, it will be able to find the drive no matter which type it is.

To a GW-BASIC program, all disks are treated the same. You just tell the program which drive contains a file you want, and it looks on that drive. The current drive is the one currently active. At the DOS level, a prompt such as C> or C:\> indicates that C is the current drive.

DOS Disk Directories

Every disk contains at least one directory, the root directory. All files are stored in directories. If a disk contains additional directories, you may have to specify a path to clearly identify a file. The directories can be used to group files for easy access or to change the files listed on the screen.

One directory is always current. If you haven't changed the directory, the root directory (named \ [backslash]) is current. Suppose the root directory contains two directories named GWBASIC and TEXTS; their full names are \GWBASIC and \TEXTS, since both start at the root directory. A file named FIRST.BAS stored in the GWBASIC directory has the full file specification of \GWBASIC\FIRST.BAS; this is often referred to as the file path. If you include the drive name, it would be specified as C:\GWBASIC\FIRST.BAS.

Like file names, directory names are limited to eight characters, with a three-character extension. While extensions are permitted in directory names, most people omit them. The current directory on each disk is the one DOS has set as the default. If your DOS prompt looks like C:\>, the root directory is current. If it looks like C:\GWBASIC>, the GWBASIC directory is current. Each drive has a current directory.

Creating and Changing Directories

You can use several commands within GW-BASIC to manipulate directories; these commands are much like the corresponding DOS commands, but you can't abbreviate them in GW-BASIC. Here are the formats:

> MKDIR *pathstring*
> CHDIR *pathstring*
> RMDIR *pathstring*

In all cases, the path is specified as a string. If you use an actual path, enclose it in double quotation marks. If you use a string variable containing the path, of course, you won't need the quotes. The GW-BASIC command `MKDIR "EXERCISE"` creates a directory named EXERCISE under the current directory; that's probably the one containing your GW-BASIC interpreter. The command `CHDIR "EXERCISE"` makes the directory current; any programs you save go to this directory and any programs you load must be in it, unless you specify a path. The command `RMDIR "EXERCISE"` removes the directory; you'll get an error message unless the directory is empty.

The command `CHDIR "\"` makes the root directory on the current drive the current directory. `CHDIR "\GWBASIC"` makes that directory current. You can change directories then try the FILES command to see what files it contains. Whenever you save a file, however, it goes automatically to the current directory. To save to a different directory, include the path in the SAVE command, as in `SAVE "\GWBASIC\EXERCISE\MICHAEL.BAS"`. If the directory is on another drive, include the drive name (with the colon) at the beginning of the path.

DOS Files

When your system stores data on a disk, it creates files. Each file is stored in a particular directory on a particular disk. The file names must be unique in each directory; you could have files named FIRST.BAS in two different directories, since the paths make the full file specifications unique. In the DOS system, each file name is limited to eight characters, with an extension of up to three characters.

If you want to change a file name, you can use the NAME command. Here is its format:

NAME *oldname* AS *newname*

The effect is to change the file name without making any other changes. The GW-BASIC command NAME "INVFILE" AS "TESTFILE" changes the name of the file named INVFILE in the current directory. The command NAME "CONVERT.BAS" AS "CHANGES.BAS" changes the name of CONVERT.BAS to CHANGES.BAS. If you use the FILES command again, you won't see INVFILE or CONVERT.BAS, but you will see the new names. You can use the NAME command to rename a stored file to save a different file under the original name.

Program Files. Each basic program that you save is stored in a file. You provide the file name when it is saved. A program file is stored in a special format by default. You have seen earlier how to store it in ASCII, or printable, format with the A parameter. The command SAVE "CONVERT" saves the current program file as CONVERT.BAS in the default format. The command SAVE "CONVERT", A saves the same file as CONVERT.BAS in ASCII format.

An ASCII-formatted file can be typed at the keyboard under DOS or after the SHELL command (with a command such as TYPE *filename*) and edited by most word processors. It can also be used as a data file and processed by a GW-BASIC program.

GW-BASIC programs can create and process two types of data files: sequential and random. Both files contain records, which are independent sets of data. How the records are constructed and how the file can be processed differ in both types of file.

Sequential Files. Each line in a sequential file (up to 255 characters, terminated by a carriage return) is a separate record. Each record can be a different length, but they are stored in a specific sequence. When such a file is processed, each record must be accessed in sequence. Suppose a file contains 100 lines. A program that creates the file must create first record 1, then record 2, and so on in order. A program that reads the file must read all records in sequence; if it only wants record 72, it must read the first 71 to get to it. A program file is an example of a sequential file. A GW-BASIC program could access records in a program stored as an ASCII file.

The records in the simplest sequential files contain a single variable each. That is, when you read one record, you have one variable name to deal with. Other sequential files contain multiple variables per record. You'll learn to handle both types in this chapter.

Data stored in sequential files is always in ASCII form. These files can always be viewed under DOS or after SHELL with the TYPE command.

Random Files. A random file is structured so that its records can be accessed randomly if desired. That is, if you want to read record 72, you can go straight to it without reading the first 71 records. To make this possible, all the records in a random file are the same length. The position of each record can be calculated from its record number, so that you can refer to a particular record by its number. Random file creation and access is more complex and more time consuming, but it is easier for users. Chapter 8 covers random file creation and use in detail.

Sequential Data Files in Programs

Before a GW-BASIC program can use a file, the file must be prepared for use so that the program can recognize it. And after the program is finished with it, the file must be put away neatly so that any changes or additions to the file are saved as part of it.

The OPEN Statement

The OPEN statement makes a file ready for use. Here are two formats and a few examples:

```
OPEN filename FOR mode AS #number
OPEN "m",#number, filename
OPEN "NEWFILE.OUT" FOR OUTPUT AS #1
OPEN FILEIN$ FOR INPUT AS #2
OPEN "C:\HSG\CHECKS" FOR APPEND AS #3
OPEN "O", #1, "NEWFILE.OUT"
OPEN "I", #2, FILEIN$
OPEN "A", #3, "C:\HSG\CHECKS"
```

The two sets of three statements have the same effect. Many versions of GW-BASIC allow you to omit the number sign (#), but we include it for documentation.

File Specification. The file name provides the file to be opened as a constant enclosed in quotes or as a string variable that contains the name of the file to be opened. The string can include the drive and path if the file is not in the current directory.

File Modes. The mode for sequential files can be INPUT, OUTPUT, or AP-PEND in the full format, or "I", "O", or "A" in the abbreviated format. Use INPUT or "I" if the file already exists and the program will use it for input data. Use OUTPUT or "O" if the file does not exist and the program will create it by writing records to it. If you use mode OUTPUT, any already existing file of the specified name will be erased and a new one of that name created. Use APPEND or "A" if the file already exists and the program will add records to the end of it. When you use APPEND, the file is opened for output, but the existing records are not erased.

If you use INPUT mode for a file that doesn't exist, you'll get the message File not found and the program will be terminated. If you use OUTPUT mode for a file that already exists, the file contents will be erased (without any warning) and the file will be used for new data. If you use APPEND mode for a file that doesn't exist, GW-BASIC will create the file and let you add records to it. Some programmers like to use APPEND instead of OUTPUT so as not to destroy existing data unwittingly.

Once a file is opened for a specific mode, any input or output statements must be of the correct type. That is, you can use input statements only for a file opened as INPUT. You can use output statements only for a file opened as OUTPUT or APPEND. A sequential file cannot be used for both input and output while it is opened. If the program must use it for both purposes, it must be opened one way, used, then closed and reopened for the other purpose.

File Number. The file number assigned in the OPEN statement remains associated with the file until it is closed. Any input or output statement specifies that number. If the program uses only one file, use number 1. If it uses three files, use numbers 1 through 3. A specific memory area, called a buffer, is also associated with the file number; GW-BASIC uses the buffer in doing file input and output.

By default, GW-BASIC lets a program have up to three open files at a time. A program could easily use more. For example, it could open three files, close two, then open two more. If the program must have more than three open at a time, you must use the /F switch when you start up GW-BASIC. You must also use the /I switch; it tells GW-BASIC to pay attention to switches that change file-related features. The command GW-BASIC /I/F:6 lets you have up to six files open at a time. The GW-BASIC command switches can be in any sequence.

1. Bring up GW-BASIC if it isn't up. Load any file.
2. Use the MKDIR command to create a directory named CHECKS under the current directory.
3. Use the CHDIR command to make the new directory current.
4. Save the loaded file as NEWONE.BAS.
5. Use the FILES command to see the files listed in the current directory.
6. Change the name of the file in the current directory to CHANGED.BAS. Check with FILES that it has changed.
7. Now write an OPEN statement to create NEWDATA.OUT as the only file referenced in a program.
8. Write an OPEN statement to use ACTIVITY.REC as the second input file referenced in a program.
9. Write an OPEN statement to add new records to the NEWDATA.OUT file. The program already has a #1 and #2 file.

If you have trouble with the MKDIR and CHDIR commands, be sure you enclosed the directory name in quotes. Once CHECKS is the current directory, it should contain no files until you save NEWONE.BAS. Change its name with NAME "NEWONE.BAS" AS "CHANGED.BAS" and it stays in the new directory under the new name.

Each of your OPEN statements should look like one of these pairs:

```
OPEN "NEWDATA.OUT" FOR OUTPUT AS #1
OPEN "O", #1, "NEWDATA.OUT"

OPEN "ACTIVITY.REC" FOR INPUT AS #2
OPEN "I", #2, "ACTIVITY.REC"

OPEN "NEWDATA.OUT" FOR APPEND AS #3
OPEN "A", #3, "NEWDATA.OUT"
```

You may have included a line number.

Record Length. The records in a sequential file can be any length, and each record can be a different length. However, by default, GW-BASIC assumes the record length will be 128 characters and it reserves a memory buffer of that size. If you place more than 128 characters in the buffer, you'll see an error message and the program will terminate. If you want to use longer records, use the /I and /S switches when starting GW-BASIC.

The /S:n switch lets you specify a different size buffer to hold the record in memory. If you start up with GW-BASIC /I/S:180, the interpreter can handle records up to 180 characters long for each file that is opened. If you use multiple switches on the GW-BASIC command, they can be in any sequence, but each must be preceded by the slash (/) character. For example, to run a program that uses four files with the largest record being 168 characters long, use the command GWBASIC /I/F:4/S:168 to start the GW-BASIC program.

The CLOSE Statement

When a program is finished using a file, it must close the file so that it is properly stored with an end-of-file mark and an updated file entry in the DOS directory. Here's the CLOSE statement format:

CLOSE #*filenumber*[,#*filenumber*]

All you really need is the word CLOSE; it closes all files that are open. In fact, execution of the END statement also closes all open files. For documentation, however, most programs include the number of each file being closed. This is essential only when you are closing one or more files and leaving others open for later use in the program. If you include a file number on the CLOSE statement, it must match one used in an OPEN statement. You can close several files in one statement; just separate them with commas. You can omit the number sign (#) in many versions of GW-BASIC, but it is included here for documentation.

File OPEN and CLOSE Examples

Suppose a program is going to create a file to be named ALLTAPES; the program uses only one file. The file would be opened and closed with statements like these:

```
OPEN "ALLTAPES" FOR OUTPUT AS #1
CLOSE #1
```

Another program uses a file named NEWTAPES and adds the records in it to the end of the ALLTAPES file. The program would use two OPEN statements and a CLOSE statement, for example:

```
OPEN "ALLTAPES" FOR APPEND AS #1
OPEN "NEWTAPES" FOR INPUT AS #2
CLOSE #1, #2
```

File Input Statements

The input statements for a file are similar to those used to get input from the keyboard, with the addition of a file number. You can use either of these formats:

LINE INPUT #*filenumber, string-variable*
INPUT #*filenumber, variable-list*

Aside from the file number, which must match the file number in the appropriate OPEN statement, the rules for using these statements for input from files are the same as at the keyboard.

The statement LINE INPUT #1, INFO$ reads a record containing a single string variable from the file opened as #1 and stores it in the string variable INFO$. The statement INPUT #2, CUSTOMER, CONTACT$, BALANCE reads a record from the file opened as #2 and stores the first field in the CUSTOMER numeric variable, the second in the CONTACT$ string variable, and the third in the BALANCE numeric variable.

File Output Statements

While it is possible to use a statement similar to PRINT for file output, most programs use the WRITE statement instead. The only difference is that the WRITE statement puts double quotation marks around each string variable individually and separates them with commas, while PRINT does not. The quotation marks and commas become part of the sequential file, taking up character positions. Double quotes aren't essential in many data files, but if there is any possibility that your data will include such characters as commas or unprintable characters, the quotes become necessary when later programs try to access the data. Most programmers just use WRITE to create all sequential files unless saving space on disk is a major concern. Here are the statement formats:

PRINT #*filenumber,*[USING *strings;*] *list*
WRITE #*filenumber, list*

The PRINT # and PRINT # USING statements work just like the keyboard equivalents, except that they send the information to the specified open file.

The WRITE # statement automatically includes double quotation marks around each value and puts a comma between them. It doesn't leave an extra space before numeric values. And it inserts a carriage return at the end of the output.

The statement WRITE #2, CUSTOMER, CONTACT$, BALANCE sends a record containing three fields to the file opened as #2. The data record might look like this: "DuoTech, Inc.", "R. Ashley", 2345.75. Notice that the numeric variable doesn't have quotes.

Creating a Sequential File

Several steps are involved in creating any file. First, you have to set up the file. You have to get the values to put in the file. And you have to send the records to it. Finally, you have to put the file away. Figure 7.1 shows an example of a GW-BASIC program that creates a simple sequential file.

The program does a little more than creating a file; it also counts the number of records sent to it. Lines 20 through 70 do some housekeeping before the real work starts; they clear the screen, remove the function key line display to give a cleaner screen, initialize a counter, and tell the user how to enter data.

Line 80 opens the file for output and assigns file number 1. Any statements in the program that refer to the file will reference this same number.

Line 100 prompts the user to input a line at the keyboard, then stores it in the string variable INFO$. As soon as the user presses ↵ before typing any data on a line, the program branches to the part of the program that closes the file and ends the program.

If any data is entered on a line, the WRITE #1 statement sends it to the file as a record, then adds 1 to the counter. Line 140 then transfers control back to line 90 to get another record.

The ending routine displays the number of records stored in the file, then closes the file and ends the program. At this point, the file is an ASCII file

```
10 ' Create a sequential file
20 CLS
30 KEY OFF
40 COUNT = 0
50 PRINT "Enter lines at => mark. Press Enter when
line complete."
60 PRINT "To end file creation, press Enter at =>
mark."
70 PRINT
80 OPEN "tapes" FOR OUTPUT AS #1
90 ' Begin getting data for records
100    LINE INPUT "=>"; INFO$
110    IF INFO$ = "" THEN GOTO 150
120    WRITE #1, INFO$
130    COUNT = COUNT + 1
140 GOTO 90
150 ' ending routine
160 PRINT "The file contains"; COUNT; "records."
170 CLOSE #1
180 END
```

Figure 7.1. Program to Create a Sequential File

stored in the default directory. You can use it with DOS commands such as TYPE and PRINT, or access it under SHELL or your word processor.

Sample Run

Figure 7.2 shows the screen when the user is about to enter the 12th record. Notice that the prompt from the LINE INPUT statement appears on each line. One line contains more characters than fit across the screen to show you how it works. As long as you don't press ⏎ or exceed 255 characters, all the data goes in a single record.

Once the program is ended, and you have left GW BASIC, you can use the SHELL command, then type TYPE TAPES to see the contents of the new file. Remember to type EXIT to return to GW-BASIC. Here's how the first several lines look:

```
"The Tin Star"
"The Lion, the Witch, and the Wardrobe"
"The Wizard of Oz"
"Cat on a Hot Tin Roof"
```

```
Enter lines at => mark. Press Enter when line complete.
To end file creation, press Enter at => mark.

=>The Tin Star
=>The Lion, the Witch, and the Wardrobe
=>The Wizard of Oz
=>Cat on a Hot Tin Roof
=>A Funny Thing Happened on the Way to the Forum
=>Collection of excerpts from Monday Night situation comedies recorded in the sp
ring of 1991
=>Faulty Towers
=>The Treasure of the Sierra Madre
=>Chinatown
=>Indiana Jones and the Temple of Doom
=>Gone with the Wind
=>_
```

Figure 7.2. Program in Progress

The quotes are a permanent part of the file. Each double quotation mark takes up one character position.

Adding to the File

Suppose you want to add records to the file just created. If you simply run the same program again, the original output file will be erased and new data will be used to create a new file. To add records to it without losing the records already stored in the file, change the OPEN statement mode to APPEND, like this:

```
80 OPEN "TAPES" FOR APPEND AS #1
```

The messages are now a bit misleading, although the program will work correctly. You might also want to make these line changes, although they don't affect the file being created:

```
60 PRINT "To stop adding records, press Enter at =>
mark."
160 PRINT "You added";COUNT;"records to the file."
```

1. Using Figure 7.1 as a model, write a program to create a file named FIRST.OUT that will contain a list of full names. Don't worry about counting the records just yet.
2. Try out the program. When it prompts you for input, use names of friends. Include at least one that requires a comma. Put seven or eight separate records into the file.
3. Save the program file as 7CREATE1.BAS. Then use the SHELL command so you can check the file contents.
4. Type TYPE FIRST.OUT and see if your lines are listed. If they are, your program worked. If not, you'll have to examine the program and try to find the error. Compare it to Figure 7.1.
5. Once your program works, modify it to open the file for APPEND. Add statements to count the number of records added and display it before ending the program.
6. Try it out again. Once the program works correctly, save it again as 7CREATE2.BAS.
7. You can check your output file under DOS to see what it contains.

If you have trouble with the first program, make sure you used the same file number in the OPEN, WRITE #, and CLOSE statements. If you don't use the same string variable name in the INPUT statement that gets keyboard input and WRITE # statement, you can use a LET statement to assign the value.

Be sure to change OUTPUT to APPEND before running the program a second time. Your final program will look something like this:

```
10 ' Create a sequential file
20 CLS
30 COUNT = 0
40 PRINT "Enter lines at cursor. Press Enter to End."
50 OPEN "FIRST.OUT" FOR APPEND AS #1
60 ' Begin getting data for records
70    LINE INPUT DATALINE$
80    IF DATALINE$ = "" THEN GOTO 120
90    WRITE #1, DATALINE$
100   COUNT = COUNT + 1
110 GOTO 60
120 ' ending routine
130 PRINT "You added"; COUNT; "records."
140 CLOSE #1
150 END
```

Your program could be quite different and still be correct.

```
10 ' List on printer records from a sequential file
20 COUNT = 0
30 OPEN "TAPES" FOR INPUT AS #1
40 WHILE EOF(1) = 0
50    LINE INPUT #1, INFO$
60    COUNT = COUNT + 1
70    LPRINT COUNT TAB(5) INFO$
80 WEND
90 ' ending routine
100 PRINT : PRINT "    ***** End of File *****"
110 CLOSE #1
120 END
```

Figure 7.3. Listing a File

Accessing a Sequential File

Once a file is created, you want to be able to access it under GW-BASIC. Figure 7.3 shows a program that prints all the records in a sequential file on the printer.

When the file is closed after being opened as OUTPUT or APPEND, an end-of-file mark is added. The program can use the EOF function, as in line 40, to detect the end-of-file mark. The argument refers to the file number, so EOF(1) refers to the end-of-file mark in file #1. EOF(1) has the value 0 until the program has read the last record in the sequential file.

This program opens the file as INPUT. The WHILE statement in Figure 7.3 checks for the presence of the end-of-file mark; when it is encountered the value of the function is –1. Within the WHILE loop, the program reads each record with LINE INPUT #1 and stores the record in the variable INFO$. It then increments the counter.

The LPRINT statement prints the current value of the counter and the contents of the record just read. Then the loop continues until the end of the file. The result is a printed, numbered listing of the records in the file.

Displaying a File

Suppose you want to see a file's contents on the display screen instead. You could use the same program as in Figure 7.3 and just change LPRINT to PRINT, but then the records would scroll off the screen as it fills. A better technique is to display one or more records and ask the user to press a key to

```
10 ' Display screens of records from a sequential file
20 KEY OFF
30 GOSUB 900
40 OPEN "tapes" FOR INPUT AS #1
50 WHILE EOF(1) = 0
60    LINE INPUT #1, INFO$
70    COUNT = COUNT + 1
80    PRINT INFO$
90    IF COUNT > 10 THEN GOSUB 1000
100 WEND
110 ' ending routine
120 PRINT : PRINT "    ***** End of File *****"
130 CLOSE #1
140 END
900 ' Routine to set up the screen
910 CLS
920 PRINT "This program lists 10 records then pauses."
930 PRINT "Press Enter to continue."
940 LOCATE 4,1
950 COUNT = 0
960 RETURN
1000 ' Routine to pause the screen
1010 INPUT A$
1020 GOSUB 900
1030 RETURN
```

══════════ Figure 7.4. Displaying File Records on the Screen

continue. Figure 7.4 shows a program that displays ten records, then continues. This program is a bit more complex than the one in Figure 7.3 because it worries more about screen layout and user control. Line 20 turns off the KEY line display for a clean screen appearance. Line 30 invokes the subroutine at line 900, which sets up the screen by clearing it and printing some information for the user. The subroutine also sets the counter to zero so the program can keep track of the number of records handled. Line 40 then opens the file for input, assigning file number 1.

The WHILE loop handles reading of records with the LINE INPUT # statement, incrementing the counter, and displaying records.

When the counter exceeds 10, the subroutine at line 1000 is invoked. The INPUT statement waits until the user presses ↵, then invokes the setup subroutine starting at line 900 again, then returns control to the WHILE loop. The loop itself continues until the end of the file is reached. The ending message is displayed, the file closed, and the program terminated.

1. Using Figure 7.3 as a model, write a program to list all the records from FIRST.OUT on the screen.
2. Try the program out until it works, then save the program as 7LIST1.BAS.
3. Load and run 7CREATE2.BAS again and add several records to the end of the file. Then reload 7LIST1.BAS and run it again to see if the records were added.
4. Modify 7LIST1.BAS to include a record number at the beginning of each displayed or printed line.
5. Test the program again. Then save this version as 7LIST2.BAS.

If you have a problem, be sure you opened the file as INPUT. Set up a WHILE loop to read records and check for the end-of-file mark.

Your final program will look something like this:

```
10 ' Display records from FIRST.OUT
20 COUNT = 0
30 OPEN "FIRST.OUT" FOR INPUT AS #1
40 WHILE EOF(1) = 0
50    LINE INPUT #1, DATALINE$
60    COUNT = COUNT + 1
70    PRINT COUNT,DATALINE$
80 WEND
90 CLOSE #1
100 END
```

Yours may be somewhat different and still be correct.

Multiple Fields per Record

So far, the sequential files you've seen have all used a single field per record. You can use multiple fields in much the same way. While GW-BASIC doesn't care, using a sequential file as input is much easier if you use the same number of variables in the same order in each record. And it helps to have a field that is in sequence in all records, such as a record number, an item number, a last name, or some variable that is unique in each record. Suppose a file contains records with an item code, followed by the item name, followed by the unit price; the item code is unique in each record. If each record has two string variables followed by a numeric variable, you can use the same input statement to access each record. And you can use the item code to identify records.

When a sequential file has multiple fields per record, you can process it more intensely. For example, you could look through the file to find the record you want, then display it. You could create a new file, using all or part of each record, and using only the records you want. This section shows more ways of processing sequential files.

Creating Files

To create a file with multiple fields per record, just gather the input values as needed, use several variables in the WRITE # statement, and they will all become part of the record. Figure 7.5 shows a sample program. Notice that each variable is received in a separate INPUT statement from the keyboard. The WRITE# statement then includes all three variables. Each string variable will be enclosed in quotes separately in the resulting output file, and the values will be separated by commas.

The program works much like the one in Figure 7.1. The file is opened for APPEND, so that data can be added later to the end. More screen formatting is used to make it easy for the user to enter data. The statements on lines 10 to 70 set up the screen and display beginning messages. Line 80 opens the file for APPEND. Lines 90 through 160 get data for one record; if the first field is left blank, the program branches to line 240 to end the program. Line 170 sends the record to the output file and line 180 increments the counter.

Lines 190 through 220 clear the three input lines for the next data entry, then line 230 branches back to line 90 to start building the next record.

The ending routine displays the number of records added in this run of the program, closes the file, and terminates the program.

Accessing Files

To access a record that contains multiple data items, you have to use the INPUT # statement and name the same number and sequence of variables as when the file was created. If the file was created with two numeric variables followed by four string variables, you have to use the same sequence to read them. You don't have to use the same variable names, however, when you access the file as when you created it.

To create a listing of all the records in the file created by Figure 7.5, you might use a program like the one in Figure 7.6. For more formatting and control, you can use spacing function or the PRINT # USING statement

```
10 ' Create a sequential file with multiple fields
per record
20 CLS
30 KEY OFF
40 COUNT = 0
50 PRINT "Enter data as prompted. Press Enter after
each field."
60 PRINT "To stop adding records, press Enter at
first field."
70 PRINT
80 OPEN "itemfil2" FOR APPEND AS #1
90 ' Begin getting data for records
100    LOCATE 4,5
110    INPUT "Item number: ",ITEM$
120    IF ITEM$ = "" THEN GOTO 240
130    LOCATE 5,5
140    LINE INPUT "Item name:    ";ITEMNAME$
150    LOCATE 6,5
160    INPUT "Item price:  ",PRICE
170    WRITE #1,ITEM$,ITEMNAME$,PRICE
180    COUNT = COUNT + 1
190    CLEARIT$ = SPACE$(50)
200    FOR X = 4 TO 6
210      LOCATE X: PRINT CLEARIT$
220    NEXT
230 GOTO 90
240 ' Ending routine
250 PRINT "You added "; COUNT; "records."
260 CLOSE #1
270 END
```

Figure 7.5. Multiple Variables per Record

instead. PRINT # USING works just like the basic PRINT USING statement except that it sends formatted output to the numbered file.

The primary difference between this program and the one in Figure 7.3 is in the INPUT statement. You must name a variable of the correct type to hold each field in the record.

1. Write a program similar to the one shown in Figure 7.5 that will create a file named MULT.OUT. MULT.OUT should contain three fields: a part number, a name, and a price.

```
10 ' List multiple fields from sequential records
20 CLS
30 KEY OFF
40 COUNT = 0
50 OPEN "ITEMFIL2" FOR INPUT AS #1
60 WHILE EOF(1) = 0
70    INPUT #1, ITEM$, ITEMNAME$, ITEMPRICE
80    COUNT = COUNT + 1
90    PRINT COUNT, ITEM$, ITEMNAME$, ITEMPRICE
100 WEND
110 PRINT : PRINT "   ***** End of File *****"
120 CLOSE #1
130 END
```

Figure 7.6. Accessing Multiple Variable Records

2. Run the program and place these values in it. Be sure to keep the part number field in sequence.

Item	Description	Price
A333	hammer, 2 pound	9.98
A334	hammer, 1 pound	7.98
A450	wrench, 5 inch	10.50
A590	wrench, 15 inch	29.98
B111	nails, 10p	0.25
B120	nails, 9p	0.24

3. Add another group of records, then save the program as 7MAKEMUL.BAS. Start your new part numbers with C and keep the digits in ascending sequence as you add records.

4. Modify your program 7LIST2.BAS to list the records in your MULT.OUT file. After you try it, save this program as 7LISTMUL.BAS.

Your 7MAKEMUL.BAS program should look something like this.

```
10 ' Create a sequential file with multiple fields per record
20 PRINT "Enter data as prompted. Press Enter after each field."
30 PRINT "To stop adding records, press Enter at first field."
40 PRINT
50 OPEN "MULT.OUT" FOR APPEND AS #1
60 ' Begin getting data for records
70    INPUT "Item number: ",ITEMCODE$
80    IF ITEMCODE$ = "" THEN GOTO 130
90    LINE INPUT "Item name:    ";ITEMNAME$
```

```
100  INPUT "Item price:  ",PRICE
110  WRITE #1,ITEMCODE$,ITEMNAME$,PRICE
120 GOTO 60
130 ' Ending routine
140 CLOSE #1
150 END
```

You probably used different variable names in your file creation program. The program to list the records is very much like 7LIST2.BAS. At least three lines will be different:

```
30 OPEN "MULT.OUT" FOR INPUT AS #1
50 INPUT #1, ITEMCODE$, ITEMNAME$, PRICE
70 PRINT COUNT, ITEMCODE$, ITEMNAME$, TAB(40);PRICE
```

You may have done additional formatting for the printed output. Your program may be quite different and still be correct.

Searching a Sequential File

If records in a sequential file have a unique identifier field, a program can read records until it locates a specific record, then display the information, and continue to locate other records.

Searching Unsequenced Records

If the records are in no particular order, you tell the program which record you want, then have it check each record in the file, using a routine like this:

```
180 INPUT "What item do you want to find"; FINDITEM$
190 OPEN "ITEMFILE" FOR INPUT AS #1
200 WHILE EOF(1) = 0
210   INPUT #1, ITEMCODE$, ITEMNAME$, PRICE
220   IF ITEMCODE$ = FINDITEM$ THEN GOTO 260
240 WEND
250 PRINT FINDITEM$, "Not found in file" : GOTO 270
260 PRINT ITEMCODE$, ITEMNAME$, TAB(40);PRICE
270 CLOSE #1
```

The routine gets a value from the keyboard, opens the file, checks through all the records for a matching one. If it finds a match, the information is displayed. If not, control falls through to line 250 which prints a message. In

```
10 ' Search for a record in a sequential file
20 CLS
30 KEY OFF
40 ' Find out which record to locate
50 INPUT "Type the five digit item number or press
Enter ",FINDITEM$
60 IF FINDITEM$ = "" THEN END
70 '   Look for record to match FINDITEM$
80 OPEN "itemfil2" FOR INPUT AS #1
90 WHILE EOF(1) = 0
100    INPUT #1, ITEM$, ITEMNAME$, PRICE
110    IF FINDITEM$ > ITEM$ THEN GOTO 140   ' Look at
next item
120    IF FINDITEM$ < ITEM$ THEN GOTO 180   ' Location
past; won't be found
130    IF FINDITEM$ = ITEM$ THEN GOTO 150   ' Item
found
140 WEND
150 ' Matching item found
160 PRINT "Item: ";ITEM$;"   Item name: ";ITEMNAME$;"
Price :";PRICE
170 GOTO 200
180 ' Item not found in file subroutine
190 PRINT : PRINT "Item number "; FINDITEM$ ; " not
in the file."
200 ' Get ready for next item
210 CLOSE #1
220 PRINT "Press Enter to continue" : PRINT
230 GOTO 40
```

━━━━━━━━━━ Figure 7.7. Searching Sequenced File

either case, the file is closed. The next search request will start over and OPEN the file again.

Searching Sequenced Records

If the records in the file are arranged so that the identifier field is in ascending or descending sequence, the search for a record is more efficient. The program doesn't have to check every record when the desired record is missing; it just checks until it reaches a record that would be past the requested one. Most files are sequenced in ascending order. The program in Figure 7.7 displays a specified record at the monitor. Notice that the file is opened for each request, the records are read and compared to the identifier, and then the file is closed.

The heart of this program is in the WHILE loop. The field that is in sequence in the record (ITEM$ here) is compared to the desired value (FINDITEM$ here). If they are the same, of course, the record has been located. If the field in the record just read (ITEM$) is less than the one you are looking for (FINDITEM$), the program must read the next record from the file and compare again. If the field in the record just read is greater than the one you are looking for, you have missed it—it isn't in the file. The program handles both these events very briefly. In a program you expect to do real work in your business, you would include more processing in each step.

1. Suppose you want to display selected records from your sequential file. Modify 7LISTMUL.BAS to do this.
   a. Load the program.
   b. Add lines to ask for the part number to be located.
   c. After the file is opened, add lines to read records and compare the item code to the number entered at the keyboard, then display the record if it is found.
   d. If the record isn't found, display a message for the user.
   e. Add lines to cause the program to repeat until the user is finished looking up records.
2. Test the program. When it works, save it as 7FINDMUL.BAS.

Your program might look something like this:

```
10 ' show selected records on screen
20 FINDIT$="AAAA"
30 WHILE FINDIT$<>""
40    INPUT "Enter the code of the item you want: ",FINDIT$
50    OPEN "mult.out" FOR INPUT AS #1
60    WHILE EOF(1) = 0
70       INPUT #1, ITEMCODE$, ITEMNAME$, PRICE
80       IF FINDIT$<>ITEMCODE$ THEN GOTO 100
90       PRINT ITEMCODE$;"   ";ITEMNAME$;TAB(50); PRICE
100   WEND
110   IF EOF(1) = 0 THEN GOSUB 1000
120   CLOSE #1
130 WEND
140 END
1000 ' Subroutine to print not found message
1010 PRINT "Record "; FINDIT$; " not found."
1020 RETURN
```

Line 20 sets a value so that the WHILE loop will get started. Each time it executes, a new value of FINDIT$ is input. Your program might be different and still be correct.

Updating Sequenced Files

If you want to see, print, or change information on several records from a sequenced file, you can put the unique fields in a separate sequential file, in the same sequence as in the main file, and gather the information that way. Figure 7.8 shows an example in which changes are made to the master sequential file based on changes specified in a smaller file.

Suppose a file contains customer numbers, customer names, and current balance. You have another file that contains the customer number and a charge or credit amount. To update the master file, you'll have to create a new file. The new file will contain many unchanged records, as well as changed records for any customers that were included in both files. If a customer was included in the change file, but not in the master file, you'll have to print an error message. In the sample data we've been using, you might want to change the prices on many items in the file. The change file might include just the item number and the new price. The program in Figure 7.8 accomplishes this.

The program uses two sequential files as input and produces an updated master file as output. The heart of the program again is record matching, but this time it involves records from two input files. Before the main record-matching routine, the program reads a record from each file (lines 90 and 100). Each time it enters the main WHILE loop (lines 120 through 160), the program has a record from each file available.

In the main loop, the sequence fields are compared. If the value of the field in the changes file (CHANGEITEM$) is greater than the value in the master file (ITEM$), the subroutine at line 2500 is processed. Since the program knows it hasn't reached the right master record yet, the subroutine copies the current master record over to the new master file (#3), reads another record from the old master file (#1), and returns control to the main WHILE loop.

Again it has two records to compare, since the change record read earlier is still available to compare with the new master record. At the point of return, the program branches to line 160 (WEND) and starts the loop again. If the value of CHANGEITEM$ is still greater than the value of ITEM$ in the new master record, the same thing happens again. It continues until the value CHANGEITEM$ is either equal to or less than ITEM$.

If the value of CHANGEITEM$ is less than the current value of ITEM$, the subroutine at line 3000 is executed. Now the program knows that it has passed

```
10 ' Program to update a master sequential file
20 ' using a sequential file to hold the changes.
30 ' It creates a third file as a new master file.
40 CLS
50 OPEN "ITEMFIL2" FOR INPUT AS #1     ' Original file
60 OPEN "CHANGES" FOR INPUT AS #2      ' Changes file
70 OPEN "NEWITEMS" FOR OUTPUT AS #3    ' New master
80 ' Read the first records for comparison
90 INPUT #1, ITEM$, ITEMNAME$, PRICE
100 INPUT #2, CHANGEITEM$, CHANGEPRICE
110 ' Start the comparisons
120 WHILE EOF(1) = 0 AND EOF(2) = 0
130    IF CHANGEITEM$  ITEM$ THEN GOSUB 2500 : GOTO 160
140    IF CHANGEITEM$  ITEM$ THEN GOSUB 3000 : GOTO 160
150    PRICE = CHANGEPRICE
152    GOSUB 2500
155    INPUT #2, CHANGEITEM$, CHANGEPRICE
160 WEND
170 WHILE EOF(2) = 0                         ' Finish up file #2
180    GOSUB 3000
190 WEND
200 WHILE EOF(1) = 0                         ' Finish up file #1
210    GOSUB 2500
220 WEND
225 WRITE #3, ITEM$, ITEMNAME$, PRICE 'Write last one
230 CLOSE #1, #2, #3
240 PRINT : PRINT "File updated"
250 END
2500 ' Copy a master record
2510 WRITE #3, ITEM$, ITEMNAME$, PRICE
2520 INPUT #1, ITEM$, ITEMNAME$, PRICE
2530 RETURN
3000 ' Handle unmatched change record
3010 LPRINT CHANGEITEM$, CHANGEPRICE, "  Not found"
3020 INPUT #2, CHANGEITEM$, CHANGEPRICE
3030 RETURN
```

Figure 7.8. Sequential File Update

the location in the master file where the record that matches the change record should be located. So the change record must be an error. The program prints an error message, then reads another record from the change file (#2), returns to the main WHILE loop, and jumps to WEND.

Eventually, a change record will match a master record. At this point, the change is made to the record, then subroutine 2500 is executed to send the changed record to the new master file and read a new master record, as well as a new change record. Then the cycle continues comparing the two new records.

Finally, the end of one of the input files is reached. Then control leaves the main WHILE loop. If the end of the master file was reached, the value of EOF(2) is still 0, so lines 170 through 190 are executed. Any records remaining in the change file at this point are errors, since they don't match a master record. A WHILE loop executes the subroutine at line 3000 until all the change records are processed.

If the end of the change file was reached first, all the records still remaining in the master file must be copied to the new master file to complete it, so lines 200 through 220 are executed. The subroutine at line 2500 does most of this, but it ends with reading the last record. When control finally leaves the final WHILE loop, the final record is written to the new master file, all files are closed, and the program terminates.

In this Self-Check, you'll consider some of the decisions required in maintaining sequential files. The questions ask you to write statements and make decisions for a program that requires file matching.

1. Suppose you want to combine records from files named MULT.OUT and MULT.MOR into one file while keeping the records in sequence. The program will put records from the two input files into an output file, depending on the values in the ITEMCODE$ field. Write OPEN statements for all three files; call the new one MULT.ALL.
2. The main processing loop needs a record from each input file to compare. Write statements to read records from each file.
3. The MULT.ALL file is to contain all records that occur in either input file. If the same code field value appears in both files, the record from MULT.OUT should be placed in MULT.ALL and the record from MULT.MOR flagged as a possible problem. What should the program do if the code value in the current record in MULT.OUT is less than the value in the current record in MULT.MOR?
4. Suppose the values of the code variable are the same in the two records being compared. What should the program do?
5. What should be done if the value in the current record in MULT.OUT is greater than the value in the current record in MULT.MOR?

For item 1, your OPEN statements should look like these:

```
OPEN "MULT.OUT" FOR INPUT AS #1
OPEN "MULT.MOR" FOR INPUT AS #2
OPEN "MULT.ALL" FOR OUTPUT AS #3
```

For item 2, your INPUT statements might look like these. Your variable names may be different; they must be different in the two statements.

```
INPUT #1, ITEMCODE$, ITEMNAME$, PRICE
INPUT #2, MORECODE$, MORENAME$, MOREPRICE
```

In item 3, the program should write the record from MULT.OUT to the output file, then read a new record from MULT.OUT before comparing again; it always writes the record with the lower number. In item 4 the values are equal. The record from MULT.OUT is written to MULT.ALL, the record from MULT.MOR is handled as an error, and a new record is read from each file before comparing again. In item 5, the program should write the record from MULT.MOR to the output file, then read a new record from MULT.MOR before comparing again.

Your decisions should be similar. A program to solve this problem must handle the file matching correctly and handle end of file processing for both input files.

Debugging Techniques

Programs that handle files frequently encounter problems. You'll be able to tell if the main record-matching portion of the program is correct by examining the output file under SHELL. If the records in the output file aren't in the correct sequence, you'll have to modify your record-matching statements.

If the last record in each input file doesn't get recorded correctly in the output file, look at your end-of-file processing. Remember that the EOF function stops being 0 when the last record has been read. This record remains available and may have to be processed by the program.

If you can't tell what is going wrong, add a few extra print statements. Try printing the variables you are matching just before the record-matching routine. You'll be able to see them on the screen. If that doesn't help you find the problem, put a PRINT statement as the first line of each subroutine, so the screen gives you a trace of which subroutines are entered. You can compare what you expect with this listing.

If these techniques don't work, use TRON to get a complete trace. You can add TRON at the point in the program where you see the problem, if you can narrow it down a bit.

File Handling Functions

You have already seen how to use the EOF function to identify when the last record in a file has been read. GW-BASIC has two additional functions you can use in programs that manage files.

The LOF Function

The LOF function returns the length of file in bytes. Here's the format:

n = LOF(*filenumber*)

The file number is the number assigned to the file in the OPEN statement. Since a sequential file is stored in ASCII form, one byte is used to store each character. The default maximum record length is 128 in sequential files.

The statement A=LOF(2) assigns the number of bytes in file #2 to the variable A. If that file contains 100 records, each 128 bytes long, A has the value 12,800. If all the records in the sequential file are the same length, you can get the number of records in the file, by dividing the result by the length of the record. A=LOF(2)/128 gives the number of records in the file when the default record length is used.

The LOC Function

The LOC function gives the location of the pointer in file, or the number of the record that will be written or read next. Here's the format:

n = LOC(*filenumber*)

As with the LOF function, the file number specifies the number assigned to the file in the OPEN statement. The LOC function returns the number of records read or written to file since opened.

When a sequential file is opened for input, GW-BASIC places the first record in its buffer, so the value of LOF for an input file is 1 as soon as it is opened. A program could check to see if a file is opened with IF LOC(2)=0 THEN GOSUB 3000. A search program might use the LOC function to report on the location of a record after it is found, rather than counting records. The value can then be used in other processing.

Summary

This chapter covered various statements and techniques useful in manipulating files under GW-BASIC, as well as those needed for creating and maintaining sequential files.

The MKDIR, CHDIR, and RMDIR commands let you make, change, and remove directories while in GW-BASIC. They work much as under DOS, but require double quotes around the string.

The NAME command lets you rename files to avoid overwriting them when you save a new file with the same name.

The OPEN statement prepares a sequential file for use as OUTPUT or INPUT. APPEND lets you add to the end of an output file.

The CLOSE statement stores a sequential file on disk.

The WRITE# statement lets you send fields to a sequential output file. PRINT# and PRINT# USING also work with sequential output files.

The INPUT# and LINE INPUT # statements let you read variables from a sequential input file.

The EOF function detects the end of a sequential file; use it to avoid reading past the end of an input file.

The LOF function gives the length (in bytes or characters) of a sequential file.

The LOC function gives the position of the current record in the sequential file.

Exercise

In this exercise, you'll write programs to create and list another sequential file. This file should contain five variables: the last name, first name, state, home phone, and work phone. Feel free to modify programs you wrote earlier in this chapter if you like.

1. Write a program to create the file. Use LINE INPUT for any fields that might include a comma.
2. Try out the program and add at least eight records. Keep the last names in alphabetical order if you can. Save this program as 7CHAPEX1.BAS.

3. Write a program to list some of the data from the records on the screen. Display up to three records in this format:
   Name: *firstname lastname*
   State: *state*
   Home: *number*   Work: *number*
   After each display, the user should be able to press Enter to see the next batch.
4. Test the program. Modify it to position the output if you like. Save this program as 7CHAPEX2.BAS.
5. If you want, write a program to locate a record by last name and display it on the screen. Assume the records aren't in any particular sequence. After you test it, name this program 7CHAPEX3.BAS.

Your program to create the file should look something like this:

```
10 ' Chapter 7 Exercise, program
20 KEY OFF
30 COUNT = 0
40 OPEN "PHONEDIR" FOR APPEND AS #1
50 ' Begin getting data for records
60    CLS
70    PRINT "Enter the values as requested. "
80    INPUT "First name: ",FIRSTNAME$
90    IF FIRSTNAME$ = "" THEN GOTO 170
100   LINE INPUT "Last name:   ";LASTNAME$
110   INPUT "State:       ",STATE$
120   INPUT "Home phone: ",HPHONE$
130   INPUT "Work phone: ",WPHONE$
140   WRITE #1,LASTNAME$,FIRSTNAME$,STATE$,HPHONE$,WPHONE$
150   COUNT = COUNT + 1
160 GOTO 50
170 ' Ending routine
180 PRINT "You added "; COUNT; "records."
190 PRINT "Number of bytes in file: "; LOF(1)
200 CLOSE #1
210 END
```

Your program to display the records should look something like this:

```
10 ' List records from PHONEDIR file
20 CLS
30 KEY OFF
40 GOSUB 190
50 OPEN "PHONEDIR" FOR INPUT AS #1
60 WHILE EOF(1) = 0
70    INPUT #1, LASTNAME$,FIRSTNAME$,STATE$,HPHONE$,WPHONE$
80    COUNT = COUNT + 1
90    PRINT
100   PRINT "Full name: ";FIRSTNAME$;" ";LASTNAME$
110   PRINT "From the state of "; STATE$
120   PRINT "Home phone: ";HPHONE$;"  Work phone: ";WPHONE$
```

```
130    IF COUNT = 3 THEN GOSUB 250
140 WEND
150 ' ending routine
160 PRINT : PRINT "    ***** End of File *****"
170 CLOSE #1
180 END
190 ' Routine to set up the screen
200 CLS
210 PRINT "This program lists 3 records then pauses."
220 LOCATE 4,1
230 COUNT = 0
240 RETURN
250 ' Routine to pause the screen
260 PRINT : INPUT "Press Enter to continue ",A$
270 GOSUB 190
280 RETURN
```

If you wrote a program to display records, it should look something like this:

```
10 REM This program locates a record by last name and
20 REM displays it on the screen"
30 KEY OFF
40 CLS
50 COUNT=0:FOUND=0
60 OPEN "PHONEDIR" FOR INPUT AS #1
70 INPUT "What last name: ";LASTNAME$
80 WHILE EOF(1)=0 AND FOUND=0
90    INPUT #1, LNAME$, FIRSTNAME$, STATE$, HPHONE$, WPHONE$
100    IF LASTNAME$=LNAME$ THEN GOSUB 140
110 WEND
120 IF FOUND=0 THEN PRINT "Sorry, couldn't locate that name."
130 END
140 PRINT
150 PRINT "Full name: ";FIRSTNAME$;" ";LNAME$
160 PRINT "State:     ";STATE$
170 PRINT "H. Phone:  ";HPHONE$
180 PRINT "W. Phone:  ";WPHONE$
190 FOUND=1
200 RETURN
```

Your program could be quite different. The one here uses a separate variable (FOUND) to indicate when a record was found. You could have used some other technique.

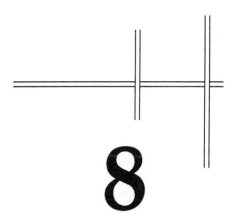

8

Random Files

This chapter deals with programs that create and use random files. Random files have the advantage over sequential files that any individual record can be accessed, as long as you know the position of the record in the file. Records can be added to a random file at any position. And random files can be updated in place; you don't have to create a new file to make changes. In this chapter, you will learn to:

- Determine the structure of records in a random file
- Use OPEN statements to prepare random files for use
- Use FIELD statements to describe the layout of data in records in a random file
- Use LSET and RSET statements to place values in field variables
- Use PUT statements to place records in random files
- Use GET statements to access records from random files
- Use CLOSE statements to save sequential files
- Use MKI$, MKS$, and MKD$ functions to convert numeric values for placement in fields for storage in random files
- Use CVI, CVS, and CVD functions to convert fielded numeric variables for use in GW-BASIC programs
- Write and execute complete programs to create and access random files
- Debug programs

193

Random File Structure

The records on a random file are stored in sequence on a disk, but there the similarity to a sequential file ends. The same amount of space is allocated to each record in a random file, so there aren't any end-of-record indicators. Since GW-BASIC knows how many characters are allocated to each record, it can find any individual record on request. If each record is 100 bytes long, requesting record 40 gets the 100 bytes starting at the 3,900th byte. If each record is 50 bytes long, requesting record 40 gets the 50 bytes beginning at the 1,950th byte. And since the records are all the same length, they can be updated in place; the program can make changes to a record, then write it back to the same location. Actually, although the specified amount of space is set aside per record, the program doesn't have to use all of it.

Unlike sequential files, a random file can be used for both input and output once it is open. This makes programs easier to handle and allows a program to accomplish more functions. For example, a program could open a file for random access, then let the user add some records, look at other records, and even update some.

When the file is opened, GW-BASIC provides an input/output (I/O) buffer the size of an individual record. When the program executes an input statement, GW-BASIC copies the appropriate record from the file to the buffer so the program can access it. When an output statement is issued, GW-BASIC sends the current contents of the buffer to the appropriate position in the file.

Like sequential files, random files must be opened before use and closed afterward. Before you can use random files in a program, however, you must learn more about the data and how it is stored. Special commands are necessary to describe the data in a record in a random file.

Random File Records

The length of each record in a random file is the same. That is, GW-BASIC reserves the same amount of space on disk for each record that is sent to the file. The record can contain several different fields, but each record for the file must contain the same number of fields, and each field must contain the same number of bytes.

The characters in a random file record are stored in string format, so you can TYPE them at the terminal under DOS. Unlike sequential files, however, random files don't automatically have a carriage return at the end of each record. So if you use the DOS TYPE command to list the file, the records won't be evenly arranged on your screen. Later in this chapter, you'll see how you can add a carriage return to the end of each record while placing a record in a random file.

A file contains space for all records up to the highest numbered one. All that space might not contain valid information, however. If a program adds record number 350, a record is added in the 350th position, even though the highest number before that might have been 240. The highest numbered record in the file determines the length of the random file.

Setting up the Record

GW-BASIC sets up an I/O (input/output) buffer to hold each record as it is used with a random file. The OPEN statement specifies the record length for records to be used with the file; the buffer is this exact size. A program may use just part of the record, if appropriate. The program uses a FIELD statement to define a template specifying how many bytes in the record are part of each data item. For string data, each character occupies one byte of memory. Numeric data must be converted to a special type of string before being placed in a random file; it must be converted back to standard numeric form for use by the program.

String Data

String data is stored in a random file record in its usual form. A record might contain a 7-character customer number, a 23-character customer name, 50 characters of address information, a 12-character city, a 2-character state, and a 10-character postal code field. All these are standard string data. The sum of the lengths of these fields (7+23+50+12+2+10=104) is the record length. Every record occupies 104 bytes on disk, even if the customer name is "AAA" and the city is "Lodi." Spaces fill out any unused positions in a field.

The FIELD Statement

The FIELD statement specifies the length, sequence, and name of each field in the file's record. Here's the format of the FIELD statement:

FIELD #*filenumber, n* AS *fieldstring* [*, m* AS *fieldstring*]

Like other file-related statements, the FIELD statement includes the number assigned to the file in the OPEN statement. Each element of the form *n* AS *fieldstring* describes a field in the record; *n* gives the number of bytes, while *fieldstring* gives the string variable name the program will use to refer to those bytes in the buffer. You can use as many of the elements as you wish; they must not be greater than the record length. All the items included in one FIELD statement describe a single record; like other statements, this one can be up to 255 characters long. If yours is longer, you'll have to use shorter field names.

Actually, you can use as many FIELD statements as you wish; a second FIELD statement for the same file describes an alternate layout of data in a record; this is called redefining the record. Each FIELD statement starts defining data at the beginning of the record, but it need not describe data to the very end. If your program will not refer to all the fields, the FIELD statement can stop when it defines the last one. As you'll see, the OPEN statement still specifies the full record length.

The FIELD statement that describes the longest record (often the only FIELD statement) defines the layout for the full record. Other FIELD statements might define just part of the data. The following statement defines the record described above:

```
FIELD #1, 7 AS FCUSTNO$, 23 AS FCUSTNAME$, 50 AS FCUSTADD$, 12
AS FCUSTCITY$, 2 AS FCUSTSTATE$, 10 AS FCUSTPOSTAL$
```

According to the FIELD statement, the first 7 bytes are referenced as FCUSTNO$, the next 23 as FCUSTNAME$, and so on. A total of 104 bytes are assigned. Once you decide how many fields and the length of each, you can calculate how long the records are for the file. You'll have to specify the record length in the OPEN statement; it must not be less than the total of the lengths specified for fields in FIELD statements for the file, or the file won't be created or accessed correctly. You'll get a Field Overflow message if the FIELD statement calls for more bytes than allocated in the OPEN statement.

Notice that we used an F as the first character in each field variable; this is not required, but it serves as a reminder. Field variables aren't handled quite the same as other variables. If you specify a field variable in an INPUT or as the destination in a LET (assignment) statement, you may get strange results. You use special statements to assign values to a field variable. Be careful, however, not to start a variable name with FN. As indicated in Appendix A, GW-BASIC reserves words starting with FN as user functions and doesn't interpret them as user variables.

The record number is not an integral part of the record in a random file. If you wish, you can include it as a separate field.

FIELD Definition Variations

Once a random file is established with a particular record structure as specified in FIELD statements, that record structure is fixed for the file. Later programs that refer to it must use the same general layout. Their FIELD statements must account for all the bytes and the data, but they can be a bit flexible. For example, a program that refers to the postal code in two parts might define it as 5 AS FZIP$, 5 AS FEXTENDED$ to account for the 10 bytes and allow the program to refer to just the first 5 characters.

If the program won't refer to all the data, it can use dummy field names for some of it. If a different program refers only to the customer number and the state, it might use this FIELD statement:

```
FIELD #1, 7 AS FCUSTNUM$, 85 AS FMISC1$, 2 AS FSTATE$, 10 AS
FMISC2$
```

The fields the program will use must be defined in the correct location in the record. The names of the field variables, however, can be different in different programs, as long as the positions are the same. Any bytes unused at the end of the buffer need not be defined, as long as the program never refers to them. All the fields are generally needed when the file is originally created to make sure each part of the record contains the correct data.

---

1. A record contains an item code in positions 1 through 6, a name in positions 7 through 20, and a description in positions 21 through 40. It ends with carriage return and line feed characters. Write a FIELD statement to describe the record for file #2.
2. Another record starts with an eight-character code, followed by eight ten-character names. Describe this record for file #1.

Your statements should look something like these:

```
FIELD #2, 6 AS FITEM$, 14 AS FITEMNAME$, 20 AS FDESC$, 2 AS
ENDSTUFF$
FIELD #1, 8 AS FCODE$, 10 AS F1NAME$, 10 AS F2NAME$, 10 AS
F3NAME$, 10 AS F4NAME$, 10 AS F5NAME$, 10 AS F6NAME$, 10 AS
F7NAME$, 10 AS F8NAME$
```

You probably used different field names. The commas are all required.

LSET and RSET Statements

Since you can't use a field variable as the target of an INPUT, LET, or assignment statement, GW-BASIC provides other statements just for this purpose. You'll need to use LSET and RSET to place values in the I/O buffer before writing the record to the random file. If the program uses a variable called CUSTNUM$ and the record variable in the FIELD statement is defined as FCUSTNUM$, the statement LSET FCUSTNO$ = CUSTNUM$ assigns the value to the field variable. Here are the statement formats:

> LSET *fieldvariable* = *string- expression*
> RSET *fieldvariable* = *string-expression*

The target string (the field variable) is on the left of the equal sign, just as in standard assignment statements. The *string-expression* can be a single string variable, a string constant, or any expression that returns a string value.

If the string value is shorter than the defined field variable, the value is left (LSET) or right (RSET) justified in the field variable; the variable is padded with spaces on the other end. If the value is the same length as the field variable, LSET and RSET have the same effect. If you use LSET or RSET with a standard string variable name on the left of the equal sign, the assigned string will be left or right justified in the receiving field.

You can also use the PRINT #, PRINT # USING, and WRITE # statements to refer to the random file, but they place the data in the I/O buffer, not in the file. The LSET and RSET statements give you more control over how and where data appears in the record.

Setting the Carriage Return

A field to hold the carriage return and linefeed characters occupies two bytes. Here's one way to set them up:

```
LSET FENDCHAR$ = CHR$(13) + CHR$(10)
```

The field FENDCHAR$ now contains the carriage return (ASCII 13) and linefeed (ASCII 10) characters. So whenever you access the file under a DOS TYPE command, each record starts on a new line. If the FIELD statement ends with 2 AS FENDCHAR$, you can follow it immediately with the LSET statement shown. If a program is doing only output to create the file, FENDCHAR$ will remain fixed throughout the program. If a record is input into the buffer, it will overlay these positions.

Numeric Data

Numeric data in a random record must be stored in a special string format. Once converted into a string, numbers take up a fixed number of bytes, which is seldom the same as the number of characters they display or print.

Numeric data can be in one of three forms: integer, single precision, or double precision. An integer has no decimal portion and has a value in the range −32,768 to 32,767. As a string, it takes up two bytes of memory. Single-precision numbers can be integers or can have a fractional part; they contain up to 7 significant digits and, as strings, take up four bytes of memory. A double-precision number can have up to 16 digits; the string is stored in eight bytes. A variable can be made double precision by appending # to the variable name. Most of the numeric variables you've used so far have been single precision; however, you can use integer and double-precision numeric data also. The numeric strings cannot be used for arithmetic or display; you have to convert them back to numbers for use in the program.

Converting numbers to strings results in some loss of precision. If you convert values to strings, then back to numbers again, a few thousandths may be off. For example, converting the value 8 to a string as a single-precision number, then back to a number for arithmetic or display, may result in 7.999999. If your value is an integer, treat it as one if you will convert it. Just use the % symbol at the end of the variable name.

Converting Numeric Data to Field Data. You use special functions to convert standard numeric variables into appropriate field variable strings. The functions correspond to the three numeric data forms. Here are their formats:

MKI$(*value*)   Convert integer to 2-byte field string
MKS$(*value*)   Convert single-precision number to 4-byte field string
MKD$(*value*)   Convert double-precision number to 8-byte field string

Any of these functions can take a numeric variable or value; if you aren't sure what form a variable is, treat it as single precision, since that is the default form. The result of the conversion is a 2-, 4-, or 8 byte string; it is not printable but GW-BASIC can read and store it just fine. The strings produced by these functions are not standard strings; we'll call them "numeric strings" so that they are not confused with standard string data.

The field variable that will hold the data should be defined as a string 2, 4, or 8 bytes long. The program can use LSET or RSET to place the numeric string in the field variable. Figure 8.1 shows an example. The conversion can be done in a separate statement or as part of the LSET (or RSET) assignment.

```
FIELD #1, 2 AS FCOUNT$, 14 AS FLNAME$
FIELD #1, 12 AS FFNAME$, 4 AS FBALANCE$
...
INPUT "Enter last name, first name: ";LNAME$, FNAME$
INPUT "Enter count, balance";INCOUNT, INBALANCE
CONVCOUNT = MKI$(INCOUNT)
LSET FCOUNT$ = CONVCOUNT
LSET FBALANCE$ = MKS$(INBALANCE)
LSET FLNAME$ = INLNAME$
LSET FFNAME$ = INFNAME$
```

Figure 8.1. Converting Numeric Display Variables

Converting Numeric Strings to Standard Numeric Format. When a program accesses a record from a random file, all fields are in string format. Any numeric strings must be converted if you want to do anything with them in the program other than write them back into a random file. There are three functions you can use to convert numeric strings back to standard numeric form. Here are the formats:

CVI(*fieldstring*)	Convert 2-byte string to integer
CVS(*fieldstring*)	Convert 4-byte string to single-precision
CVD(*fieldstring*)	Convert 8-byte string to double-precision

The returned value is a standard numeric variable and can be used as such in a program.

Storing the Record Number. Suppose you want to store the record number as the first variable in a random file record. Record numbers are always whole numbers, so you'll use it as an integer. An integer string occupies 2 bytes, so you would start the field description like this:

```
FIELD #1, 2 AS FRECNUM$, ...
```

Suppose the record number is stored in memory in the integer variable RECNUM%. This statement converts it into a numeric string for storage in the output record:

```
LSET FRECNUM$ = MKI$(RECNUM)
```

When you have to convert the value later for use by the program, use the function CVI(FRECNUM$).

1. You have a record described as FIELD #2, 6 AS FITEM$, 14 AS F1NAME$, 20 AS FDESC$. The program has just used INPUT statements to get values for ITEMCODE$, ITEMNAME$, and ITEM-DESC$. Write statements to put the input values in the field variables.
2. The record should also contain variables to hold the unit price and the quantity on hand, received into INPUT variables UPRICE and QONHAND (single-precision variables). Extend the FIELD statement to describe field variables for these.
3. Write statements to convert the numeric input values into numeric strings and place them in the field variables.
4. Write statements to convert the numeric string variables into standard numeric form as UNITPRICE and QUANTITY.

Your statements will look something like these:

```
1. LSET FITEM$ = ITEMCODE$
   LSET F1NAME$ = ITEMNAME$
   LSET FDESC$ = ITEMDESC$
2. FIELD #2, 4 AS FPRICE$, 4 AS FQUANT$
3. LSET FPRICE$ = MKS$(UPRICE)
   LSET FQUANT$ = MKS$(QONHAND)
4. UNITPRICE = CVS(FPRICE$)
   QUANTITY = CVS(FQUANT$)
```

You may have used different field variable names. And you may have used RSET instead of LSET statements for the numeric strings. Be sure you used strings for all variable names in the FIELD statements and on the left of the equal sign in LSET or RSET statements.

Opening and Closing Random Files

Now that you know a bit more about handling the data in random files, it's time to get into other aspects of programming them. Like other files, random files must be opened before use and closed afterward. The total number of files that can be opened at a time while a program is running defaults to three. You can specify more files with the /I/F:*n* parameter when starting up GW-BASIC. The value you supply for n sets the maximum number of files open at a time. Of course, programs can still use fewer.

The default maximum record length of each file, sequential or random, is 128 bytes. If one or more files uses a longer record, you can increase the maximum length with the /I/S:*m* parameter when starting up GW-BASIC. The value you supply for *m* sets the maximum record length. Of course, all files may use a shorter length.

If you want to use both parameters, you can type it as /I/F:*n*/S:*m* or as /I/S:*m*/F:*n*. The order of the switches makes no difference.

Opening Random Files

The OPEN statement for random files is similar to that for sequential files, but the options are a bit different. Here are the formats:

OPEN *filename* FOR RANDOM AS #*filenumber* [LEN=*recordlength*]
OPEN "R", #*filenumber,filename*,[*recordlength*]

Opening the file FOR RANDOM or with "R" tells GW-BASIC the file is a random file. This also tells it about the structure and permitted usage of the file, allocating an I/O buffer of the correct size. Once a file is opened for random access, it can be used for both input and output operations, using special statements that apply only to random files. The filename and filenumber are specified as with sequential files.

The recordlength parameter is specified only for random files. If you omit the recordlength parameter, GW-BASIC uses 128 as the default record length.

Recordlength Parameter

The recordlength parameter must not be shorter than the length specified by the fields in the FIELD statement that defines the longest record for that file. In most cases, you'll use a single FIELD statement and the OPEN statement will specify the exact record length. If the records are 110 bytes long, you might open the file like this:

```
OPEN "CUSTFILE" FOR RANDOM AS #1 LEN = 110
OPEN "R", #1, "CUSTFILE", 110
```

Both statements have the same effect. You can omit the record length parameter if you like; it will default to 128 characters. That is, the I/O buffer will be 128 characters long, as will the records. The fields you define begin at the first byte in the record. There may be unused bytes at the end, but if they aren't in a FIELD statement, they won't be available to the program. If you specify a length less than 128, the records will be shorter and you'll save space on the disk. If you use a length longer than 128, you must use the special parameter when you start up GW-BASIC before running the program.

Describing the Record

The FIELD statement (or statements) to describe a record in a random file must follow the OPEN statement for the file. Every file opened for RANDOM access must have at least one associated FIELD statement.

Closing Random Files

Random files are closed just as sequential files are. You can use a separate CLOSE statement for each file, or combine all in a single CLOSE statement. The statement CLOSE #1, #2, #3, #4 closes four files, in any combination of sequential and random.

Creating Random Files

Random files are created with the PUT statement, which writes a record from the I/O buffer to the file. GW-BASIC uses the record number, which the program supplies, to decide where to put the record in the file. If the record number is 1, the record becomes the first record in the file. If the record number is 25, the record becomes the 25th record in the file. You can put record 145 in the file, even if there aren't already 144 records to precede it. The file gets large quickly this way. Record numbers that represent records that haven't yet been added may contain garbage rather than printable data.

Creating a random file consists of building each record in the buffer using LSET or RSET statements, setting the record number, and issuing the PUT statement. The same process is used to change records in a random file.

The PUT Statement

Output to a random file is done with the PUT statement; it takes whatever is currently in the I/O buffer and sends it to the file as a record. If you use PRINT

or WRITE # statements, they send data only to the buffer. Before the PUT statement is executed, the program must build the record in the I/O buffer; most programs use LSET and/or RSET statements, but you could use PRINT # or WRITE # for this step. Here's the PUT statement format:

PUT #*filenumber, recordnumber*

The statement PUT #1, 6 sends the data in the buffer, established by the FIELD statement and placed there with LSET and/or RSET statements earlier in the program, as record number 6 to the file. If no record 6 existed, it creates one. An existing record 6 is overwritten. Most PUT statements use a variable to hold the record number; the variable must represent a positive whole number. PUT #2, ITEMNO sends the record in the buffer for file #2 as the record number indicated by ITEMNO. If you omit the recordnumber value, the record is placed in the next position in the file after the last one put there.

A Sample Program

Figure 8.2 shows a program that defines and creates a random file, using a sequential file as input. After setting up the screen in lines 20 and 30, the program sets variable RECNUM to zero; this variable will be used to manipulate the record number. Line 50 tells the user what the program does. Line 60 opens the random file as #2 and sets the record length at 29. Line 70 opens the sequential file as #1; data read from this file will be used to build records for the random file. Line 80 is a FIELD statement that sets up the fields in the record for the random file. Notice that there are only two fields; these are both standard, rather than numeric, strings.

The WHILE loop from lines 100 through 160 creates the random file. The condition is the end of the sequential file (#1). The record number is set to next value in sequence. Then the INPUT #1 statement gets the next record from the sequential file and stores it in three fields. Two LSET statements place the two string values in the buffer. The PUT statement specifies the random file and the variable that holds the record number. When the loop has read the last record in the sequential input file, control branches out of the loop. The ending routine displays a message showing how many records were added, then it closes both files and ends the program.

A random file could be created from keyboard input as well. In that case, you define only one file and prompt for the appropriate input. The program can create record numbers in sequence or ask the user to provide them.

```
10 ' Create a random file
20 CLS
30 KEY OFF
40 RECNUM = 0
50 PRINT "This program creates a random file from a
sequential one"
60 OPEN "ITEMFILE" FOR INPUT AS #1
70 OPEN "RANFILE" FOR RANDOM AS #2 LEN = 29
80 FIELD #2, 5 AS FITEM$, 24 AS FITNAME$
90 ' Begin getting data for records
100 WHILE EOF(1) = 0
110    RECNUM = RECNUM + 1
120    INPUT #1, ITEM$, ITEMNAME$, PRICE
130    LSET FITEM$ = ITEM$
140    LSET FITNAME$ = ITEMNAME$
150    PUT #2, RECNUM
160 WEND
170 ' Ending routine
180 PRINT "You added "; RECNUM; "records."
190 CLOSE #1, #2
200 END
```

Figure 8.2. Program to Create a Random File

A More Complex Program

Figure 8.3 shows another program that creates a random file. This program includes numeric data in the random file record.

The first part of the program, lines 20 through 60, gets the program started and sets up the screen. Lines 70 and 80 open both files, while line 90 is a FIELD statement to set up the random file record. Notice that it has four fields; the last two represent 4-byte numeric string items. The record length is the same in both the OPEN and FIELD statements.

The loop beginning at line 110 gets input data, formats it, and places it in the random file. First, it gets three fields from the input sequential file. Then it gets another field from the user at the keyboard. Lines 150 and 160 place the string data in the I/O buffer. Lines 170 and 180 convert the numeric data and place it in the I/O buffer. Line 190 sends the entire record from the I/O buffer to the random file, at the location indicated by COUNT, then COUNT is incremented and the loop continues until the end of the sequential input file is reached.

The ending routine displays a count of the number of records written to the random file, then closes both files and ends the program.

```
10 ' Create a random file with numeric fields
20 CLS
30 KEY OFF
40 COUNT = 1
50 PRINT "This program creates a random file from a
sequential one"
60 PRINT "You enter the quantity during each record
addition."
70 OPEN "ITEMFILE" FOR INPUT AS #1
80 OPEN "INVFILE" FOR RANDOM AS #2 LEN = 37
90 FIELD #2, 5 AS FITEM$, 24 AS FITNAME$,  4 AS
FPRICE$, 4 AS FQUANT$
100 ' Begin getting data for records
110 WHILE EOF(1) = 0
120    INPUT #1, ITEM$, ITEMNAME$, PRICE
130    PRINT "For item # "; ITEM$; " "; ITEMNAME$
140    INPUT "Please enter the quantity on hand ",QUANT
150    LSET FITEM$ = ITEM$
160    LSET FITNAME$ = ITEMNAME$
170    LSET FPRICE$ = MKS$(PRICE)
180    LSET FQUANT$ = MKS$(QUANT)
190    PUT #2, COUNT
200    COUNT = COUNT + 1
210 WEND
220 ' Ending routine
230 PRINT "You added "; COUNT-1; "records."
240 CLOSE #1, #2
250 END
```

Figure 8.3. Random File Creation with Numeric Data

1. Suppose you want to write a program that contains a numbered listing of all your videotapes. Allow 4 bytes to store each number and 70 characters per title. Write (on paper) the OPEN and FIELD statements needed for the program.
2. Continue to work on paper until you reach item 5 in this Self-Check. Write a short routine to ask for the data at the keyboard and store it in the field variable.
3. Write statements to initialize a record number variable, store it in the buffer, and place the record in the file at the current record number.
4. Write a statement to close the file.
5. Now write a short program that incorporates the statements you have just written to create a random file named "MYTAPES". The program

should set up the screen, ask for input at the keyboard, and create the file. Have the user indicate when no more input is needed.

6. Test your program and add at least ten records to the MYTAPES file. Save the program as RANTAPE.BAS.

7. Check the resulting file contents under SHELL with TYPE MYTAPES at the DOS prompt. Notice that the records are not lined up nicely. If you add a carriage return to the end of each record, they will produce a better ASCII listing.

Your program should look something like this; it includes all the statements in steps 1 through 4.

```
10 ' Create a random file
20 CLS
30 KEY OFF
40 COUNT = 0
50 PRINT "Enter lines at = mark. Press Enter when line complete."
60 PRINT "To end file creation, press Enter at = mark."
70 PRINT
80 OPEN "MYTAPES" FOR RANDOM AS #1 LEN = 74
90 FIELD #1, 4 AS FRECNO$, 70 AS FTAPENAME$
100 ' Begin getting data for records
110    COUNT = COUNT + 1
120    PRINT "For record #" COUNT ;
130    LINE INPUT " ="; INFO$
140    IF INFO$ = "" THEN GOTO 190
150    LSET FRECNO$ = MKS$(COUNT)
160    LSET FTAPENAME$ = INFO$
170    PUT #1, COUNT
180 GOTO 100
190 ' ending routine
200 PRINT "The file contains "; COUNT - 1 ; "records."
210 CLOSE #1
220 END
```

Your program may use different logic, but the structure of the statements should be as shown here. If your program creates a file, you did it right.

Accessing Random Files

Once a random file is created, you can access it whenever it is open. The OPEN statement is the same no matter how the file is used in a program. The FIELD statement can be the same as well. You can use any field names; they don't have to match the ones used when the file was created. You should use the same field lengths as were used when the file was created because the data will be interpreted as you specify.

For example, suppose the program included FIELD #1, 10 AS FPHONE$, 14 AS FLASTNAME$, 12 AS FFIRSTNAME$ when it created a random file. You could use FIELD #1, 3 AS FAREA$, 7 AS FPHONE$, 26 AS FFULLNAME$ when you use the file some other time. As long as the fields are standard strings, you won't have any trouble. Don't define numeric strings created with the conversion functions such as MKS$ any differently than when they were placed in the record, however; numeric strings can't be subdivided or combined unless the program won't refer to these values in any way.

The GET Statement

To read a record from a random file, you use the GET statement, which is much like the PUT statement. Here's the format:

GET #*filenumber, recordnumber*

The *filenumber* is the number assigned to the file in the OPEN statement. The *recordnumber* is the number of the record to be accessed; if you omit the recordnumber, the next record in the file will be accessed. The GET statement copies the appropriate record from the file into the I/O buffer. You must use the defined field names to refer to the data. If you want to remove all the data from the buffer with one statement, you can use an INPUT # statement to read data from the buffer into the standard variables you name.

To read all the records in sequence, you can increment the record number in a loop, as shown in Figure 8.4. This program creates a printed listing of all the records in the file created by the program in Figure 8.3. The program includes a few new components: locating the end of a random file and converting numeric strings back to their standard numeric form.

For access, the file is opened (line 70) just as for creation. The FIELD statement (line 80) again defines the structure of the buffer. Line 100 sets TOTRECS to the calculated number of records in the file. (The LOF function is explained in the next section.) Then the loop increments the record counter, gets each record in turn, converts any numeric fields to a printable form, and sends the record to the printer with LPRINT. When the record number (COUNT) exceeds the number of records in the file (TOTRECS), the loop ends. This method of accessing all the records in sequence is only effective if all the records are filled and printable. The program thinks it has real records up to the highest record number; it doesn't know if you have placed valid data in them all or not.

```
10 ' List records in a random file
20 CLS
30 KEY OFF
40 COUNT = 0
50 PRINT "This program lists a random file"
60 PRINT
70 OPEN "INVFILE" FOR RANDOM AS #1 LEN = 37
80 FIELD #1, 5 AS FITEM$, 24 AS FITNAME$,  4 AS
FPRICE$, 4 AS FQUANT$
90 ' Begin getting data to list
100 TOTRECS = LOF(1)/37     ' check # of records
110 WHILE COUNT < TOTRECS    ' process each record
120    COUNT = COUNT + 1
130    GET #1, COUNT
140    PRICE = CVS(FPRICE$)
150    QUANT = CVS(FQUANT$)
160    PRINT COUNT;" ";FITEM$;"   ";FITNAME$;TAB(38);
PRICE;TAB(46);QUANT
170 WEND
180 ' Ending routine
190 CLOSE #1
200 END
```

Figure 8.4. Listing a Random File

The LOF Function

The end of the file is located with the LOF (length of file) function. The function returns the number of bytes in the entire file; the argument gives the number assigned to the file in the OPEN statement. Dividing that value by the record length (37 in this case) gives the number of records in the file. Line 110 in Figure 8.4 tests whether the value of COUNT is still lower than the total number of records in the file (TOTREC). When it isn't, the loop is ended.

The LOC Function

As with sequential files, the LOC function returns the position of the record in the file. In random files, it returns the record number of the record just accessed with GET or written with PUT.

Be sure to convert numeric strings before using them for anything; they can't be used in expressions, calculations, or printing until you do.

1. Write a GET statement to read the current record from the random file.
2. Write a statement to determine the number of records in your file.
3. Modify the RANTAPE program so it will let you add records to the end. It must first calculate the number of records in the file and set the record counter to start at the next record. Then it can write records.
4. Test the new version and add at least five more records to MYTAPES. Save this version as RANTAPE2.
5. Modify the ending routine of your RANTAPE2 program to list all the records in the file before terminating.
6. Test the newest version, adding two more records. Save this version as RANTAPE3.

Your final program should look something like this:

```
10 ' Create a random file
20 CLS
30 KEY OFF
40 PRINT "Enter lines at = mark. Press Enter when line complete."
50 PRINT "To end file creation, press Enter at = mark."
60 PRINT
70 OPEN "MYTAPES" FOR RANDOM AS #1 LEN = 74
80 FIELD #1, 4 AS FRECNOS, 70 AS FTAPENAME$
90 COUNT = LOF(1)/74
100 ' Begin getting data for records
110    COUNT = COUNT + 1
120    PRINT "For record #" COUNT ;
130    LINE INPUT " ="; INFO$
140    IF INFO$ = "" THEN GOTO 190
150    LSET FRECNOS = MKS$(COUNT)
160    LSET FTAPENAME$ = INFO$
170    PUT #1, COUNT
180 GOTO 100
190 ' ending routine
200 PRINT "The file contains"; COUNT - 1; "records."
210 GOSUB 1000
220 CLOSE #1
230 END
1000 ' Routine to list all records in MYTAPES file
1005 COUNT = 0
1010 TOTCOUNT = LOF(1)/74
1020 WHILE COUNT < TOTCOUNT
1030    COUNT = COUNT + 1
1040    GET #1, COUNT
1050    TAPENO = CVS(FRECNOS)
1060    PRINT TAPENO TAB(6) FTAPENAME$
1070 WEND
1080 RETURN
```

Line 90 calculates the number of records currently in the file. The loop 100-180 starts adding records at the next available location. The subroutine starting at line

1000 lists the records in the file. Your logic may be a bit different. Make sure the first and last records are listed in the result.

Random Access

Random files can be accessed in any sequence. Once a random file is opened, it can be used in any way. You can read any record by specifying its record number. You can add a new record anywhere in the file by specifying its record number. You can change any record by changing data in one or more of its fields and putting it into the file again without changing its record number.

Figure 8.5 shows a program that accesses and displays a record when the user enters the record number. It first checks the file length, then tells the user what the acceptable range is. If the user enters a record number that isn't in the file, the program terminates.

```
10 ' Locate a specific record in a random file
20 CLS
30 KEY OFF                        ' To clear the screen
40 FIND = 1                       ' To force the WHILE loop
50 OPEN "INVFILE" FOR RANDOM AS #1 LEN = 37
60 FIELD #1, 5 AS FITEM$, 24 AS FITNAME$,  4 AS
FPRICE$, 4 AS FQUANT$
70 TOTRECS = LOF(1) / 37
80 PRINT "The file contains " TOTRECS "records."
90 PRINT "If you enter a record number not in the
file, the program ends"
100 ' Begin one item request
110 WHILE FIND >= 1 AND FIND <= TOTRECS
120    INPUT "Enter the record number you want ",FIND
130    IF FIND < 1 OR FIND > TOTRECS THEN GOTO 180
140    GET #1, FIND
150    PRICE = CVS(FPRICE$)
160    QUANT = CVS(FQUANT$)
170    PRINT FITEM$;"  ";FITNAME$;TAB(30);PRICE;
TAB(46);QUANT
180 WEND
190 ' Ending routine
200 PRINT "Ended because you asked for record "; FIND
210 CLOSE #1
220 END
```

Figure 8.5. Random File Access

When a valid record number is entered at the keyboard (line 110), the GET statement (line 130) uses that value to access the record. The numeric values are converted, and the record displayed. Figure 8.6 shows a variation in which random updates are made. The user is asked if changes are needed (subroutine 1000). Then, if they are, new values are gathered from the keyboard and the record is written back. Since the value of the record number (FIND) isn't changed, the new values replace the old ones in the file, updating the record.

Figure 8.7 shows still another variation. In this one, the user is asked if a new record should be added to the file. Another subroutine (line 500) handles adding a new record and assigning a new record number at the end of the file. Notice that the file length is changed in the process, so the message to the user is changed.

1. Write a new program to do keyboard access of your MYTAPES file. Use Figure 8.5 as a model if you like.
2. Test the program, examining several different records. Then save this program as RANLOOK.BAS.

Your program should look something like this:

```
10 ' Locate a specific record in a random file
20 CLS
30 KEY OFF
40 PRINT
50 OPEN "mytapes" FOR RANDOM AS #1 LEN = 74
60 FIELD #1, 4 AS FRECNO$, 70 AS FTAPENAME$
70 TOTRECS = LOF(1) / 74
80 PRINT "The file contains"; TOTRECS; "records."
90 PRINT "If you enter a record number not in the file, the pro-
gram ends"
100 ' Begin one item request
110   INPUT "Enter the record number you want to see ",FIND
120   IF FIND < 1 OR FIND > TOTRECS THEN GOTO 180
130   GET #1, FIND
140   RECNO = CVS(FRECNO$)
150   PRINT
160   PRINT RECNO; TAB(5); FTAPENAME$
170 GOTO 100
180 ' Ending routine
190 PRINT "Ended because you asked for record"; FIND "."
200 CLOSE #1
210 END
```

Your logic may be somewhat different, but the effect should be the same.

```
 10 ' Locate and update a record in a random file
 20 CLS
 30 KEY OFF
 40 FIND = 1
 50 OPEN "INVFILE" FOR RANDOM AS #1 LEN = 37
 60 FIELD #1, 5 AS FITEM$, 24 AS FITNAME$,  4 AS
FPRICE$, 4 AS FQUANT$
 70 TOTRECS = LOF(1) / 37
 80 PRINT "The file contains"; TOTRECS; "records."
 90 PRINT "If you enter a record number not in the
file, the program ends"
100 ' Begin one item request
110 WHILE FIND >= 1 AND FIND  <= TOTRECS
120    INPUT "Enter the record number you want ", FIND
130    IF FIND < 1 OR FIND > TOTRECS THEN GOTO 190
140    GET #1, FIND
150    PRICE = CVS(FPRICE$)
160    QUANT = CVS(FQUANT$)
170    PRINT FITEM$;" ";FITNAME$;TAB(38);PRICE;
TAB(46);QUANT
180    PRINT: GOSUB 1000
190 WEND
200 ' Ending routine
210 PRINT "Ended when you asked for record"; FIND; "."
220 CLOSE #1
230 END
1000 ' Subroutine to see if changes are needed
1010 PRINT "Press 1 to change the price"
1020 PRINT "   or 2 to change the quantity"
1030 PRINT "Any other key continues"
1040 CHANGE$ = INPUT$(1)
1050 IF CHANGE$ = "1" THEN GOSUB 1500
1060 IF CHANGE$ = "2" THEN GOSUB 2000
1070 RETURN
1500 ' Subroutine to change the price
1510 PRINT: INPUT "Type the new price: ", NEWPRICE
1520 LSET FPRICE$ = MKS$(NEWPRICE)
1530 PUT #1, FIND
1540 RETURN
2000 ' Subroutine to change the quantity
2010 PRINT: INPUT "Type the new quantity: ",NEWQUANT
2020 LSET FQUANT$ = MKS$(NEWQUANT)
2030 PUT #1, FIND
2040 RETURN
```

═══════════════ Figure 8.6. Random File Update

```
10 ' Randomly access or add records to a random file
20 CLS
30 KEY OFF
40 FIND = 1 : RECLEN = 37
50 OPEN "INVFILE" FOR RANDOM AS #1 LEN = RECLEN
60 FIELD #1, 5 AS FITEM$, 24 AS FITNAME$,   4 AS
FPRICE$,  4 AS FQUANT$
70 TOTRECS = LOF(1) / RECLEN
80 PRINT "The file contains " TOTRECS "records."
90 PRINT : PRINT "Press 1 to add records to the file"
100 PRINT "Any other key accesses records randomly."
110 CHOICE$=INPUT$(1)
120 IF CHOICE$ = "1" THEN GOSUB 500
130 PRINT
140 PRINT "If you enter a record number not in the
file, the program ends"
150 ' Begin one item request
160 WHILE FIND >= 1 AND FIND <= TOTRECS
70   INPUT "Enter the record number you want ",FIND
180   IF FIND < 1 OR FIND > TOTRECS THEN GOTO 230
190   GET #1, FIND
200   PRICE = CVS(FPRICE$)
210   QUANT = CVS(FQUANT$)
220   PRINT FITEM$;"   ";FITNAME$;TAB(38);PRICE;
TAB(46);QUANT
230 WEND
240 ' Ending routine
250 PRINT "Ended when you asked for record " FIND "."
260 CLOSE #1
270 END
```

Figure 8.7. Random File Processing (Part 1)

Random File Techniques

If you expect to create a large random file and add records to various parts of it, a good technique is to first initialize all the records in it. You can do this by creating the file and writing a record full of spaces to each location. Then the records contain valid data and won't produce data errors. You might even place the record number in one field or use a value that indicates an empty record in the first field, so programs can test to see if a record has been placed in a given position yet.

Many programmers like to define a one-character field as the first variable in each record. The value in this field can indicate the status of the record. You

```
500 ' Routine to add records to file
510 ITEM$ = " "
520 WHILE ITEM$ <> ""
530     PRINT
540     INPUT "Enter the new item number: ", ITEM$
550     IF ITEM$ = "" THEN GOTO 650
560     INPUT "  Enter the new item name: ", ITEMNAME$
570     INPUT "           Enter the price: ", PRICE
580     INPUT "        Enter the quantity: ", QUANT
590     LSET FITEM$ = ITEM$
600     LSET FITNAME$ = ITEMNAME$
610     LSET FPRICE$ = MKS$(PRICE)
620     LSET FQUANT$ = MKS$(QUANT)
630     TOTRECS = TOTRECS + 1
640     PUT #1, TOTRECS
650 WEND
660 PRINT "The file now contains"; TOTRECS; "records."
670 RETURN
```

Figure 8.7. Random File Processing (Part 2)

might use "E" for Empty, "D" for Deleted, "M" for Modified, and so on depending on the use made of the file.

Problems with Random File Access

The major problem with random file access is in knowing the record number. If there is some correlation between a field in the record and the record number, it helps. So if the records in the file are in sequence by employee number, for example, the record numbers will also be in sequence. You need some sort of calculated, manual, or printed system of referring to records. In Chapter 11, you'll learn one way to do this using an index that the program builds in memory.

Controlling Multiple File Access

If you write a program to run in a network environment, the program must make sure that only one user at a time tries to change a record in the file. You can do this with the LOCK and UNLOCK statements. Before reading a record, the program can lock it so no other program can get access. If no changes are being made, the program should immediately unlock it so the record is available to other programs. Before writing a changed record back to the file, the program should lock it so that no other program can access the record. After it is written safely, the program unlocks it again.

If a program is working with a block of records or even all of them, it can lock the file itself to prevent any other access of the particular record or a seqence of records. In either case, the program should unlock the file or records as soon as possible.

The LOCK statement specifies the file number and perhaps one or more record numbers. Here are the formats:

LOCK #*filenumber*
LOCK #*filenumber,recordnumber*
LOCK #*filenumber,recordnumber* TO *recordnumber2*

The UNLOCK statement has the same formats. If just the *filenumber* is specified, as in LOCK #2, no other program can access the file until UNLOCK #2 is issued by that program. If the *filenumber* and *recordnumber* are specified, as in LOCK #1, RECNUM, no other program can access that particular record in the specified file until UNLOCK #1, RECNUM is issued by that program. The value of RECNUM must not change between the LOCK and UNLOCK statements. A series of records can be locked with a statement like LOCK #1, RECNUM TO RECNUM2. A corresponding UNLOCK statement is needed to release the records.

If a program tries to LOCK a record or file that is already LOCKed by another program, it gets the message Permission Denied.

The UNLOCK statement must specify the same parameters as the corresponding LOCK. LOCK and UNLOCK always work in pairs. If the program uses an UNLOCK statement that doesn't match the previous LOCK statement, the message Permission Denied arises; this is the same message that appears when a program tries to access a LOCKed file. It doesn't interrupt the running of the program, but it will probably produce incorrect results.

Summary

This chapter has covered the basics of describing and using random files in GW-BASIC programs.

Records in a random file are all the same length, which allows reading or writing a particular record if you know its position in the file.

The OPEN statement prepares a file for RANDOM mode and specifies the size of record to be associated with the file; the CLOSE statement closes the file. Once a random file is open, it can be used for input, output, or both.

The FIELD statement describes the layout of a record in a random file, specifying the number of bytes reserved for each field or variable in the record.

The LSET and RSET statements position data in a specific field in a random file record. If the value is shorter than allowed for the field, it is aligned on the left (LSET) or right (RSET).

The GET statement accesses a record from the random file by record number and stores it in the I/O buffer allocated for the file.

The PUT statement sends the values stored in the I/O buffer to the random file and stores it at the position indicated by the current record number.

The MKI$, MKS$, and MKD$ functions convert a numeric integer, single-precision, or double-precision values to a numeric string form which occupies 2, 4, or 8 bytes, respectively, in the I/O buffer. All values in the buffer must be strings.

The CVI, CVS, and CVD functions convert numeric strings to standard integer, single-precision, and double-precision numeric forms so they can be used in calculations and for display.

Records in a random file can be updated in place; a program can GET a record, make changes to it, and PUT it back in the same location.

Exercise

In this exercise, you'll write programs to create and access another random file. You'll create it from the sequential file (PHONEDIR) you created at the end of Chapter 7, plus one field added at the keyboard. Each record in the random file will include the last name (14 characters), the first name (12 characters), the state (2 characters), the home phone number (13 characters), and the work phone number (13 characters) from the sequential file. In addition, you'll supply the age (an integer) from the keyboard. If you used more than two characters in the state field in your sequential file, use more here as well. Feel free to modify programs you wrote earlier in this chapter if you like.

1. Write a program to create the file. You'll have to open both files. Use COMMITEE as the name for the new random file. Remember to use a name like AGE% for the keyboard input and convert it to an integer 2-

byte string.
2. Try out the program, supplying the age for each record. Save the program as 8CHAPEX1.BAS.
3. Write a program to list the data from the records in three lines on the screen. Put the name on the first line, the state and age on the second line, and the two phone numbers on the third line. Be sure to convert the age string back to numeric form.
4. Test the program. Modify it to position the data readably on the screen. Save this program as 8CHAPEX2.BAS.
5. If you want, write a program to add records in sequence to the end of the file or locate a record by record number. It can do either or both operations, depending on how much practice you want using random files. After you test it, save this program as 8CHAPEX3.BAS.

Your program to create the random file should look something like this:

```
10 ' Chapter 8 exercise; create file
20 CLS
30 KEY OFF
40 RECNUM = 0
50 PRINT "This program creates a random from a sequential file"
60 OPEN "PHONEDIR" FOR INPUT AS #1
70 OPEN "COMMITEE" FOR RANDOM AS #2 LEN = 56
80 FIELD #2, 14 AS FLNAME$, 12 AS FFNAME$, 2 AS FSTATE$, 13 AS
FHPHONE$, 13 AS FWPHONE$, 2 AS FAGE$
100 ' Begin getting data for records
110 WHILE EOF(1) = 0
120    RECNUM = RECNUM + 1
130    INPUT #1, LNAME$, FINAME$, STATE$, HPHONE$, WPHONE$
140    PRINT "Enter the age for ";FINAME$;" "; LNAME$;"."
150    INPUT AGE%
160    LSET FAGE$ = MKI$(AGE%)
170    LSET FLNAME$ = LNAME$
180    LSET FFNAME$ = FINAME$
190    LSET FSTATE$ = STATE$
200    LSET FHPHONE$ = HPHONE$
210    LSET FWPHONE$ = WPHONE$
220    PUT #2, RECNUM
230 WEND
240 ' Ending routine
250 PRINT "You added "; RECNUM; "records."
260 CLOSE #1, #2
270 END
```

Your program to display the records should look something like this:

```
10 ' List records in a random file
20 CLS
30 KEY OFF
40 COUNT = 0
50 PRINT "This program lists a random file"
```

```
60 PRINT
70 OPEN "COMMITEE" FOR RANDOM AS #1 LEN = 56
80 FIELD #1, 14 AS FLNAME$, 12 AS FFNAME$, 2 AS FSTATE$, 13 AS
FHPHONE$, 13 AS FWPHONE$, 2 AS FAGE$
90 ' Begin getting data to list
100 TOTRECS = LOF(1)/56       ' check number of records in file
110 WHILE COUNT < TOTRECS    ' process every record in file
120    COUNT = COUNT + 1
130    GET #1, COUNT
140    AGE = CVS(FAGE$)
150    PRINT "Full name: "; FFNAME$; " "; FLNAME$
155    PRINT "State: "; FSTATE$; "    Age: "; AGE
160    PRINT "H: "; FHPHONE$; "    W: "; FWPHONE$
170 WEND
180 ' Ending routine
190 CLOSE #1
200 END
```

*If you wrote a program to access and add records, it should look something like
the following program. Yours might perform only one function.*

```
10 ' Randomly access records or add new ones to a random file
20 CLS
30 KEY OFF
40 PRINT
50 OPEN "COMMITEE" FOR RANDOM AS #1 LEN = 56
60 FIELD #1, 14 AS FLNAME$, 12 AS FFNAME$, 2 AS FSTATE$, 13 AS
FHPHONE$, 13 AS FWPHONE$, 2 AS FAGE$
70 TOTRECS = LOF(1) / 56
80 PRINT "The file contains"; TOTRECS; "records."
90 PRINT : PRINT "Press 1 to add records to the file"
100 PRINT "Any other key lets you access records randomly."
110 CHOICE$=INKEY$: IF CHOICE$ = "" THEN GOTO 110
120 IF CHOICE$ = "1" THEN GOSUB 280
130 PRINT
140 PRINT "If you enter a record number not in the file, the pro-
gram ends"
150 ' Begin one item request
155    PRINT
160    INPUT "Enter the record number you want to see ",FIND
170    IF FIND < 1 OR FIND > TOTRECS THEN GOTO 240
180    GET #1, FIND
190    AGE = CVS(FAGE$)
200    PRINT "Full name: ";FFNAME$;" ";FLNAME$
210    PRINT "State: ";FSTATE$;"    Age: ";AGE
220    PRINT "Home: "; FHPHONE$; "    Work: ";FWPHONE$
230 GOTO 150
240 ' Ending routine
250 PRINT "Ended because you asked for record " FIND "."
260 CLOSE #1
270 END
280 ' Routine to add records to file
290 LNAME$ = " "
300 WHILE LNAME$ <> ""
310    PRINT
320    INPUT "    Enter the new last name: ", LNAME$
330    IF LNAME$ = "" THEN GOTO 470
340    INPUT "  Enter the new first name: ", FINAME$
350    INPUT "             Enter the state: ", STATE$
```

```
360    INPUT "      Enter the home phone: ", HPHONE$
370    INPUT "      Enter the work phone: ", WPHONE$
380    INPUT "            Enter the age: ", AGE%
390    LSET FLNAME$ = LNAME$
400    LSET FFNAME$ = FINAME$
410    LSET FSTATE$ = STATE$
420    LSET FHPHONE$ = HPHONE$
430    LSET FWPHONE$ = WPHONE$
440    LSET FAGE$ = MKI$(AGE%)
450    TOTRECS = TOTRECS + 1
460    PUT #1, TOTRECS
470 WEND
480 PRINT "The file now contains "; TOTRECS; "records."
490 RETURN
```

Your programs may be different and still be correct. If you have trouble with the logic of your programs, compare them to the ones shown here.

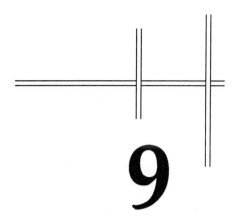

9

Introduction to Graphics

In this chapter, you'll learn to use the GW-BASIC graphics commands to draw lines, circles, and shapes on your screen. You'll learn to control pixels and apply color to graphics output. The statements covered in Chapter 6 help you control the colors available. Like colors, use of graphics requires that you have the appropriate equipment installed. You can create graphics on any color monitor or on a monochrome monitor if the system has a graphics display adapter. In this chapter you'll learn to:

- Use the DRAW statement in interactive mode to draw on the screen
- Use the DRAW statement in a program to create and position graphics on the screen
- Use the LINE statement to position straight line segments on the screen
- Use the CIRCLE statement to position curved segments on the screen
- Control the use of graphics and color in a program

GW-BASIC Graphics

So far, you have been using text on the screen. Most of the time you have been using screen mode zero, which supports only text. Other screen modes (1, 2, 7, 8, 9, and 10) support graphics as well; all except 10 support color too. Screen modes 1 and 7 support medium-resolution graphics, 2 and 8 support high-resolution graphics, and 9 and 10 support ultra-high-resolution graphics, although 10 uses monochrome shading instead of color.

Pixels

A graphics screen consists of many pixels; a pixel is the smallest point that a graphics command can use on that screen. Each text character on the screen is made up of pixels; the number of pixels allowed per character depends on the resolution of the screen.

Each pixel is at a specific location, identified with coordinates such as (50,100). The first coordinate specifies a location across the horizontal dimension of the screen. The second coordinate specifies a location down the vertical dimension of the screen. Different resolution screens contain different numbers of pixels. Table 9.1 shows the number of pixels in the different screen modes. Since the number varies, the center of the screen is at a different location on each screen mode.

If you are writing programs to be used only on your own system, you can use the highest resolution available. If your programs will be used on other systems as well, you'll want to use a mode that will work on all the systems. Systems that have just monochrome with no graphic display adapter cannot use graphics. CGA screens can handle modes 1 and 2, while EGA can handle modes 7, 8, and 9. Screen mode 10 is reserved for monographic (monochrome with graphic capability) monitors with EGA adaptors. A VGA system can handle anything an EGA system can.

Specifying Coordinates

You can specify coordinates by number or by a variable containing a number. Each set of coordinates has the horizontal or x coordinate followed by the vertical or y coordinate; they are separated by a comma. Some statements

Table 9.1. Graphic Coordinates

Resolution	Mode	Across	Down	Center
Medium	1,7	0-319	0-199	(160,100)
High	2,8	0-639	0-199	(320,100)
Ultra	9,10	0-639	0-349	(320,175)

require that each set be enclosed in parentheses. The coordinates are absolute; that is, each set of coordinates represents a specific point on the screen.

You can also specify relative coordinates in most statements; relative coordinates can include a sign. Relative coordinates are calculated based on the last point drawn or referenced.

Where Graphics Start

When GW-BASIC draws a line, it starts at the last point referenced; where that is depends on several factors. When a program first starts, the center of the screen is the default point. Everytime you use LOAD, NEW, RUN, or CLS, the last point referenced is set to the center of the screen.

Once you start using graphics, the last point referenced changes. It is usually at the end of the last line or curve drawn. You can control this to some extent in your statements. In some cases, you might ask for something to be drawn without changing the last point referenced. You can also ask to move the point without drawing; this places the last point referenced where you specify.

The Graphics Statements

Several different statements are available for creating graphics. The LINE statement draws separate straight lines, based on specified start and end locations. The CIRCLE statement draws curved lines, also based on points you specify. The DRAW statement lets you draw connected straight lines; it includes a complete macro language for graphics.

Other statements let you control the colors of your graphics. Arguments within the graphics statements also give you some control over color. The PAINT statement lets you fill an area. The COLOR statement (see Chapter 6) allows you to set in advance the color to be used for drawing on the screen.

The DRAW Statement

The DRAW statement has many features that let you create line drawings on the console. It depends on a set of macro commands used in a string to create the effects you need. The DRAW statement has an extensive Graphics Macro

Language (GML) that you can use in creating expressions for your program's graphic effects. Here's the format:

DRAW *string-expression*

You can use a constant, as in DRAW "U7 L12 D7 R12", to create a rectangle. Or you can use a string variable that has the value you want, as in the statement DRAW RECT$.

Line Directions

The command you use in the DRAW statement sets the direction of the line. Table 9.2 shows all the macros for the DRAW statement; notice the basic directional commands at the top. The commands for the up, down, left, and right lines start with their initial letters. D10 means a line straight down, 10 pixels long. L50 means a line straight to the left, 50 pixels long. The commands for diagonal lines are somewhat arbitrary. The command G75 means a line

Table 9.2. DRAW Graphics Macro Language

Directional Commands	
U*n*	Up *n* pixels
D*n*	Down *n* pixels
R*n*	Right *n* pixels
L*n*	Left *n* pixels
E*n*	Up and right *n* pixels
F*n*	Down and right *n* pixels
G*n*	Down and left *n* pixels
H*n*	Up and left *n* pixels
M*x,y*	Move to coordinate *x,y*
B	Move, but don't draw points
N	Move, but return to original position
A*n*	Set angle 0 to 3 (0, 90, 180, 270)
TA*n*	Turn to specified angle (−360 to 360)
S*n*	Scale diferently (1 to 255); default is 4, scaled *n*/4
X*string; variable*	Include variable in string
C*n*	Set color *n* (as established earlier)
P*paint, boundary*	Specifies colors and creates filled in figure

```
10 ' Set up direct mode draw
20 INPUT "Enter Screen mode 1, 2, 7, 8, 9, 10 ", SMODE
30 SCREEN SMODE
40 CLS: KEY OFF: A$="0"
50 WHILE A$ <> ""
60    A$=INPUT$(1)
70    DRAW A$
80 WEND
90 END
```

Figure 9.1. Drawing on the Screen

from the last point referenced toward the lower left at a 45-degree angle, 75 pixels long.

The string of macros in the DRAW statement must be enclosed in double quotes. You can include spaces or semicolons to separate macro commands if you like, but they aren't necessary. The value of *n* can range from 1 up, but if it exceeds the number of pixels remaining on the screen in that direction, only the ones that fit will be drawn. You won't get any error messages, but you won't see the entire line either. If you want to draw a line just one pixel long, you can omit the 1 following the directional macro; U1 and U have the same effect; they draw a line toward the top of the screen one pixel long.

Interactive Drawing. Figure 9.1 shows a program that lets you try out the directional DRAW macros interactively. If you enter and run this program, you'll be asked to specify the screen mode; you can't do graphics in the default screen mode 0. Enter one of the others. The screen is set as you specify, then it is cleared. Since line 60 uses the INPUT$ function, you won't see a cursor on the screen. However, if you press one of the keys U, D, R, L, E, F, G, or H and hold it for a moment, you'll see a line. Then press another of these keys. You'll be able to use all the directional keys to draw on the screen.

If you press any key other than these eight, you'll get an Illegal function call message and interrupt the program. You can also interrupt it with Ctrl-Break or Ctrl-ScrollLock.

Notice that the first line you draw starts at the center of the screen. Each direction you choose starts where the last one ended. Using this program is much like using a classic Etch-a-Sketch® to create drawings!

In a Program. You can use the directional macros in a program. For example, the command DRAW "U50 L100 D50 R100" draws a rectangle, with the lower-right corner at the center of the screen. The command DRAW "E50 F50

`L99"` draws a triangle with the lower-left corner at the center of the screen. Both the rectangle and the triangle will have a somewhat different size and shape on different resolution screens.

You can use variables instead of constants in the directional macros. The variables require that you specify the macro, followed by an equal sign and the variable, followed by a semicolon. If variable WALL has the value 40, the statement `DRAW "U=WALL; R=WALL; D=WALL; L=WALL; "` draws a rectangle with each side 40 pixels long; whether that is a square depends on the screen mode. Notice that the semicolon following the variable is needed even after the last one in the string.

Suppose you want to draw a series of rectangles, all starting at the center of the screen. Figure 9.2 shows a program that does that. The size of the rectangles depends on the resolution of the screen. Medium resolution (1 and 7) produces squares, but the larger ones extend off the top of the screen. High resolution (2 and 8) produces rectangles, which also extend off the top of the screen. Ultra-high resolution (9 and 10) produces rectangles that fit nicely in the upper-right quadrant of the screen.

The FOR statement sets the value of the variable used in the directional macros in the DRAW statement.

Suppose you want to draw a diamond on the screen with sides of length SIDE; the last point referenced is the top of the diamond. The program assigns a value to SIDE, then issues this command:

```
DRAW " F=SIDE; G=SIDE; H=SIDE; E=SIDE; "
```

Affecting the Last Point Referenced

Drawing a line changes the last point referenced from its beginning point to its end point. If you want gaps in your drawing, or if you don't want to start at midscreen, you need to make some changes.

If you precede a macro with the character B, GW-BASIC calculates the line, but doesn't draw it. It simply positions the last point referenced at the end point of the undrawn line. So the command `DRAW "BU40 U90 R90 D90 L90"` draws a rectangle with its lower-left corner 40 pixels above the center of the screen. No line is drawn by `"BU40"`; it just resets the last point referenced. If you add the line `15 DRAW "BD80"` to the program in Figure 9.2, it will move the last point referenced down toward the bottom of the screen. Now the entire graphic fits on any screen. The character B must be repeated before each macro it is to affect.

If you want to draw a line without changing the last point referenced, you can use the prefix N. Suppose you want to draw three lines extending from a

```
10 ' Draw nested rectangles
20 CLS
30 FOR X = 10 TO 150 STEP 10
40   DRAW "u=x; r=x; d=x; l=x;"
50 NEXT
60 END
```

Figure 9.2. Nested Rectangles

single point. You could do it like this: DRAW "NU90 NG90 NF90". The three line segments are all drawn from the point that is the last point referenced when the DRAW command begins. And when it is drawn, that point is still the last point referenced.

It doesn't make any sense to use both B and N before a macro, since using B has the effect of just moving the reference point and N has the effect of keeping it in the same place. If you happen to use both, whichever occurs last will be in effect.

The following program draws a house on the screen when executed with the mode set to 1.

```
10 ' Draw a line figure
20 CLS : KEY OFF
30 DRAW "BU50 BL50 NF80 NG80 BF60 D80 L120 U80 BD20
BR40 ND60 L20 D60 R40 BU30 U30 R50 D30 L50"
40 END
```

Figure 9.3 shows the effect of running this short program. Notice that the house is entirely created using one DRAW statement with directional macros. If multiple DRAW statements are used, the effect is the same. The B character is used to position the last point referenced when the lines should not connect. The N character is used to draw a line segment without changing the last point referenced.

1. If you haven't yet tried out the interactive drawing program from Figure 9.1, enter it now and see how it works. Save it as ETCH.BAS.
2. Enter the program from Figure 9.2 and test it in SCREEN 1.
3. Test it in all other screen modes available to you. To make it fit on the screen, use BD60 and BL60 at the beginning of the macro string to move the reference point. Save this program if you want it.
4. Enter the program that produced Figure 9.3 and test it.

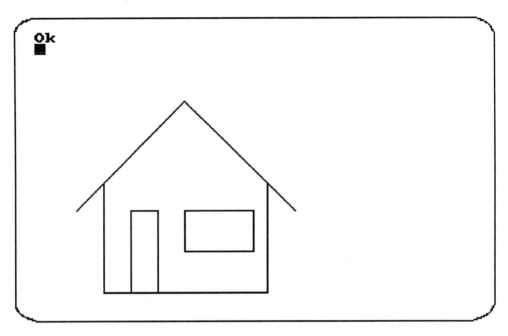

Figure 9.3. Line Drawing of House

5. Test it in all other screen modes available to you. Save this program as HOUSE.BAS.

You shouldn't have any problems if you enter the macro commands carefully. Once your programs work, you can use them as models for other programs.

Specifying a Line Precisely

The M macro lets you specify that a line be drawn from the last point referenced to the exact coordinates you specify. The statement DRAW "M 90,90" draws a line to the point represented by 90,90; the exact location on the screen depends on the resolution, of course. You can set the last point referenced to an exact coordinate position with a command such as DRAW "BM 0,0"; this command doesn't plot any points, but it ends up with the last point referenced at the end of the undrawn line, which is the upper-left corner of the screen in this case. You can also use the N character preceding M to keep the last point referenced from changing when a line is drawn.

```
10 ' Figure 10.4
20 CLS
30 DRAW "BM 20,0"
40 FOR X = 20 TO 200 STEP 20
50    DRAW "M = X;,= Y;"
60    Y = Y + 10
70    DRAW "BM =X;,=Y;"
80  NEXT
90 END
```

Figure 9.4. Using the M Macro

You can use variables in the M macro much as in the directional ones. Here too you have to use the equal sign and follow each variable with a semicolon. Figure 9.4 shows an example. This program draws a series of stepped lines on the screen, controlled by the FOR...NEXT loop. The first DRAW statement sets the last point referenced at point (20,0). The FOR...NEXT loop includes two DRAW statements. The first draws a line from the last point referenced to the point (X,Y). Each time the loop increments X, the line will be further to the right. The last DRAW statement moves the pointer without drawing a line. The increased value of Y steps the line down to the next location on the screen.

Notice that each variable in a DRAW statement is preceded by an equal sign and followed by a semicolon. A comma separates the variables indicating the two coordinates. You can combine variables and constants in the same M macro if you like.

You can also use relative coordinates in the M macro. The starting point is still the last point referenced. The relative end point is calculated from that location. A plus sign on a coordinate increases the value, while a minus sign decreases it. Suppose the last point referenced is 100,150. The statement DRAW "M +30,50" draws a line from point 100,150 to point 130,50. The statement DRAW "M +50,-50 draws the next line from point 130,50 to point 180,0.

As you can see, a plus sign on the first coordinate moves the point to the right, while a minus sign moves it toward the 0 point on the left. A plus sign on the second coordinate moves the point down on the screen, while a minus sign there raises the point on the screen toward 0 at the top. Omitting a sign on either coordinate means that the absolute coordinate is used.

To make variable coordinates relative, you still use the plus and minus sign. The sign must precede the equal sign or GW-BASIC won't recognize the entity as a relative variable coordinate.

Controlling Angles

So far, we've been considering the default orientation of graphics created with the DRAW statement. You can tilt or rotate these graphics on the screen with either of two additional macros. The A*n* macro lets you rotate the figure 0 degrees (none), 90 degrees (so the former top now points to the right), 180 degrees (upside down), or 270 degrees. The value of *n* must be from 0 to 3 for the four rotations. If the statement specifies A1 or A3 to rotate the figure sideways, GW-BASIC maintains the same aspect ratio so it won't appear distorted on the screen.

The TA*n* macro lets you specify the amount of rotation. You can specify from –360 to 360 degrees to get an exact rotation. A negative value rotates the figure counterclockwise, while a positive value rotates it clockwise. The TA*n* macro doesn't do as good a job at maintaining the aspect ratio as the A macro does.

When you change the rotation, the directional macros have different effects. For example, if the program in Figure 9.2 includes the line 25 DRAW "A2", then later appearances of the macros U, D, R, and L have reversed effects and the nested rectangles are drawn upside down—the reverse of their original position. Macros E and G, and F and H also have reversed effects. Using M macros following an angle change also causes the lines to be drawn as specified in the rotation. If 180 degrees is in effect (A2 or TA180), position 0,0 is considered to be in the lower-right corner of the screen instead of its usual upper-left corner.

The rotation you set stays in effect through other DRAW statements until you change it or run another program.

Sizing the Graphic

By default, each graphic line is drawn to the default scale. The S macro lets you change the scale by specifying a number from 1 to 255. If you have created program lines that create a figure in the wrong size, you can insert an S macro to make it larger or smaller. What ever you specify is divided by four to get the new scale. The statement DRAW "S8 BU40 U90 R90 D90 L90" creates a rectangle whose sides are twice as long, because the scale is evaluated at 8/4 or 2. The scale you set stays in effect through other DRAW statements until you change it or run a new program. To create a half-size graphic, use S2. S1 creates a graphic one-quarter the size of the original.

1. Load your HOUSE.BAS program if it isn't loaded. Add a macro at the beginning of the string that will display the house upside down. Test the program.
2. Now change that macro so that the house is displayed with the roof pointing to the left. Test the program.
3. Now change that macro so that the house is at a 45-degree angle from the normal position. Test it again.
4. Without changing the angle, add a macro to the string that will cause the house to be drawn half size. Test the program, then try a double-size house.

To invert the house, use the macro A2. A3 causes it to point to the left. The macro TA45 produces a 45-degree angle. The macro S2 produces a half-size house, while S8 produces a double size.

Macro String Variables

You can set a macro string to a variable and execute it by naming the variable in a DRAW statement after it has been given the desired value. The following statements show how:

```
40 BOX$ = "U90 R130 D90 L130"
50 DRAW BOX$
```

If you want to use the variable within a larger string, you must precede the variable name with X and follow it with a semicolon, as shown here:

```
60 DRAW "S8 BL50 XBOX$;"
```

You can use variables whenever you want to use the same string several times in a program. Figure 9.5 shows a program that stores the description of an organization chart element in a variable, then uses it at different points in a string.

Notice that each reference to AREA$ in the DRAW statement quoted string is preceded by X and followed by a semicolon. Figure 9.6 shows the result of running this short program in screen mode 2.

```
10 ' create an organization chart
20 CLS
30 AREA$="D15 R40 D20 L80 U20 R40 BU15"
40 DRAW "BM 50,30 XAREA$; R100 XAREA$; R100 XAREA$;"
50 END
```

Figure 9.5. The Organization Chart Program

Example

The program shown in Figure 9.7 expands the use of the house drawing. The HOUSE description itself is in line 1020 in the subroutine. It has been scaled to half size here, since the program prints several of them on the screen. Line 1010 is used to set the location where the house drawing begins.

After setting up the screen, the program initializes the variable Y for positioning the graphic. The FOR statement increments X, while the following statement increments Y. The ANGLE is incremented to tip the house 30 degrees further each time. So each time the subroutine is executed, the house starts in a different position and tips over a bit further.

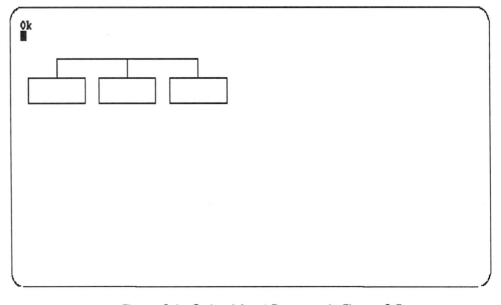

Figure 9.6. Output from Program in Figure 9.5

```
10 ' Expand the HOUSE drawing
20 CLS : KEY OFF
30 Y = 30
40 FOR X = 100 TO 420 STEP 80
50    Y = Y + 40
60    ANGLE = ANGLE + 30
70    DRAW "TA =ANGLE;"
80    GOSUB 1000
90 NEXT
100 END
1000 ' Basic house description
1010 DRAW "BM =X;, =Y;"
1020 DRAW "S2; BU50 BL50 NF80 NG80 BF60 D80 L120 U80
BD20 BR40 ND60 L20 D60 R40 BU30 U30 R50 D30 L50"
1030 RETURN
```

Figure 9.7. The Expanded HOUSE program

The output from the program in screen mode 9 is shown in Figure 9.8. Lower-resolution screens show fewer complete houses, but the program still works. You might want to resize the drawing by changing S2 to S1 at the beginning of the string so more of it fits on your screen.

Color in Drawing

The colors available to a graphics command depend on the screen mode and what COLOR and PALETTE statements may be in effect. Those statements establish the background color and often the foreground color as well. You can also use the C macro to specify what color a line will appear in. The color numbers, or attributes, are the same here as in the COLOR and PALETTE statements. (They are listed in Table 6.2 on page 138; the colors available depend on the screen mode.) The command DRAW "C2 BU40 U90 R90 D90 L90" draws a rectangle in color 2 on the screen. The specified color will be used for all DRAW statement output until another DRAW statement changes the color.

The C macro has no effect in screen mode 2. In screen 1, it is limited to 0, 1, 2, and 3. The background color is 0, so you have only three choices for drawing colors. The effect of each depends on the palette that is the current default. Screen modes 7, 8, 9, and 10 can use up to 15 colors.

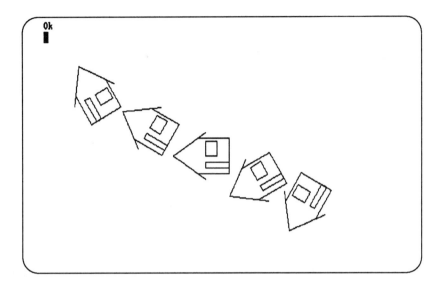

Figure 9.8. Graphic Output

Creating Your Own Graphics

When you create your own graphics, take time to plan them first. Make sure the graphic is possible with the commands at your disposal; so far you can just do straight lines. First, decide on the screen mode so you know how many pixels are available. Then take a piece of plain or graph paper and mark the coordinates of the four corners and the center of the screen. If you will have a fairly complex graphic, you might want to mark several lines on a grid so you can tell approximately what points are included on each line. Sketch the graphic or tape down a copy of it. Determine the points at each end of each line. Figure out if there are any repeating elements that you can code as variables and include in strings. Decide where the drawing cannot be continuous and figure out what starting point to use.

1. If you have a simple line drawing in mind, sketch it out on paper. Then create DRAW statements to draw it. If not, at least modify your HOUSE.BAS program to see how it appears in color.
2. Check your program after each change. You will know when it is doing what you want.

3. Add various other macros to change the size, the angle, and the color of your graphic. Test it in various screen modes.

You will know when your graphic is as you want it. Take time to play with other macros as well. Remember that you can use as many separate DRAW statements as you wish; as long as no other graphic statements intervene, GW-BASIC treats them as one continuous stream of macros.

The LINE Statement

You've seen how to use the DRAW statement to create straight lines and line segments on the screen. You can also use the LINE statement to draw separate line segments in which you can specify both beginning and ending points, regardless of the last point referenced. You can include other features as well in the LINE statement. Here's the format:

LINE [(x1,y1)]-(x2,y2) [,[color attribute][,B[F]][,style]]

The final parameter, *style*, has special effects that are not covered in this book.

Drawing a Basic Line

The basic LINE statement includes two sets of coordinates, each in parentheses. The first gives the starting point of the line; you can omit this set if you want the line to start at the last point referenced. The second set of coordinates specifies the ending point of the line; this becomes the last point referenced after the line is drawn. The coordinates are the same as the ones used in the DRAW statement; which ones are available depends on the screen mode in effect.

The statement LINE (0,0)-(319,199) draws a line from the upper-left corner to the lower-right corner on a screen in mode 1 or 7. It draws a line from the upper-left corner to the center of the bottom of the screen in mode 2 or 8. If you want the line to start at the last point referenced, you could use LINE -(319,199); this specifies a line starting wherever the last point referenced is located and extending to the pixel at coordinates 319,199. It is equivalent to DRAW "M 319,199".

Using Relative Coordinates

Relative coordinates in a LINE statement are specified with the word STEP preceding the set of coordinates. The statement LINE STEP (50,50) – STEP (-50,-50) uses relative coordinates for both sets. You can use a plus sign if you wish, but omitting the sign following STEP is treated as relative plus; a minus sign means relative minus. The amount in the first set is added to or subtracted from the last point referenced. The amount in the second set is used to adjust the calculated value for the first set. The prior example draws a line from a point 50 pixels down and to the right of the last point referenced back to the original point.

Either or both coordinates can include STEP. If the first set of coordinates is relative, it is calculated in relationship to the last point referenced. If the second set of coordinates is relative, it is calculated in relationship to the set of coordinates that defines the starting point of the line.

Specifying a Color

The next parameter is an attribute; this is a color number. If you don't specify a color, the current foreground color is used. The color may be the default assigned to that attribute or it may have been changed with the PALETTE statement. The color you specify here turns on the color only for the specific line being drawn. You can draw several lines in different colors by specifying different color number parameters. If you want to draw several lines in the same color, you must include the attribute in each or change the current foreground color with a COLOR statement.

In mode 1, the statement LINE (0,0) – (319,199), 2 draws the same line described above, this time in color 2, which is green. The statement LINE (0,319) – (199,0), 4 draws the other diagonal on the screen, in red. Of course, the exact color depends on the screen mode and the attribute settings.

If you omit the color attribute from the LINE statement and use a later parameter, you must include the comma to mark its position. You'll see some examples of this as you continue.

Creating a Box from LINE

The B parameter lets you draw a box with a single LINE statement. It uses the two sets of coordinates as diagonally opposite corners of the rectangle. The statement LINE (50,50)- (100,100),2,B draws a box with the corners (50,50), (50,100), (100,100), and (100,50); the box is drawn in color 2. To cause it to appear in the default foreground color, use the statement LINE (50,50)- (100,100),,B. A comma marks the color parameter position.

If you want the box to be solid, you can follow B with F to fill it. The box will be filled with the color used to draw it. The statement LINE (50,50)- (100,100),2,BF draws a solid green box on the screen. Notice that there is no comma between B and F. Use the B parameter to create a rectangle outline with the specified corners; use BF to create a filled rectangle.

After the LINE statement is executed, the second (or only) set of parameters specified becomes the last point referenced, no matter whether the LINE statement created a line or a box.

1. Figure 9.9 (on the next page) shows a diagram of a teepee, with several coordinates marked. Write a program that uses LINE commands to draw the basic tent shape. Use screen mode 8 if you can, otherwise use screen mode 2. You can't use the colors in mode 2.
2. Test the program. When the basic shape is correct, add LINE statements to put in the door.
3. Add parameters to make the door borders appear in a different color.
4. Add a LINE statement to create a filled colored box as long as the base of the TEEPEE and 20 pixels high that appears 10 pixels below the base of the TEEPEE.
5. Test the program. When it looks the way you want, try it out in different screen modes. Save the program as TEEPEE.BAS.

Here's how our program looks:

```
10 ' Practice using LINE statement
20 CLS : KEY OFF
30 LINE (50,150)-(190,150)
40 LINE (50,150)-(150,50)
50 LINE (190,150)-(90,50)
60 LINE (120,50)-(120,80)
70 LINE (65,150)-(110,120),4
80 LINE (110,120)-(155,150),4
90 LINE (50,160)-(190,180),2,BF
100 END
```

Your program may be different and still be correct, especially if you used a different screen mode. Line 30 draws the base. Lines 40 through 60 form the outer edges and "sticks" of the teepee. Lines 70 and 80 form our door, while line 90 creates the

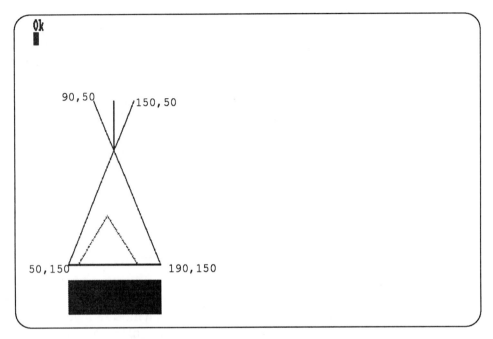

Figure 9.9. Output from TEEPEE Program

box at the base.

The CIRCLE Statement

Both the DRAW and LINE statements let you create and position straight line segments. Many graphics, however, require curved segments. The CIRCLE statement lets you create and position circles and ellipses or arcs representing part of a circle or ellipse. We'll cover the complete figures first.

Creating Circles and Ellipses

To create a circle, you have to specify the coordinates of the center and the size of the radius (in pixels). If you omit the center coordinates, the last point referenced is used. Here's the format for a creating a circle:

CIRCLE (*x,y*),*radius*

To create a circle with the center at point 100,100 with a 15-pixel radius, use the statement CIRCLE (100,100),15. After the CIRCLE statement is executed, the last point referenced is the center of the figure drawn.

The center coordinates in the CIRCLE statement can be absolute or relative; if you want to use relative coordinates, you'll need the STEP form as in LINE. The statement CIRCLE STEP (-100,50),25 draws a circle with the center at a point 100 pixels down and 50 to the right of the last point referenced.

An ellipse or oval is a circle with a varying radius, from a shortest length to a longest length. The ellipse is described in GW-BASIC by specifying the center point and the ratio of the shortest radius to the longest, which is called the aspect ratio. To create an ellipse, use this format:

CIRCLE (x,y),radius,,,,aspect

For an ellipse, the *radius* parameter gives the length of the longest radius. The aspect ratio gives an expression used to calculate the length of the shortest radius. The default aspect ratio for most screens is 4:3. That means that 4 pixels across is about equal in length to 3 pixels down. On some monitors, you may find that an aspect ratio of 1 gives a better-shaped circle. To create an ellipse at location 100,100 with the longest radius 50 pixels and the shortest half that, use the statement CIRCLE (100,100),50,,,,.5.

Circle Drawing

The program in Figure 9.10 draws five circles on the screen. Notice that the first one uses absolute coordinates, then the others are a bit smaller and positioned with relative coordinates. The LINE statement near the end of the program draws a small box to show the last point referenced.

Figure 9.11 shows the output of the program on screen mode 2. Notice the effects of the relative coordinates and the position of the small box. This shows that the last point referenced, used as a corner of the box, is the center of the last circle figure drawn.

Adding Color to a Circle

You can draw a circle or ellipse in color with the parameter following *radius* in the statement. Here's an expanded CIRCLE statement format:

CIRCLE (x,y),radius,[color],,[aspect]

```
10 ' create circles
20 CLS
30 KEY OFF
40 CIRCLE (60,20),30
50 FOR X = 150 TO 310 STEP 40
60    Y = Y + 30
70    CIRCLE (X, Y), 25
80 NEXT
90 LINE - STEP (10,5),,B
100 END
```

Figure 9.10. Drawing Circles

You've already seen that four commas must be included if you use the aspect ratio. If you use the color attribute, only three intervening commas are needed to specify an ellipse. The statement CIRCLE (50,100),40,2 draws the specified circle in green. The statement CIRCLE (150,70),30,4,,,.7 draws the specified ellipse in red. The color attribute here has the same effect as in the other graphics statements.

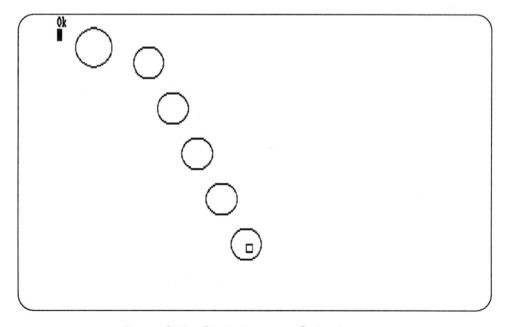

Figure 9.11. Circle Program Output

1. Load your TEEPEE.BAS program if necessary. In this exercise, you'll replace the triangular door with a circular entrance.
2. Figure out where the center of the circle should be to place the circle just above the base of the teepee.
3. Enter the necessary statement and test it.

At this point, our program looks like this:

```
10 ' Practice using CIRCLE statement
20 CLS : KEY OFF
30 LINE (50,150)-(190,150)
40 LINE (50,150)-(150,50)
50 LINE (190,150)-(90,50)
60 LINE (120,50)-(120,80)
70 CIRCLE (120,135),30
80 LINE (50,160)-(190,180),2,BF
90 END
```

Your CIRCLE statement may be different. If the circle looks like a door into the teepee, it is just fine.

Drawing Curved Lines

Sometimes you don't want a complete circle or ellipse. You might want an arc (part of a circle) or a sector that includes lines, such as a pie wedge. The CIRCLE statement lets you draw an arc or include the wedge lines. Here's the complete format:

CIRCLE (*x,y*),*radius*,[*color*][,[*start*],[*end*][,*aspect*]]]

The start and end parameters specify the portion of the circle or ellipse you want created. These are expressed in radians.

Calculating Radians. Each complete circle or ellipse contains 360 degrees or exactly 2π radians; this is approximately 6.28 radians. One fourth of a circle is 1.57 radians, one half is 3.14 (that's 1π!), and so forth. If your drawing needs mathematical accuracy rather than a good apearance on the screen, you'll have to use more decimal places in your calculation. You have to be able to figure out how many radians make up the portion you want drawn. If you know how many degrees you want, multiply the number of degrees by $\pi/180$ (.01745 is close).

Specifying Arcs or Sectors

The 0 point on a circle or ellipse is the point nearest the top edge of your screen, and the CIRCLE statement counts radians and draws counterclockwise. The statement CIRCLE (100,100),80,,0,1.57 draws an arc from the right to the top, or the upper-right quadrant of the circle. The statement CIRCLE (100,100),80,,-1.57,-3.14 draws an arc of the upper-left quadrant, with both ends of the arc connected to the center. The minus sign causes the radius line to be drawn. If both start and end values are negative, the wedge is created. If only one is negative, just that end has a line connecting it to the center. The meaning of the radian value doesn't change.

One slight problem is that – 0 doesn't have the effect we want here. To draw a line to the center from the rightmost point of the circle, use –.000001 or –6.28.

Example

Figure 9.12 shows the HOUSE with a curved path leading up to it and a half moon in the sky.

Figure 9.12. The House with Curved Elements

```
10 ' Draw a line figure
20 CLS : KEY OFF
30 DRAW "S2 BU50 BL50 NF80 NG80 BF60 D80 L120 U80
BD20 BR40 ND60 L20 D60 R40 BU30 U30 R50 D30 L50"
40 CIRCLE (250,70),20,3,-2,-5.14
50 CIRCLE (115,168),30,2,6.1,1.15
60 CIRCLE (102,168),30,2,6.1,1.15
70 END
```

Figure 9.13. Program for Figure 9.12

Figure 9.13 shows the program. Line 30 is the basic house drawing. Line 40 adds the moon; notice the minus signs that control the drawing of the radius line from each end of the arc to the center. Lines 50 and 60 add the path. Trial and error helps you determine where to place the center and how much of an arc to use. One technique to use when adding a graphic element to the screen is to use a direct mode command. Just keep making changes to the statement until it is what you want. Then insert a line number so that it becomes part of the program in progress.

The PAINT Statement

The graphics statements may create closed figures on the screen. Any combination of LINE, DRAW, and CIRCLE may be involved, creating figures of any shape. The PAINT statement lets you fill the closed figure with a color. The figure must be completely closed with a border of the same color; even one border pixel in a different color lets all the "paint" leak out to fill the entire screen and obliterate whatever else is on it. A box, circle, or ellipse is closed, unless you set a pixel on its border to a different color. Even crossing it with a line has this effect. Here's the PAINT statement format:

PAINT (x,y)[,color[,border]]

The closed figure to be filled is assumed to have an outline or border around it that is all the same color; the color number (or attribute if you used PALETTE to change the color) already applied to this outline is specified as *border*. The color to be filled is specified before the border color. The coordinates must specify a point that is within the closed figure; it can't be on the border. If it is, PAINT will probably fill the entire screen and obliterate the graphics.

Which parameters are required depends on the figure to be filled. The statement PAINT (100,100) fills the closed figure that contains the point with the default foreground color; this works even in screen 2. The statement PAINT (100,100), 2 fills it with whatever color attribute 2 indicates; this depends on the screen mode and any previous PALETTE statements.

Suppose a point is within several different closed figures. You can specify the continuous color of the border to be filled with a statement such as PAINT (100,100), 2, 4; In mode 8 this statement fills the closed figure bordered in color 4 (red) with color 2 (green). In screen mode 2, the only colors available are 0 (the background) and 1 (the foreground); the statement above has different effects on different resolution consoles. You can fill the area with the border color on an EGA console, but it is difficult on a CGA console. Use screen 1 for best color control on CGA consoles. Remember than only one background color is valid at a time in modes other than 1.

1. Reload your TEEPEE program. You are going to put a half moon in the sky, then color it appropriately.
2. Decide where to put the moon, and enter the CIRCLE statement.
3. Modify the CIRCLE statement to use a color you haven't used yet to border the moon.
4. Add a PAINT statement to fill the door with a color.
5. Test the program. Then save it if you like.

We added this statement:

```
95 CIRCLE (280,50),40,3,-5.14,-2
```

You may have located the moon somewhere else. Both start and end point must have a minus sign. We used 3 as the color number. Your moon may be very different, of course.

Summary

This chapter has covered many of the statements you can use to create graphics on your computer screen.

The DRAW statement provides a set of macro commands that let you create graphics made up of straight line segments. Other macros permit sizing and tilting of the graphic. They also allow you to control the position of the last point referenced.

The LINE statement draws straight lines or rectangles; you can specify that a rectangle be filled. LINE also allows you to specify a color to be used for lines or fill.

The CIRCLE statement draws a circle or ellipse, using a color if you want. If you specify begin and end points on the arc, it will draw a segment; it will connect the end of an arc to the center point of the full figure if you want.

The PAINT statement fills an area completely enclosed by a line with the color you specify; the area can be made up of the output of several different statements, as long as the lines bordering the space are all the same color.

Exercise

In this exercise, you'll write a program to create a graphic like the one in Figure 9.14. Use screen mode 1 or 7. The parts of the drawing must be done in a particular sequence, so later parts don't overlay and remove early elements of the picture. Test each graphic statement as you add it to the program.

1. Write statements to set up the screen and set the value of PI at 3.1416.
2. Write statements to draw a line across the screen at about the mid-point, then paint the top half of the screen blue.
3. Write statements to draw a box that forms the trunk of the tree. It can extend well above the "leaves," since the upper part can be overlaid by the ellipse.
4. Write statements to draw an ellipse to form the tree leaves (it needn't be positioned and shaped exactly like ours). Then paint the leaves a different color than the sky.
5. Write statements to draw the bird in the upper-right part of the sky. Use two arcs, one starting at 0 radians and extending to PI/2, the other starting at PI/2 and extending to PI radians.
6. Use a LINE command to draw a point to set the last point referenced in the lower-right portion of the screen (we used (220,110)). Use your HOUSE coding to draw a house in this area; you may want to use a size macro to make it smaller.
7. Add any other elements to the drawing that you want. Then save it.

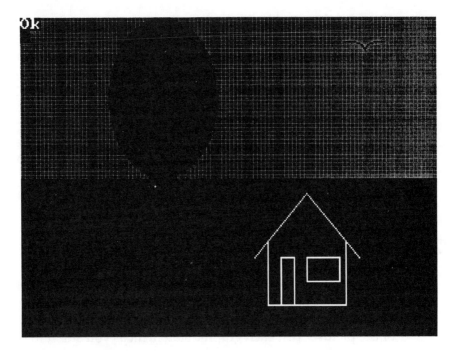

Figure 9.14. Drawing for Exercise

Your program should look something like this:

```
10 ' Graphic for Chapter 9 Exercise
20 CLS : KEY OFF
30 PI=3.1416
40 LINE (0,100)-(319,100),1
50 PAINT (1,1),1,1
60 LINE (100,50)-(120,175),2,BF
70 CIRCLE (110,50),50,2,,,1.2
80 PAINT (110,45),2
90 CIRCLE (250,20),15,0,0,PI/2,.35
100 CIRCLE (280,20),15,0,PI/2,PI,.35
110 LINE (220,110)-(220,110),1
120 DRAW "S2 NF80 NG80 BF60 D80 L120 U80 BD20 BR40 ND60 L20 D60
R40 BU30 U30 R50 D30 L50"
130 END
```

Lines 40 and 50 create the sky. Line 60 creates the tree trunk. Lines 70 and 80 create the leaves. Lines 90 and 100 create the bird. Line 110 sets the last point referenced. Line 120 creates a half-size house. Your statements could be a bit different and still be correct.

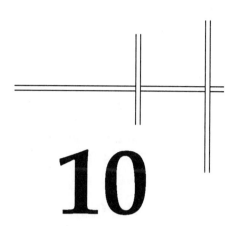

10

Working with Strings and In-Program Data

Y ou have already learned to use strings in your GW-BASIC programs. This chapter looks more closely at strings; you'll learn to specify the type of variable so you aren't limited to the character suffixes to define the type. You'll also learn to combine strings and manipulate them in programs. In particular, you'll learn to:

- Use DEF*type* statements to specify variable name types
- Use the STR$ and VAL functions to convert data between string and numeric types
- Use the LEN function to determine the length of a string
- Use the LEFT$, RIGHT$, and MID$ functions to extract substrings from larger strings
- Use the MID$ statement to replace part of a string with another string
- Use the DATA statement to define data for use within the program
- Use the READ statement to assign data from DATA statements to variables
- Use the RESTORE statement to control data in DATA statements

Review of Strings

Strings in a program are made up of series of characters, any characters at all. Strings can be from 1 to 255 characters long. A string constant must be enclosed in double quotation marks. Strings can be used for comparison, display, and printing, but they can't be used in arithmetic.

Typing Variables

You can already specify the type of variable by appending the appropriate type declaration character to the variable name: $ indicates string, ! indicates single precision, % indicates integer, and # indicates double precision.

As you know, all variable names must start with a letter, and each name can include letters, numbers, and the period. By default, all variable names without a type declaration character represent single-precision variables. You can set aside variable names beginning with certain letters to automatically define other types of variables with the DEF*type* statement. Here's the format:

DEF*type letters*

The type can be INT, SNG, DBL, or STR. DEFINT I reserves all variables beginning with I as integers; you won't need to use the % character to indicate that ITEM contains an integer. DEFSNG A, X, Z reserves variable names beginning with A, X, or Z as single-precision variables. DEFDBL B-H reserves variable names beginning with letters B, C, D, E, F, G, and H for double-precision variables. DEFSTR I-L, N-P reserves variable names beginning with letters I, J, K, L, N, O, and P for string variables.

Adjacent letters can be connected with a hyphen; separated letters can be indicated with a comma. You can combine both types in one statement as in DEFSTR A, S, X-Z. However, each DEF statement defines only one type of variable.

Once a letter is defined for a particular variable type, variables beginning with that letter default to the variable type. You can override this for any variable by using the appropriate type specification character as a suffix on the variable name. The characters always take precedence over the DEF*type* specification. If the program contains DEFINT I-N, the variable ITEM contains an integer, but INVOICE! contains a single-precision value. If the program contains DEFSTR X-Z, the variable X contains a string, but X% contains an integer value.

Converting between String and Numeric Variables

Often a string contains a numeric value. Keyboard characters entered via INKEY$ or INPUT$(*n*) could be digits as well as letters. If your program needs such input in numeric form, you can convert it with the VAL function. If it needs numeric values in standard string form, you can convert it with the STR$ function. Here are the formats:

VAL(*x$*)
STR$(*n*)

These functions are not equivalent to the functions you use to convert numeric values to numeric strings for storage in random file records. A string created by the STR$ function is a standard string.

Converting to Numeric

Suppose variable ITEMNO$ contains only digits in the form "12345". The program wants to do calculations using the value. The statement ITEMNUM = VAL(ITEMNO$) converts the string into a numeric quantity of the precision of the receiving variable.

The VAL function automatically removes any leading spaces, tabs, or line feeds. If the resulting first character is not numeric, the function returns the value 0. The result of VAL("$15.98") is 0, since the first character other than a space, tab, or line feed is $; the effect is the same if the value is contained in a variable.

Converting to String

Suppose the zip code is received from the keyboard into a numeric variable as five digits and stored as ZIP. Your program needs to process it later as a string. The statement ZIPCODE$=STR$(ZIP) converts the value so you can use various string functions and operators on it. At this point, the value is stored in two places; the variable named ZIP is numeric and the variable named ZIPCODE$ is a string. If you print the string value, you will see that the resulting string includes a significant leading space; that is, the position reserved for a sign in the numeric value.

Length of Strings

When a string variable has a value, the program may need to know the length. The LEN function returns the number of characters in the string. Here's the format:

B=LEN(*string-variable*)

If the value of LASTNAME$ was read in from the keyboard or a sequential file, B=LEN(LASTNAME$) assigns the number of characters in LASTNAME$ to the variable B. The value includes nonprinting characters and embedded blanks. If the string includes significant leading or trailing blanks (blanks enclosed within double quotation marks), they are included in the length as well. Figure 10.1 shows a program that converts values and prints them on the screen.

Suppose a program deals with postal codes, some of which have five digits, others have nine digits, and still others (such as those from Canada) have six characters. The program could execute a subroutine for customers from Canada with a statement such as IF LEN(POSTAL$)=6 THEN GOSUB 8000. The subroutine would handle the processing for any records that have a postal code with six characters.

```
Ok
list
10 ' demonstrate conversions
20 DEFSTR A-E
30 CHARLES = "123"
40 GEORGE = 12
50 XNUM= VAL(CHARLES)
60 PRINT "String:" CHARLES, "Numeric:" XNUM
70 GEOR$=STR$(GEORGE)
80 PRINT "String:" GEOR$, "Numeric:"GEORGE
90 PRINT "Length of numeric converted to string: ", LEN(GEOR$)
100 END
Ok
run
String:123    Numeric: 123
String: 12    Numeric: 12
Length of numeric converted to string:      3
Ok
_

1LIST  2RUN+  3LOAD"  4SAVE"  5CONT+  6."LPT1 7TRON+  8TROFF+ 9KEY    0SCREEN
```

Figure 10.1. Conversion Demonstration

1. Write a short program that defines variables starting with letters R through Z as strings. Then receive string variables to hold the name and the age from the keyboard. Use another INPUT statement to receive the height in inches as a numeric variable.
2. Print the string contained in the name variable, as well as the length of that field, on the screen. Test the program.
3. Print the string contained in the age variable, as well as its converted numeric value, on the screen. Then print the length of the string age variable. Test the program.
4. Print the string equivalent of the height value, as well as the numeric value, on the next screen line. Test it.
5. Finally, display the length of the converted height value. Display the length of each variable. Compare the numeric length to the string length of each. Test it, then save the program if you wish.

Here's our program:

```
10 ' Self check, Chapter 10
20 DEFSTR R-Z
30 INPUT "Enter your name: ",YOURNAME
40 INPUT "Enter your age: ",YOURAGE
50 INPUT "Enter your height in inches: ",INCHES
60 PRINT: PRINT "String: "; YOURNAME; "   Length: "; LEN(YOUR-
NAME)
70 PRINT "Age as string: "; YOURAGE ; "  Age as numeric: ";
VAL(YOURAGE)
80 PRINT "Length of age as string: "; LEN (YOURAGE)
90 PRINT: PRINT "Height as string: "; STR$(INCHES); "  Height as
numeric: "; INCHES
100 PRINT "Length of height as string: "; LEN (STR$(INCHES))
110 END
```

Yours may be quite different and still be correct. Make sure you converted the values correctly. Notice that the length of the string is longer than just the digit positions.

Finding a Substring

You may want to find a value within a string. For example, suppose you want to search the name field to see if the characters "Dr" occur, and if they are a title. You could search for "Dr" within any string variable. The INSTR function

```
10 ' Find substring in TAPES records
20 CLS
30 KEY OFF
40 INPUT "Enter the string you want to search for:
",FINDIT$
50 OPEN "TAPES" FOR INPUT AS #1
60 WHILE EOF(1) = 0
70    LINE INPUT #1, INFO$
80    COUNT = COUNT + 1
90    IF INSTR(INFO$,FINDIT$) THEN PRINT COUNT; INFO$
100 WEND
110 ' ending routine
120 PRINT : PRINT "   ***** End of File *****"
130 CLOSE #1
140 END
```

Figure 10.2. Character Search Program

lets you name a substring, then search for it in a larger string. It returns the position in the string where the substring begins. Here's the format:

B=INSTR([n,]x$,y$)

If you use a value for *n*, it specifies a starting point for the search; otherwise INSTR starts at the beginning. The value of *n* must be between 1 and 255. Generally, an Illegal function call error exists if *n* has an invalid value, but a value of 0 gets the message Illegal function call in *nnnnn*, so you can check the line number.

The string you are searching in is specified as *x$*, while the string you are searching for is specified as *y$*. Either can be specified as a string constant, a string variable, or a string expression. (String expressions are covered later in this chapter.) To search for Dr in CUSTNAME$, you might use the following sequence of statements:

```
60 SUB$="Dr"
70 SPOT=INSTR(CUSTNAME$,SUB$)
```

Alternatively, you could use 60 SPOT=INSTR(CUSTNAME$,"Dr").

If the value of CUSTNAME$ is "Dr. Michael Jordan", the value assigned to SPOT is 1. If the value of CUSTNAME$ is "Rueben Drainage Contractors", the value assigned to SPOT is 8.

The INSTR function returns 0 if the substring (*y$*) can't be found. It will also return 0 if the value *n* is greater than the length of the main string (*x$*) or

```
10 ' try to count all things in loop
20 COUNT = 1
30 COUNTSTRING = 0
40 STOPIT = 2
50 INPUT "Main string: ", MAIN$
60 INPUT "Sub string: ", SUBS$
70 WHILE STOPIT   0
80    FOUNDIT = INSTR(COUNT,MAIN$,SUBS$)
90    IF FOUNDIT = 0 THEN STOPIT = 0 : GOTO 120
100    COUNT = FOUNDIT+1
110    COUNTSTRING = COUNTSTRING + 1
120 WEND
130 PRINT "Number of occurrences is "; COUNTSTRING
140 END
```

Figure 10.3. Counting Occurrences

if the main string is null. If the substring (*y*$) is null, INSTR returns the value of *n*; that's 1 if you don't specify it.

The INSTR function starts at the position you specify (or at position 1) and searches until it finds a match for the substring. At that point, it stops searching; it won't notice if you have more than one substring unless you set up a loop to keep it going. Figure 10.2 shows a program that checks each record in a file, looking for the character you specify.

This program looks through the records in the TAPES file. If the records in the file contained more fields, it could search through characters in one or more variables.

Figure 10.3 shows how you can use INSTR to count the occurrences of a character in a string. The program has to locate one occurrence, then add 1 to the occurrence counter, increment the position number, and execute INSTR again until it reaches the end of the string. Line 40 sets the value of STOPIT to 2 so it won't have the value 0 at the start.

Combining Strings

You can already combine strings for output by having them printed adjacent to each other. There are times when you want to actually combine two or more strings to create a different one. The easiest way is with concatenation. Concatenation simply joins two strings end to end. It is accomplished with the plus sign. To combine the values of ZIP5$ and ZIP4$ into POSTAL$, you would use the statement POSTAL$=ZIP5$+ZIP4$. To combine the values of strings named LAST$ and FIRST$ with a separating space between them into a variable named FULL$, use the statement FULL$=FIRST$+" "+LAST$. There's no limit to the number of strings you can concatenate, as long as the result is not longer than 255 characters. You can include constants anywhere you need them in a concatenated string.

1. Write the first few lines of a program that clears the screen, reserves variable names beginning with N for strings, and gets the first, middle, and last names as NAME1, NAME2, and NAME3.
2. Use concatenation to combine the strings into a variable called NAMEFULL; include spaces to separate the components. Display the concatenated result. Test the program at this point.
3. Write statements to determine which position in the concatenated string starts the last name. Be sure to account for the first and middle name lengths, as well as the inserted spaces.
4. Print the length of the concatenated string and the position containing the first letter of the last name on the screen.
5. Test the program, and correct it until it works. Then save it as 10STRINGS.BAS.

Your program should look something like this:

```
10 ' Use strings
20 CLS
30 DEFSTR N
40 INPUT "Enter your first name:   ",NAME1
50 INPUT "Enter your middle name: ",NAME2
60 INPUT "Enter your last name:    ",NAME3
70 NAMEFULL=NAME1+" "+NAME2+" "+NAME3
80 PRINT : PRINT NAMEFULL
90 PRINT
100 POSITION = LEN(NAME1)+LEN(NAME2)+2
110 PRINT : PRINT "Length of full name is"; LEN(NAMEFULL)
120 PRINT "Your last name starts in position"; POSITION
130 END
```

Your program may be different and still be correct. Make sure you combined the strings into a new one and used INSTR to locate the position of the embedded character.

Finding Pieces of String

Several functions let you extract substrings from other string variables. LEFT$ extracts a string starting at the left end, RIGHT$ extracts a string starting at the right end, and MID$ extracts a string from some point in the middle.

A String on the End

The LEFT$ and RIGHT$ functions both extract a string of the number of characters you specify from a larger string variable. Here are the formats:

LEFT$(*x$,number*)
RIGHT$(*x$,number*)

In both cases, *x$* specifies a string variable and *n* specifies the number of characters to be extracted. If *n* is greater than LEN (*x$*), the entire string *x$* is returned. If *n* is 0, the null string is returned. The length of *n* must be between 0 and 255 or a fatal error occurs.

The function removes a string of length *n* from the beginning (LEFT$) or end (RIGHT$) of the string variable *x$*. To extract the first three characters from the string variable PHONENUM$, use a statement such as AREACODE$ = LEFT$ (PHONENUM$,3). To remove the last seven characters from the string, use a statement such as LOCAL$ = RIGHT$ (PHONENUM$,7).

The system variable DATE$ returns a 10-character string in the form 12-18-1990, while TIME$ returns a string in the form 13:42:18. You can use the string functions to extract portions, like this:

```
MONTH$=LEFT$(DATE$,2)
YEAR$=RIGHT$(DATE$,4)
HOUR=VAL(LEFT$(TIME$,2))
SECOND=VAL(RIGHT$(TIME$,2))
```

In the first two examples, the result is a string. In the last two, the extracted string is converted to its numeric equivalent with the VAL function.

A Substring from the Middle

Sometimes the substring you want isn't at either end; at least, you may not be sure where the string is located. The MID$ function lets you extract a substring beginning at the character number you specify. To use MID$, you have to specify the character position at which to begin, as well as the number of characters to extract. Here's the format:

MID$(*x$*,*start*[,*number*])

The start position must be in the range of 1 to 255. The number of characters to extract must be in the range of 0 to 255. If either is out of range, you'll get an Illegal function call message. If you omit the number of characters to extract, the rest of the string is extracted. If the number of characters to extract is larger than the number of characters remaining in the string *x$*, the rest of the string is extracted.

For example, to extract the third through sixth characters of an item number, you might use a statement such as CODE$=MID$(CUSTNUM$,3,4).

You can combine the INSTR function with MID$ to find a value. For example, suppose a string uses spaces to separate several different values of variable lengths. You want to extract the second value. You could use statements like these:

```
100 FIND1=INSTR(BIGSTRING$," ")
110 FIND2=INSTR(FIND1+1,BIGSTRING$," ")
120 VARLENGTH=FIND2-FIND1
130 KEEP$=MID$(BIGSTRING$,FIND1,VARLENGTH)
```

Line 100 locates the first space in BIGSTRING$ and assigns its position number to FIND1; the character following that will be the first character to be extracted. Line 110 locates the second space in BIGSTRING$. Line 120 finds the number of characters between those two spaces; that will be the length of the substring to be extracted. Line 130 extracts the desired string.

You can use the MID$ function with the DATE$ and TIME$ system variables as well. Here are some examples:

```
DAY$=MID$(DATE$,4,2)
MINUTE=VAL(MID$(TIME$,4,2))
```

As before, we've converted the result of the time value to show you how to get numerical output from a string.

Replacing a Substring

Instead of extracting a substring from a larger string variable, you may want to replace it with other characters. For example, suppose you wish to replace a zip code or an area code in a string. The MID$ statement (not to be confused

```
190 ' Statements in the main read loop
200 OLDAREA$ = MID$(PHONENUM$,2,3)
210 IF OLDAREA$ = "619" THEN GOSUB 1000
220 ' Program continues
 ...
 ...
1000 ' Replace the area code
1010 MID$(PHONENUM$,2,3)="708"
1020 PUT #2, RECNUM
1030 RETURN
```

Figure 10.4. Replacing String Components

with the MID$ function), lets you overlay a part of a string with another one. Here is the format:

MID$(*string-expression1,n[,m]*)=*string-expression2*

In the format, *string-expression1* is the original string. The substring starting at position *n* will be replaced with the first *m* characters in *string-expression2*. Both *n* and *m* are integer expressions. If you omit *m*, the characters up to the end of *string-expression1* are replaced if there are that many characters in *string-expression2*. The length of the original string never changes. Suppose PHONENUM$ contains strings in the form (619)555-1425. You could use this series of statements to change the area code to 708:

```
100 NEWCODE$="708"
200 MID$(PHONENUM$,2)=NEWCODE$
```

You could include the length of NEWCODE$ if you wish, but it isn't necessary since you know for sure that it is three characters long. You could use the actual replacement string as a constant rather than a variable if you prefer. If the PHONENUM$ field is in a file, you might use a routine like the one in Figure 10.4 to find and replace all the values.

1. Load 10STRINGS.BAS, if necessary. Delete the statements that ask for the initial and extract the position of it in the concatenated result.
2. Write statements to get the initials from NAME1, NAME2, and NAME3. Then print the three initials as a concatenated value. Test the program at this point.

3. Extract and print the last three characters of the middle name. Test the program again.
4. Extract and print the second through fourth characters of the last name. Test it again.
5. From NAMEFULL, replace the six characters beginning in the fifth position with "123456" and print the resulting value of NAMEFULL. Test it again and save it if you wish.

Your complete program should look something like this:

```
10 ' Use strings
20 CLS
30 DEFSTR N
40 INPUT "Enter your first name:  ",NAME1
50 INPUT "Enter your middle name: ",NAME2
60 INPUT "Enter your last name:   ",NAME3
70 NAMEFULL=NAME1+" "+NAME2+" "+NAME3
80 PRINT : PRINT NAMEFULL
90 PRINT
100 INIT1$ = LEFT$(NAME1,1)
110 INIT2$ = LEFT$(NAME2,1)
120 INIT3$ = LEFT$(NAME3,1)
130 PRINT: PRINT "Your initials are "; INIT1$+INIT2$+INIT3$
140 ' Extract portions
150 X2$=RIGHT$(NAME2,3)
160 PRINT: PRINT "Last three characters of middle name are :
";X2$
170 X3$=MID$(NAME3,2,3)
180 PRINT: PRINT "The 2nd thru 4th characters of last name are:
";X3$
190 MID$(NAMEFULL,5,6)="123456"
200 PRINT: PRINT "The new name is "; NAMEFULL
210 END
```

Lines 40 through 130 accomplish item 2. Lines 140 through 180 accomplish items 3 and 4. Lines 180 and 190 accomplish item 5. Your program may be somewhat different and still be correct.

Using Data within a Program

While many programs use files, it is often convenient to include data within a program. GW-BASIC provides the DATA statement to define constant data and the READ statement to access it for the program. In addition, you can use the RESTORE statement to manage your data. This section shows you how they all work. Figure 10.5 shows how a simple program might use READ and DATA statements.

```
10 ' Demonstration to use DATA
20 WHILE CLASS$ <> "ZZZ"
30    TOTUNITS = TOTUNITS + UNITS
40    READ CLASS$, UNITS, GRADE$
50 WEND
60 PRINT "Total units completed: "; TOTUNITS
70 END
1000 ' Start DATA statements here
1010 DATA LIT133, 4, B
1020 DATA LIT134, 4, B
1030 DATA LIT136, 4, B-
1040 DATA MATH2A, 5, A-
1050 DATA MATH2B, 5, B+
1060 DATA MATH2C, 5, B
1070 DATA PE17, 1, C
1080 DATA ZZZ, 9, Z
```

Figure 10.5. Using DATA in a Program

The DATA statements each contain three constant values, a string, followed by a numeric value, followed by another string. The last set of three constants is a dummy; it is used to mark the end of the list. The WHILE...WEND loop accumulates the total of the numeric fields. The READ statement reads three constants and assigns them to variables. When the last three constants are read, the value of CLASS$ is "ZZZ", so the PRINT statement is executed and the program ends.

Defining Program Data

The DATA statement contains a list of constants, separated by commas. Here's the format:

DATA *constant list*

You can use any type of constant, either numeric or string. The DATA statements in Figure 10.5 include both numeric and string values. If a string contains commas, colons, or spaces at the beginning or end that you want to keep, enclose the string in double quotation marks. You can see examples of numeric, unquoted string, and quoted string data in Figure 10.6. You can combine types in a single DATA statement.

```
1000 DATA Adios, Hasta la vista, Hasta luego, Buenos
noches
1100 DATA "Goodbye, Columbus", 1492, "The Lion, the
Witch, and the Wardrobe"
1200 DATA run, jump, speed, hop, jog, trot, amble,
stroll, stray
1300 DATA 15.2, 18.7, 19.6, 12.9, 16.5, 18.3
```

Figure 10.6. Sample DATA Statements

Constants in DATA statements are treated as if they are one continuous list. You can use as many DATA statements in a program as you like, and each can be as long as you want (up to 255 characters, of course). Each constant is accessed in sequence; it makes no difference to GW-BASIC whether you use 12 DATA statements with a single constant each or one DATA statement with 12 constants.

If the data isn't all the same type (numeric or string), you have to be consistent in where the different constants occur; when the program accesses each constant, it must know whether to expect a string or a numeric value.

Most programmers group all their DATA statements together at the end of the program, but that isn't really necessary. You can insert DATA statements anywhere you want in the program. When the program runs, GW-BASIC assumes the DATA statements create one long list of constants in line number order. So where you place the individual DATA statements makes no difference as long as the overall sequence is as you want it.

When a program begins, the first READ statement starts accessing constants at the first constant in the first DATA statement in the program. Constants are accessed in sequence through all DATA statements unless the sequence is changed with a RESTORE statement.

Accessing Program Data

To access constants from a DATA statement, you use a READ statement. Each READ statement includes a list of variables to be accessed from DATA statements, starting where the last READ statement left off. Here's the format:

READ *variable-list*

The variables in the list can be separated by commas or not; the choice is up to you. When READ is executed, it accesses constants from the DATA

```
10 ' To demonstrate use of DATA
20 READ SIGNAL$, ITEM$, PRICE
30 WHILE SIGNAL$<>"X"
40    IF SIGNAL$<>"S" THEN GOSUB 1000 ELSE GOSUB 2000
50    PRINT ITEM$; TAB(20);
60    PRINT USING "####.##"; SALEPRICE;
70    PRINT MARKER$
80    READ SIGNAL$, ITEM$, PRICE
90 WEND
100 END
1000 ' Set regular price
1010 SALEPRICE = PRICE
1015 MARKER$= SPACE$(8)
1020 RETURN
2000 ' Set sale price
2010 SALEPRICE = PRICE * .9
2015 MARKER$= " On sale"
2020 RETURN
5000 DATA R,"Sweatshirt, hooded",14.98
5010 DATA S,"T-shirt",8.98, S,"Shorts, Gym",5.98
5020 DATA R,"Sweatpants",19.98, S,"Cap, baseball",6.75
5030 DATA X,"dummy",0
```

Figure 10.7. Multiple READs per DATA Statement

statement. If this is the first READ, the first constant on the first DATA statement is assigned to the first variable in the READ statement, the second constant to the second variable, and so forth. If this is a later READ statement, it starts assigning constants with the first unread constant. Each constant must be of the same type as the variable it is assigned to or a Syntax error occurs, just as with INPUT statements. If READ statements don't read all the data constants, the extra values are ignored.

The program in Figure 10.5 shows a very simple use of READ and DATA. The DATA statements include unquoted string and numeric values. The WHILE...WEND loop goes through all the data and does some calculations. The READ statement reads three variables; we placed three constants on each DATA statement, but that isn't necessary. Statement 30 adds the values in one field as each set of data is read.

When GW-BASIC tries to READ beyond the end of the data, it gets an Out of data error. You can avoid this by including a dummy DATA statement as we did. The loop tests for the dummy value and stops reading at that point.

Figure 10.7 shows another example. In this program, the READ statement gets three variables, but the DATA statements don't all contain three constants. And some extra strings are enclosed in double quotes; this isn't necessary but it doesn't hurt. Each time the READ statement is executed, it reads three additional constants. Notice that the constants are arranged in the DATA statements so that the numeric variables appear in the correct locations.

The program prints a report based on the data it reads. If the SIGNAL$ variable shows the item is on sale, the price is discounted and MARKER$ is set to a sale message. If it is not on sale, the standard price is used and MARKER$ is set to spaces. The final dummy variable is listed at the bottom of the list.

Changing the Data Sequence

Normally, READ statements access DATA constants in sequence. Each READ starts assigning values to variables at the next unread constant. After the last constant is assigned, an attempt to READ raises the Out of data message. You can modify this with the RESTORE statement. Here's the format:

RESTORE [*line number*]

If you use RESTORE by itself, it resets the READ so that it starts at the first DATA statement again. If you specify a line number, it resets the READ so it will start at the DATA statement on that line. If there is no DATA statement on that line, GW-BASIC finds the next DATA statement after it and points to that.

You can use RESTORE to point to certain areas of your data. A program might use a statement like this:

```
200 IF X$ = "1" THEN RESTORE 2000 ELSE IF X$ = "2" THEN RESTORE 4000
```

Based on the value of a particular variable, the program specifies which section of DATA statements is to be accessed by READ statements. When used without a line number, the RESTORE statement causes READ access to start at the first DATA statement in the program.

1. In this Self-Check, you'll write a program that contains names of people and their ages as DATA. First, write DATA statements (starting at 1000) to include a full name, then an age for ten people; use an age of under 21 for at least three people, and 21 or over for the rest.

Put a dummy set of values at the end.
2. Write another set of DATA statements (starting at 2000) that contains the words "Adult" and "Minor".
3. Write a segment of the program that will use the heading "Adult" from the second set of DATA statements and list all the names that show an age of 21 or over.
4. Write a segment to use the heading "Minor" from the second set of DATA statements and list all the names that show an age under 21. Don't print the "dummy" information.
5. Test the program; modify it until it works correctly.

Your program will look something like this:

```
10 ' Using DATA
20 DEFSTR L-N
30 RESTORE 2000
40 READ LIST1, LIST2
50 PRINT LIST1
60 RESTORE 1000
70 WHILE NAMED <> "DUMMY"
80     READ NAMED, AGE
90     IF NAMED = "DUMMY" THEN GOTO 110
100     IF AGE >= 21 THEN PRINT NAMED
110 WEND
120 RESTORE 1000
130 PRINT : PRINT LIST2
140 NAMED = ""
150 WHILE NAMED <> "DUMMY"
160     READ NAMED, AGE
170     IF NAMED = "DUMMY" THEN GOTO 190
180     IF AGE < 21 THEN PRINT NAMED
190 WEND
200 END
1000 ' DATA statements follow
1010 DATA Ruth Ashley,45,Judi N. Fernandez,46,Paul Loveland,20
1020 DATA "Michael Sloan,Jr.",24,Alice Jones,33,Mary Michaels,35
1030 DATA Steven Wagner,18,Dorothy Dawes,51,Jennifer Griffith,19
1040 DATA Marcia Melinn,34
2000 DATA Adults,Minors
```

You used different names and ages, of course. You can have one set per DATA statement or any number of constants you want. Be sure to use double quotes if any of your names includes a comma. Be sure to use RESTORE to start accessing records from the second set of data. We included just one DATA statement in the set beginning at line 2000. You could use more statements here if you prefer. The program works the same in either case.

Summary

This chapter has covered various ways of handling strings and other data in programs. The string and conversion features will come in handy in any program that uses string variables. The ability to store constants in a program with DATA statements and access them with READ statements helps you write more useful programs.

The DEFSTR statement reserves variable names beginning with specific letters for string variables. You can override DEFtype statements with the type specification characters ($, %, !, #).

The VAL function converts the contents of a string variable containing valid numeric data to numeric form, while the STR$ function converts a numeric value into a valid string.

The LEN function returns the length of a string.

The INSTR function finds a string value within a larger string. You specify the starting position, if not at the beginning, and the two strings in variable or constant form.

String concatenation is accomplished with the + sign. Join the constants or variable names in any combination with + signs to create a new, combined variable.

The LEFT$ and RIGHT$ string functions extract a string of the length you specify from the left or right edge of the string you name. The result is also a string.

The MID$ string function extracts a string of the length you specify, starting at the point you specify, from the middle of a string you name. The MID$ statement lets you replace a substring with another string, actually changing the value of the original string.

The DATA statement includes a list of constants, of any type, that can be used by the program as often as needed. A program can include DATA statements at any location, but they are read in order from the beginning of the program. Only a RESTORE statement can change the sequence.

The READ statement accesses constants from DATA statements. It can specify as many variables to hold the constants as needed; the type of the constant must match that of the variable to which it is assigned. READ always starts with the latest unread constant in the list, unless a RESTORE statement is executed.

The RESTORE statement points to a specific DATA statement for the next READ to access. Used without a line number, it resets the pointer to the first DATA statement.

Exercise

In this exercise, you'll write a program that uses many strings. It is based on constants included in DATA statements. Here are the DATA statements you will use:

```
1000 '  DATA statements follow
1010 DATA "M. Jackson", (503)555-1414
1020 DATA Steven Wagner, (503)555-1414
1030 DATA Judi Fernandez, (619)555-8684
1040 DATA Ruth Ashley, (503)555-1713
1050 DATA Mary Smithers, 555-8989
1060 DATA S. Washington, (503)555-8888
1070 DATA A. Lincoln, (555)555-6666
1080 DATA last, 555
```

The program will perform one operation on the first string in each DATA statement (the name) and another on the second (the phone number).

---

1. Enter the DATA statements shown above, starting at line 1000. You can combine the values differently on DATA statements if you like, but be sure to maintain the same sequence.
2. Reserve variable names beginning with letters M through P for use with strings. Use these letters to start all your string variables.
3. The program must extract the last name and store it in another string variable.
4. The program must check the phone number for length. If it is 13 characters, it is in standard format. The program should change the area code 503, wherever it occurs, to 666. It should use a different message for adjusted area codes, area codes it knows are OK, and numbers that are out of format.
5. Write the statements to read two variables, perform the two operations, and print a line with the last name, the phone number, adjusted if appropriate, and the message telling what was done. Don't print a line for the dummy last DATA constants.

Your program should look something like this:

```
10 DEFSTR M-P
20 READ MEMBER, PHONE
30 WHILE MEMBER <> "last"
40    FOUND = INSTR(MEMBER," ")
```

```
50      PARTNAME = MID$(MEMBER,FOUND)
60      IF LEN(PHONE) = 13 THEN GOSUB 500 ELSE GOSUB 800
70      PRINT PARTNAME; TAB(20) ; PHONE; TAB(35); FIXED$
80      READ MEMBER, PHONE
90 WEND
100 END
500 ' adjust area code for listing
510 IF MID$(PHONE,2,3) = "503" THEN MID$(PHONE,2,3)="666" :
FIXED$ = "Area code adjusted" ELSE FIXED$ = "Area code OK as is"
520 RETURN
800 ' note about area code
810 FIXED$ = "Out of format - area code not adjusted"
820 RETURN
1000 'DATA statements follow
1010 DATA "M. Jackson", (503)555-1414
1020 DATA Steven Wagner, (503)555-1414
1030 DATA Judi Fernandez, (619)555-8684
1040 DATA Ruth Ashley, (503)555-1713
1050 DATA Mary Smithers, 555-8989
1060 DATA S. Washington, (503)555-8888
1070 DATA A. Lincoln, (555)555-6666
1080 DATA last, 555
```

We used the INSTR and MID$ functions to extract just the last name. You could have used RIGHT$(PHONE,LEN(PHONE) − FOUND) instead. In line 510, MID$ as a function and as a statement are needed to replace the area code. The LEN function helps you determine if the phone number is in the correct format.

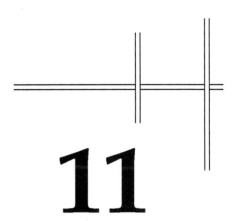

11

Defining and Using Arrays

In this chapter, you'll learn to define and use arrays in GW-BASIC. You will see how arrays are stored and how to create and use them in programs to simplify data processing and expand the power of your programs. In particular, you'll learn to:

- Use the DIM statement to set up a string or numeric array
- Use the OPTION BASE statement to eliminate the 0 element
- Use the ERASE statement to clear a named array
- Fill an array from the keyboard, DATA statements, or a file
- Access individual elements in a one- or two-dimensional array
- Access all the elements in a one- or two-dimensional array
- Use the SWAP statement to exchange values of two variables
- Use an array as an index for locating records in a random file

What Are Arrays?

An array is a set of values. A variable is like a box that holds a single value at a time. An array variable is like a set of boxes that holds a collection of values. The values in an array must all be of the same type; that is, they must be all strings, all single-precision numbers, all integers, or all double-precision numbers. An array variable name has the same restrictions as a variable name;

267

you use the same type specification character or DEF*type* statement to specify the type of data it will hold. MEMBERS$ and SALARIES might be names of a string and single-precision array.

Arrays make for very efficient storage and processing of data. FOR...NEXT loops can process every element in a table. Since the subscripts start with 0 (or 1) and increase by 1 for every element, it is easy to step through the entire array. Many applications couldn't be programmed without the use of arrays.

Array Dimensions

Arrays can come in several dimensions. A simple list is a one-dimensional array. A rectanglar arrangement of values is a two-dimensional array. A cubic arrangement is three dimensional. Arrays can have up to 255 dimensions.

All the arrays are stored linearly. This is easiest to imagine with a one-dimensional array. A multidimensional array is stored in row order; that is, all elements in the first row of the rectangular array are stored first, then all elements in the second row, and so forth. If the array has three dimensions, after the last row on the first plane, the first row on the second plane is stored, and so forth. With strings, three-byte pointers to the actual values are stored end-to-end, but it has the same effect.

Most applications of arrays use only one or two dimensions. Three are sometimes useful. Higher dimensions, while possible, are more complex to use. Programs that must use four or more array dimensions are often better written in a higher-level language. We'll concentrate on one- and two-dimensional arrays in this book. You'll see one example using a three-dimensional array so you can see how to load and access it.

Array Elements

The elements in an array are referred to with the array name followed by a subscript for each dimension. The subscript is a number (or several numbers) that refer to the position of the particular element in the array. By default arrays start with position zero, so the second element has subscript 1. MEMBERS$(2) refers to the third element in the one-dimensional MEMBERS$ array. SALARIES(8,5) refers to the element in the ninth row and sixth column of the SALARIES array. A subscript must be a whole number and must not be negative. It must be within the range of the array. In form, any subscript can be a number, numeric variable, or an expression. For example, the array reference MEMBERS$(COUNT+1) is valid.

Size of Arrays

By default, an array of up to four dimensions can use any subscript up to 10 for each dimension; that is, a one-dimensional array automatically has 11 elements, a two-dimensional array has 121 elements (11 in each direction), and so forth. The default array size reserves that much space in memory, whether you need it or not. However, you can reserve exactly the amount of space you want for each dimension. If you need a one-dimensional array of eight double-precision numbers, you can reserve exactly the right size. If you need a two-dimensional array of five rows of 16 elements each, you can reserve exactly the right size. The next section shows you how.

Each dimension can have up to 255 elements in it technically, but each element takes up space. If your array has more than four dimensions, it will run out of space very quickly. A default size three-dimensional array needs space for 121 x 11 elements, or 1,331 elements. A default four-dimensional array needs space for 11 times that many or 14,641 elements; if they are all two-byte integers they take up 29,282 bytes.

Arrays with more than four dimensions cannot use the default dimensions; the default size takes too much space. A default five-dimensional array needs space for 11 times as many as a four-dimensional array, or 161,054 elements. Since GW-BASIC can use only about 64,000 bytes, you can see that the practical limits on array size are much smaller than 255 elements per dimension.

Dimensioning Arrays

Reserving space for an array involves telling GW-BASIC how many dimensions are needed and how many elements are in each. This is often called dimensioning arrays.

Implicit

If you use an undefined variable name with subscripts, GW-BASIC treats it as implicit dimensioning for an array. It reserves the array name with as many dimensions as there are subscripts, allotting 11 elements in each dimension. You can use the array within these parameters. For example, suppose a program will use eight different names and you want them stored in an array. Figure 11.1 shows the beginning of a program that gets the names from the keyboard and stores them in the array.

```
10 ' Set up array of names
20 FOR X = 0 TO 7
30    INPUT "Please type one name: ", STORENAME$(X)
40 NEXT
```

Figure 11.1. Implicit Dimensioning and Array Loading

In the program, the first appearance of the array variable name is in line 30. The FOR...NEXT loop will execute eight times and assign eight values to the array elements. If the FOR statement used a value greater than 10 for the stop value, an error (Subscript out of range in 30) would occur.

Using the DIM Statement

You can specify the exact size of an array with the DIM statement; it must occur earlier in the program than any reference to the array variable name. In Figure 11.1, the program could use DIM STORENAME$(7) to reserve exactly the amount of space needed for the eight names. Here's the format:

DIM *variable(subscripts)* [*,variable(subscripts)*]

Here are some examples:
```
DIM PRICES(7)
DIM MEMBER$(25)
DIM STUDENTS(68), SCORES(68,10)
DIM TEMPS(24), HUMIDS(24), PRESSURE(24)
```

You can dimension several arrays in one DIM statement, or you can use as many DIM statements as you want. For each array variable, specify the highest element number, remembering that the subscript 0 refers to the first element in the array. If space isn't a problem, you could use DIM PRICES(8) to reserve an eight-element array and just ignore the first element. Once you use a DIM statement, the storage space is allocated and all variables get an initial value. Numeric array elements get value 0. String array elements get the null value.

Canceling a DIM or Explicit Dimension

Once an array is dimensioned to a specific level, it stays at that level until the program ends. To use it for a different size array, you must use the ERASE command; you can name one or more variables to be erased. Once an array variable is ERASEd, all of its elements are undefined and the variable name can be reused for any purpose. Here's the format:

ERASE *array-variable-list*

While the CLEAR statement also removes variables, it doesn't free up array variable names. You must use ERASE if the program will use the array variable name later for some other purpose.

Occasionally, a program may terminate unexpectedly and the array variable name isn't released. If you get a message such as Duplicate definition in line *nn*, try using ERASE at the Ok prompt, specifying any array variables named in the line that got the message. Then test the program again.

Starting an Array at 1

You may sometimes wish to start referencing an array with subscript 1 rather than 0. While the program can ignore the 0 position, storage is allocated for it and that can waste space, especially in multidimensional arrays. A special statement causes all arrays referred to in the program to start at 1 rather than 0. Here's the format:

OPTION BASE 1

If you include OPTION BASE 1, all array variable subscript references start at 1 instead of 0. MEMBER$(1) refers to the first element in the array instead of the second. You can't pick and choose, however; either all the arrays in the program start with subscript 1 or they all start with subscript 0. The OPTION BASE 1 statement must occur before any reference to any array variable, even in a DIM statement, or you'll get the Duplicate definition error message.

If you dimension a variable at 14 under default conditions, remember to increase the DIM by 1 if you add OPTION BASE 1 to the program later to keep the arrays at the same size.

One-Dimensional Arrays

Many programs use one-dimensional arrays. Any time a program must handle a list of data, it makes sense to build an array. The major things you do

MONTHNAME$	SALARY	CATEGORY$
January	36000	Basic
February	38000	Advanced
March	24000	Classified
April	28000	Coordinated
May	30000	PostGrad
June	32000	Remedial
July	36000	
August	42000	
September		
October		
November		
December		

Figure 11.2. One-Dimensional Arrays

with arrays are load them, access them sequentially, and locate a specific element.

Figure 11.2 shows three sample lists; any separate list could be an array. The first list represents the elements in a string array named MONTHNAME$. The 12 elements might be named MONTHNAME$(0), MONTHNAME$(1), and continuing on through MONTHNAME$(11). In this case, it would make sense to include the OPTION BASE 1 statement, so the first element in the array is MONTHNAME$(1) and the last is MONTHNAME$(12).

The second column in Figure 11.2 represents the eight elements in an array named SALARY. The last element here would be SALARY(7) unless OPTION BASE 1 is in effect. The rightmost column shows the six elements in the CATEGORY$ array.

Loading a One-Dimensional Array

To load values into an array, the program must assign a value to each element in turn. That is most easily done through a FOR...NEXT loop that starts at the lowest subscript and increments by one until it reaches the top. An example of this was included earlier in Figure 11.1. Figure 11.3 shows how the array MONTHNAME$ can be loaded from DATA statements.

Notice that OPTION BASE 1 precedes the DIM statement. When statement 60 is finished, each element has the desired value.

```
10 ' Set up array of month names
20 OPTION BASE 1
30 DIM MONTHNAME$(12)
40 FOR X = 1 TO 12
50    READ MONTHNAME$(X)
60 NEXT
100 '  Rest of program here
1000 ' Start DATA lines here
1010 DATA January, February, March, April, May, June
1020 DATA July, August, September, October, November,
December, None
```

Figure 11.3. Loading a One-Dimensional Array

You have seen how a one-dimensional array can be loaded from keyboard input or from DATA statements. It can also be loaded from a file. For example, suppose you have a random file that has records in order by six-digit customer number. You could read each record in the file sequentially and assign it to an element in a one-dimensional array. The array can function as an index. When a user wants to look up a record, the program can get the desired customer number from the keyboard, look up the element number in the array, then directly access the record in that position.

Accessing All Elements

If you want to process all elements sequentially, you have to set up a loop that processes the first, second, and on through the last element in the array. The process is much like loading the array initially. Figure 11.4 shows an example in which the array is loaded, then printed in reverse order on the console.

Notice that the array is first loaded from the DATA statements, then printed following a heading. The last DATA variable is a dummy that won't be read.

The MONTHNAME$ array (from Figure 11.3) can be printed with the following program lines:

```
70 PRINT "The month names are as follows:"
80 FOR X = 1 TO 12
90    PRINT X;" ";MONTHNAME$(X)
100 NEXT
```

The program can do as extensive processing of arrays as it needs. Figure 11.5 shows a short program that loads two arrays, one each of high and low

```
10 ' process a string array
20 DIM WORKERS$(12)
30 FOR X = 0 TO 12
40    READ WORKERS$(X)
50 NEXT
60 PRINT "Worker List"
70 FOR X = 12 TO 1 STEP -1
80    PRINT "Array element"; X; "is "; WORKERS$(X)
90 NEXT
100 END
5000 ' start data values here
5010 DATA John Smith, Harry Wash, Abraham Golden
5020 DATA Ruth Ashley, Mary Hoogterp, Anne Elwood
5030 DATA Dorothy Toto, George Bush, Saddam Hussein
5040 DATA Judi Fernandez, Paul Loveland, Jenny Gritter
5050 DATA Anthony Pernicano, Should not be in array
```

Figure 11.4. Processing an Array

temperatures for 20 consecutive time periods, then finds the average high and low temperatures.

This program ignores element 0. The first loop loads two separate one-dimensional arrays from the DATA statements. The second loop totals all elements in each array. Then the average of each array is calculated and printed. You'll be able to do the same thing in a two-dimensional array later in this chapter.

1. Start a new program that will load 15 elements into an array named PRICES. Write the DATA statements starting at line 3000, using any values you wish.
2. Write the first few lines of the program, dimensioning the array.
3. Write a routine to load all the elements into the array.
4. Write a statement to print a heading for a list of all the elements.
5. Write a routine to list all the elements in the array on the screen. Include the subscript number with each element's contents.
6. Test the program and make sure you loaded every element.
7. Modify the program so it starts with element number 1 and test it again.

Here's how our program looked at item 6:

```
10 ' Set up array of prices
20 DEFINT X
30 DIM PRICES(14)
40 FOR X = 0 TO 14
50   READ PRICES(X)
60 NEXT
70 PRINT "Price listing"
80 FOR X = 0 TO 14
90   PRINT USING "##  ####.##"; X, PRICES(X)
100 NEXT
120 END
3000 ' Start DATA lines here
3010 DATA 145.99, 178.98, 145.76, 99.50, 119.00
3020 DATA 79.99, 67.99, 95.00, 78.98, 98.50
3030 DATA 129.99, 138.75, 119.20, 87.75, 99.99
```

To modify it, we added line 15 OPTION BASE 1, changed line 30 to dimension up to 15, and changed each FOR...NEXT loop to start with 1 and stop with 15. Your program could be a bit different and still be correct.

```
10 ' Set up and process temperature values
20 DEFINT H,I,L,T
30 DIM HITEMP(19), LOTEMP(19)
40 FOR I = 0 TO 19
50   READ HITEMP(I)
60   READ LOTEMP(I)
70 NEXT
80 FOR I = 0 TO 19
90   TOTHI = TOTHI + HITEMP(I)
100   TOTLO = TOTLO + LOTEMP(I)
110 NEXT
120 AVGHI = TOTHI / 20
130 AVGLO = TOTLO / 20
140 PRINT "Average high temperature: "; AVGHI
150 PRINT "Average low temperature:  "; AVGLO
160 END
1000 ' Start DATA lines here
1010 DATA 87,58,85,57,82,52,90,61,85,62,83,57,79,59
1020 DATA 74,53 78,54,75,59,79,61,81,60,84,58,82,59
1030 DATA 79,56,75,54,77,53,76,54,76,53,72,56
```

Figure 11.5. Calculating From Arrays

Accessing a Specific Element

In most cases, a program will need to access a specific element in the array. For example, it may need to find the month represented by the variable MONTH or the worker represented by EMPNO%. The program can use any variable containing a value that represents the element needed as a subscript. The following program segment uses part of the system date to determine the month, then uses that value to access and display the month name from the array loaded by the program shown earlier in Figure 11.3.

```
120 MONTH = VAL(LEFT$(DATE$,2))
130 PRINT "The current month is "; MONTHNAME$(MONTH)
```

The following example uses the arrays loaded in Figure 11.5. The user enters the desired period at the keyboard.

```
300 INPUT "Type the period (1 to 20): ",PERIOD
310 period = period - 1
320 PRINT "The high temperature was ";HITEMP(PERIOD)
330 PRINT "The low temperature was ";LOTEMP(PERIOD)
```

Once the program has the value of the subscript it needs, it can use any variable with a nonnegative value as a subscript. If the subscript variable holds a number with a fractional component, only the integer portion is used.

Two-Dimensional Arrays

A two-dimensional array is represented on paper as a rectangular arrangement of data. The rows and columns represent the two dimensions. The first subscript will refer to the row, and the second will refer to the column. Figure 11.6 shows the values in a two-dimensional array. Each row represents a different student. Each column represents the score of that student on a different assignment.

Processing a Two-Dimensional Array

Two-dimensional arrays are loaded from any of the same sources you can load a one-dimensional array. In most cases, you'll load them from DATA statements or file records, since entering that much information from the keyboard can be tedious. Figure 11.7 shows a program that loads the score data shown in Figure 11.6 into an array, then prints out the information.

Rows						Columns						
	0	1	2	3	4	5	6	7	8	9	10	11
0	90	87	84	88	76	81	89	76	78	84	94	92
1	92	86	83	91	75	79	86	77	74	81	89	87
2	87	86	85	84	79	82	86	86	88	94	84	82
3	89	100	87	92	90	87	89	90	86	91	93	97
4	94	99	96	100	97	89	91	88	87	85	86	88
5	91	83	87	93	79	84	89	75	79	87	91	91
6	90	82	91	93	86	86	91	77	73	81	93	90
7	85	87	91	86	82	83	87	82	85	91	87	89
8	89	100	88	95	89	87	91	92	86	95	93	96
9	96	99	96	97	87	89	91	88	87	95	96	98

Figure 11.6. Two-Dimensional Array Data

In this case, each DATA statement includes values for 12 scores for one student; that is, it contains one row of values. The inner loop assigns values to SCORE(0,0), SCORE(0,1), and on through SCORE(0,11) the first time around. The next set of executions of the inner loop assigns values to student 1. The process continues until all the data values are assigned and the array is filled.

The second processing loop prints all the scores. The inner loop again handles all the scores for each student. The PRINT statement on line 140 starts a new line for the next student's scores.

Extracting Values from an Array

Suppose you want to average the scores on a particular test to find out what the relative difficulty was. You could use a routine like this:

```
160 INPUT "Test (1 through 12) to average "; TEST
170 FOR X = 0 TO 9
180     TEMPTOT = TEMPTOT + SCORE (X, TEST)
190 NEXT
200 AVETEST = TEMPTOT / 10
210 PRINT "The average on test"; TEST; "is"; AVETEST
220 END
```

In this routine, the value of TEST is received from the keyboard and used as the second subscript. The FOR...NEXT loop steps through each student (the first subscript) and adds the value of the specified test score to a running total. After all students are checked, the average is calculated and printed.

```
10 ' Use the SCORE array
20 DIM SCORE(9,11)
30 FOR X = 0 TO 9
40    FOR Y = 0 TO 11
50       READ SCORE(X,Y)
60    NEXT Y
70 NEXT X
80 PRINT "Scores for each student"
90 FOR X = 0 TO 9
100 PRINT USING "Student###"; X+1;
110    FOR Y = 0 TO 11
120       PRINT USING "####"; SCORE(X,Y);
130    NEXT Y
140    PRINT
150 NEXT X
160 END
2000 ' Start SCORE data here, one line per student
2010 DATA 90,87,84,88,76,81,89,76,78,84,94,92
2020 DATA 92,86,83,91,75,79,86,77,74,81,89,87
2030 DATA 87,86,85,84,79,82,86,86,88,94,84,82
2040 DATA 89,100,87,92,90,87,89,90,86,91,93,97
2050 DATA 94,99,96,100,97,89,91,88,87,85,86,88
2060 DATA 91,83,87,93,79,84,89,75,79,87,91,91
2070 DATA 90,82,91,93,86,86,91,77,73,81,93,90
2080 DATA 85,87,91,86,82,83,87,82,85,91,87,89
2090 DATA 89,100,88,95,89,87,91,92,86,95,93,96
2100 DATA 96,99,96,97,87,89,91,88,87,95,96,98
```

Figure 11.7. Processing a Two-Dimensional Array

1. You need a program to process salary and deduction information. For each of 12 employees, you need three values: salary, number of dependents, and employee class. Enter the DATA statements shown in Figure 11.8.
2. Write the first part of the program, to allocate space for the PAYROLL array and load it from the DATA statements.
3. Write another segment to list all the data on the screen.
4. Test the program. When it works correctly, save it as 11SELF.BAS.

Your program should look something like the one that follows. Make sure you loaded the array in row order; that is, the inner loop should load three values and the outer loop 12. If you used OPTION BASE 1, you should dimension and process the file as (12,3).

```
10 ' Load and print a two-dimensional array
20 DIM PAYROLL(11,2)
30 FOR X = 0 TO 11
40    FOR Y= 0 TO 2
50       READ PAYROLL(X,Y)
60    NEXT
70 NEXT
75 PRINT "Salary   Dependents   Class"
80 FOR X = 0 TO 11
90    FOR Y = 0 TO 2
100      PRINT USING "#####,##"; PAYROLL(X,Y),
110   NEXT
120 PRINT
130 NEXT
140 END
1000 ' start data values here
1010 DATA 24000, 5, 1, 22000, 4, 1, 25000, 2, 2, 36000, 1, 2
1020 DATA 18500, 1, 0, 32000, 3, 2, 31000, 4, 1, 29000, 1, 2
1030 DATA 20000, 1, 1, 36000, 4, 2, 28000, 3, 2, 40000, 3, 1
```

Your program may be different and still be correct.

Using Multiple Arrays

Since an array is limited to one type of data, you may have to use more than one array to store your information. For example, recall the SCORES two-dimensional array. It contains scores for 10 students for 12 different tests. If a second array contains the students' passwords, a program can work with both arrays at once. Figure 11.9 shows how.

In this program, the two arrays are first loaded. The program then sets up a loop so that students can enter a password and get the current grade. When a password is entered, the subroutine starting at line 1000 is executed to find out if it is valid, and, if so, what the subscript it. When control returns to line 200, an invalid password is handled, if necessary.

```
1000 ' start data values here
1010 DATA 24000,5,1,22000,4,1,25000,2,2,36000,1,2
1020 DATA 18500,1,0,32000,3,2,31000,4,1,29000,1,2
1030 DATA 20000,1,1,36000,4,2,28000,3,2,40000,3,1
```

Figure 11.8. DATA Statements

```
10 ' Use two arrays
20 DIM SCORE(9,11), PASSWORD$(9)
30 ' Load scores array
40 FOR X = 0 TO 9
50   FOR Y = 0 TO 11
60     READ SCORE(X,Y)
70   NEXT Y
80 NEXT X
90 ' Load student password array
100 RESTORE 3000             ' To point to correct DATA
110 FOR A = 0 TO 9
120   READ PASSWORD$(A)
130 NEXT
140 ' Start grade checking loop
150 CLS: PRINT "Type END to stop the program."
160 INPUT "Enter the password in caps: ", PWORD$
170 WHILE PWORD$ <> "END" AND PWORD$ <> "end"
180   GOSUB 1000       ' find subscript to use in SCORES
190   IF PASS = -1 THEN PRINT "Invalid password" : GOTO 280
200   TEMPTOT = 0
210   FOR Y = 0 TO 11
220     TEMPTOT = TEMPTOT + SCORE(PASS,Y)
230   NEXT
240   AVERAGE = TEMPTOT/12
250   PRINT : PRINT USING "Your average is####.##"; AVERAGE
260   PRINT "Press any key to clear screen." : A$ = INPUT$(1)
270   PRINT "Type END to stop the program."
280   INPUT "Enter the password in all caps: ", PWORD$
290 WEND
300 PRINT "Program ended. Type RUN to start again."
310 END
1000 ' Find subscript for password
1010 PASS = -1
1020 FOR A = 0 TO 9
1030   IF PASSWORD$(A) = PWORD$ THEN PASS = A
1040 NEXT
1050 RETURN
2000 ' Data for SCORE array
2010 DATA 90,87,84,88,76,81,89,76,78,84,94,92
2020 DATA 92,86,83,91,75,79,86,77,74,81,89,87
2030 DATA 87,86,85,84,79,82,86,86,88,94,84,82
2040 DATA 89,100,87,92,90,87,89,90,86,91,93,97
2050 DATA 94,99,96,100,97,89,91,88,87,85,86,88
2060 DATA 91,83,87,93,79,84,89,75,79,87,91,91
2070 DATA 90,82,91,93,86,86,91,77,73,81,93,90
2080 DATA 85,87,91,86,82,83,87,82,85,91,87,89
2090 DATA 89,100,88,95,89,87,91,92,86,95,93,96
2100 DATA 96,99,96,97,87,89,91,88,87,95,96,98
3000 ' Data for PASSWORD$ array
3010 DATA GEODE, TOUCAN, CLAMBAKE, MEERKAT, OKAPI, DOLPHIN
3020 DATA SKINK, GECKO, WALLABY, NENE
```

Figure 11.9. Using Two Arrays

The program then uses the subscript value of a valid password to find the students' grades, calculate the average, and display the information on the screen.

Notice that the information for loading the two arrays is in two different sets of DATA statements. The RESTORE statement in line 100 points to the beginning of the second set for loading the second array.

Sorting an Array

Sorting data is a common procedure. The easiest way to sort data in GW-BASIC is when it is stored in an array. While there are various ways of setting up a sort method, the easiest to handle is called a bubble sort.

The Bubble Sort

In a bubble sort, pairs of values are switched, depending on which one is larger. The entire list to be sorted is examined repeatedly, and the higher values just bubble up toward the top, while the lower values sink to the bottom. (This assumes a sort with the higher values at the top, of course. You can sort in either direction.)

In a bubble sort, the computer compares each set of two values, then switches them if the one nearer the beginning of the list is not larger. After it checks all the values once, it checks again, repeatedly switching values until they are all in sequence.

The SWAP Statement

You can always switch two values by setting up a third temporary variable to hold one during the switch. But there's an easier way. The SWAP statement specifies two variable names, and their contents are switched. You might use SWAP PRICE, NEWPRICE, for example. The two variables must be of the same type (string, single precision, double precision, or integer) or you'll get a Type mismatch error. All the elements of an array are of the same type, so any two can be switched. The statement SWAP PASSWORD$ (X), PASSWORD$ (X+1) is valid and useful.

```
10 ' Demonstrate sorting an array
20 TOTPRES = 20
30 OPTION BASE 1
40 DIM PRES$(TOTPRES)
50 FOR X = 1 TO TOTPRES
60    READ PRES$(X)
70 NEXT
80 ' Now start the bubble sort loops
90 FOR M = 1 TO TOTPRES
100    FOR N = 1 TO TOTPRES
110       IF PRES$(N)   PRES$(M) THEN SWAP PRES$(N),
PRES$(M)
120    NEXT N
130 NEXT M
140 ' Print the array in sorted order
150 FOR X = 1 TO TOTPRES
160    PRINT X, PRES$(X)
170 NEXT
180 END
1000 ' start president listing here
1010 DATA "Washington, George", "Adams, John", "Jef-
ferson, Thomas"
1020 DATA "Madison, James", "Monroe, James", "Adams,
John Quincy"
1030 DATA "Van Buren, Martin", "Jackson, Andrew",
"Harrison, William Henry"
1040 DATA "Tyler, John", "Polk, James K.", "Taylor,
Zachary"
1050 DATA "Fillmore, Millard", "Pierce, Franklin",
"Buchanan, James"
1060 DATA "Lincoln, Abraham", "Johnson, Andrew",
"Grant, Ulysses S."
1070 DATA "Hayes, Rutherford", "Garfield, James"
```

Figure 11.10. Sorting an Array

The Sort Program

Figure 11.10 shows a program that loads a one-dimensional array with the names of the first 20 presidents, then sorts them into alphabetical order. A variable holds the number of array elements to make the program easy to maintain.

Lines 50 through 70 load the array from the DATA statements and get it ready to sort. The sort itself involves a nested FOR...NEXT loop so the array can be processed completely. The outer loop is executed once for each element in the array. The inner loop performs the actual work of the sort. It compares each set of two values and swaps them if the one represented by the inner loop index is greater than the one represented by the outer loop index. When the nested loops are finished, the array is completely sorted.

When the array is printed by the last FOR...NEXT loop, you'll see the result. To sort in descending sequence, use the symbol < rather than > in a bubble sort.

Using Arrays as Indexes

One very important use of arrays is to build an index to help you locate records in a random file. You can do this whether or not the records are in a meaningful sequence. In order to do this, each record location in the file must contain valid data.

The technique involves first reading every record in the file sequentially, assigning an identification field in each record to an element in the array, corresponding to the record number. The program then accesses records in two stages. First, the desired identifier is located in the array. Then the subscript number is used as the location number in accessing the record. Figure 11.11 shows an example.

In this program, the file is opened and the record described in a FIELD statement. The calculated number of records in the file (TOTRECS) is used to set the size of the array. OPTION BASE 1 is used because the record positions start with position 1. The loop in lines 130 to 160 reads every record in the file and sets up the index array to contain the unique identifier in each record in the array element that corresponds to the position of the record in the file.

When the user enters an item number to request a record, the loop in lines 200 to 220 finds out if it is valid. If it locates the entered item number, the variable KEEP is set to the current subscript. If it isn't found, the program handles it and asks for a different number. Then it uses KEEP as the position number to access the record (see line 240) and displays the information.

1. Reload program 11SELF.BAS if necessary. You'll modify this program to use two arrays, then print out both together.
2. Add DATA statements to supply a full name for each employee.
3. Write a routine to load the new array as STAFF$ with 12 elements.
4. Modify the print routine so that it prints the employee's name on the line before the payroll information.

```
10 ' Create an index to use in finding records
20 CLS
30 KEY OFF
40 OPTION BASE 1
50 DIM RINDEX$(TOTRECS)
60 COUNT = 0
70 PRINT "This program finds records in a random file"
80 PRINT
90 OPEN "invfile" FOR RANDOM AS #1 LEN = 37
100 FIELD #1, 5 AS FITEM$, 24 AS FITNAME$,  4 AS
FPRICE$, 4 AS FQUANT$
110 ' Begin getting data to list
120 TOTRECS = LOF(1)/37   ' check number of records
130 FOR X = 1 TO TOTRECS     ' process every record
140    GET #1, X
150    RINDEX$(X)=FITEM$
160 NEXT
170 ' File access routine
180 CLS
190 INPUT "Enter the item number you want or X to
quit: ", ITEM$
200 WHILE ITEM$ <> "X" AND ITEM$ <> "x"
210    KEEP = -1
220    FOR X = 1 TO TOTRECS
230       IF RINDEX$(X) = ITEM$ THEN KEEP = X
240    NEXT
250    IF KEEP = -1 THEN PRINT "Not in file" : GOTO 280
260    GET #1, KEEP
270    PRICE=CVS(FPRICE$)
280    QUANT=CVS(FQUANT$)
290    PRINT FITEM$, FITNAME$, PRICE, QUANT
300    INPUT "Enter the item number you want or X to
quit: ", ITEM$
310 WEND
320 CLOSE #1
330 END
```

Figure 11.11. Using a Random File Array Index

5. Test the program. When it works correctly, save it again if you like.

Your program should look something like this:

```
10 ' work with two arrays
20 DIM PAYROLL(11,2), STAFF$(11)
```

```
30 FOR X = 0 TO 11
40    FOR Y= 0 TO 2
50       READ PAYROLL(X,Y)
60    NEXT
70 NEXT
80 ' Load the staff array
90 RESTORE 2000
100 FOR Z = 0 TO 11
110    READ STAFF$(Z)
120 NEXT
130 PRINT "Name";TAB(20);"Salary    Dependents   Class
140 FOR X = 0 TO 11
150    PRINT STAFF$(X); TAB(20)
160    FOR Y = 0 TO 2
170       PRINT USING "####,###"; PAYROLL(X,Y),
180    NEXT
190 PRINT
200 NEXT
210 END
1000 ' values for two-dimensional array
1010 DATA 24000, 5, 1, 22000, 4, 1, 25000, 2, 2, 36000, 1, 2
1020 DATA 18500, 1, 0, 32000, 3, 2, 31000, 4, 1, 29000, 1, 2
1030 DATA 20000, 1, 1, 36000, 4, 2, 28000, 3, 2, 40000, 3, 1
2000 ' values for one-dimensional array
2010 DATA "Davis, John", "Lincoln, Mark", "Ashley, Ruth"
2020 DATA "Fernandez, Judi", "Klein, Karen", "Albert, Sue"
2030 DATA "Quayle, W. C.", "Burton, Kris", "Gritter, Larry"
2040 DATA "Loveland, Karl", "Rosencranz, R.", "Conrad, Conrad"
```

Be sure you used the same number of elements in the STAFF$ array as in your first subscript for the other array. To cause the name to print just once, you must include it in the outer FOR...NEXT loop while the two-dimensional array elements are handled by the inner loop. Of course, you program could be quite different and still be correct.

Summary

This chapter has shown you how to define and use arrays in GW-BASIC programs. An array is a set of values referred to by an array variable name and one or more subscripts. By default, an array can use up to subscript 10 in each dimension.

An array reference needs one subscript per dimension; the subscripts must be nonnegative integers. By default, subscript 0 refers to the first element.

The DIM statement lets you define an array with the exact size you need in each dimension. It must appear before any reference to the array name.

The ERASE statement cancels an implicit or explicit definition of an array so that it can be reused with different dimensions in the same program.

The OPTION BASE 1 statement eliminates the 0 element, so storage and referencing of elements begins with subscript 1; if this statement is used, subscript 0 is out of range.

Arrays can be loaded from the keyboard, from DATA statements within the program, or from files. To load them in FOR...NEXT loops, you need one loop for each dimension, nested if there is more than one dimension.

The subscript from one array can be used to access corresponding elements in another array.

The SWAP statement exchanges the values in two variables, such as two different array elements. You can make use of this statement in sorting array elements in ascending or descending sequence.

Exercise

For this exercise, you will modify the program shown in Figure 11.5 so that it creates a two-dimensional array and does additional processing.

1. Modify the basic program so that it creates a two-dimensional array. It should then calculate and print the average high and low temperatures, as in Figure 11.5.
2. Now add a routine to calculate and print the average temperature for each period.
3. Test the program to make sure it works. Save it if you like.

Your program should look something like this:

```
10 ' Set up and process temperature values
20 DEFINT H,I,L,T
30 DIM TEMP(19,1)
40 FOR I = 0 TO 19
50    FOR H = 0 TO 1
60       READ TEMP(I,H)
70    NEXT
80 NEXT
90 FOR I = 0 TO 19
100    TOTHI = TOTHI + TEMP(I,0)
110    TOTLO = TOTLO + TEMP(I,1)
120 NEXT
130 AVGHI = TOTHI/20
140 AVGLO = TOTLO / 20
150 PRINT "Average high temperature: "; AVGHI
160 PRINT "Average low temperature:  "; AVGLO
```

```
170 ' Routine to get periodic average
180 PRINT "Period    Average Temperature"
190 FOR I = 0 TO 19
200   PERAVE = (TEMP(I,0) + TEMP(I,1))/2
210   PRINT I+1, PERAVE
220 NEXT
230 A$=INPUT$(1)
240 END
1000 ' Start DATA lines here
1010 DATA 87,58,85,57,82,52,90,61,85,62,83,57,79,59,74,53
1020 DATA 78,54,75,59,79,61,81,60,84,58,82,59,79,56,75,54
1030 DATA 77,53,76,54,76,53,72,56
```

Lines 30 through 80 build the two-dimensional array. Lines 90 through 160 calculate and print the averages. Lines 180 through 220 calculate the average for each period and print it on the screen. Line 230 pauses the screen so that all the data fits. Your program may be different and still be correct.

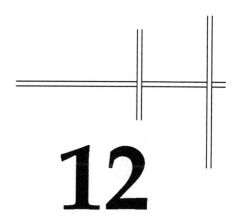

12

Handling Program Errors

In the course of this book you have learned many ways to make programs work correctly or to debug them. Once programs are ready to use, however, they may still produce errors, especially if they depend on user or file input. This chapter covers the basics of error handling in programs. You'll see how to keep such errors from terminating programs and how to recover from many errors that may occur. In particular, you'll learn to:

- Use the ON ERROR statement to set up error trapping in a program
- Use the RESUME statement to continue program execution after an error is trapped
- Use the ERROR statement to induce an error for testing purposes
- Use the ERR and ERL system variables to show the error number and the line in which the error occurred
- Use the ERDEV and ERDEV$ variables to identify errors originating from devices after DOS 3.0
- Use the EXTERR function to get expanded information after DOS 3.0

Error Handling

In Chapter 4, you learned to use the ON statement for branching (GOTO and GOSUB) and for trapping events such as key presses. You can also use ON to trap errors. When a program traps errors and tries to fix them, it helps people to use your programs more efficiently, and it keeps the program from terminating in an awkward place. For example, suppose the program gets user input for updating files. The user may enter data in the wrong format or outside the acceptable range for certain operations. When an error occurs, the program is by default terminated and file changes aren't saved, which can be extremely annoying to the user. A simple error trapping routine can avoid the abrupt termination. Even if it simply closes the files, a great deal of time can be saved because any changes are saved when the files are closed normally. In this section, you'll learn to set up and test error trapping routines.

Trapping Errors

The ON ERROR statement lets you specify a line to branch to if any error (other than Division by zero) occurs. Here's the format:

    ON ERROR GOTO *nnn*

After this statement is executed, any error causes the requested branch. Figure 12.1 shows an example. This program counts the number of elements in DATA statements. When it tries to read past the last data item, an Out of DATA error occurs. The branch to line 70 will occur no matter what the error is; in this case, we assume it is the Out of DATA error.

    In this program, the error routine simply prints the number of counted items and ends the program without an error message. If the program deals with files, you might include the statement CLOSE in the error routine; without any file numbers, this statement closes all open files and saves the data.

Error Trapping Limitations

Error trapping has no effect within an error routine; if an error occurs while the error routine is being processed, after it has been activated by an ON ERROR statement, the error terminates the program. The effect of ON ERROR GOTO continues until you issue another RUN or LOAD command. If you type LSIT to list your program, for example, the Syntax error is trapped and the error handling routine is executed again. To turn error trapping off, use ON ERROR GOTO 0 in direct mode or in a program. This works even if your program includes 0 as a valid program line.

```
10 ' Use the SCORE array
20 ON ERROR GOTO 70
30 READ VALUE
40 COUNT = COUNT + 1
50 GOTO 30
60 END
70 ' error trap result
80 PRINT COUNT; "data items"
90 END
2000 ' Start SCORE data here, one line per student
2010 DATA 90,87,84,88,76,81,89,76,78,84,94,92
2020 DATA 90,87,84,88,76,81,89,76,78,84,94,92
2030 DATA 87,86,85,84,79,82,86,86,88,94,84,82
2040 DATA 89,100,87,92,90,87,89,90,86,91,93,97
2050 DATA 94,99,96,100,97,89,91,88,87,85,86,88
2060 DATA 90,87,84,88,76,81,89,76,78,84,94,92
2070 DATA 90,87,84,88,76,81,89,76,78,84,94,92
2080 DATA 87,86,85,84,79,82,86,86,88,94,84,82
2090 DATA 89,100,87,92,90,87,89,90,86,91,93,97
2100 DATA 96,99,96,97,87,89,91,88,87,95,96,98
```

Figure 12.1. Trapping an Error

Continuing Program Execution

Programs are often ready to continue executing after an error is trapped and dealt with. Suppose a program wants to build an array and process it, without knowing in advance how many data values are present. Just as subroutines (started by GOSUB) are ended with RETURN, so can an error trapping subroutine end with the RESUME statement. RESUME can have three different formats:

RESUME
RESUME NEXT
RESUME *nnn*

The word RESUME alone returns control back to the statement in which the error occurred. If the routine solved the problem, that may be what you want. If the problem still exists, however, it might not be. For example, if the error routine in Figure 12.1 included RESTORE to point to the first DATA statement, you could safely return to the READ statement and start over.

The statement RESUME NEXT works much like RETURN; it returns control to the statement following the one that transferred control to the subroutine. The statement RESUME *nnn* transfers control to the line number you specify. For example, suppose the program has to determine the number of elements, then dimension and load an array containing all of them. Figure 12.2 shows how this can be done.

Notice that the error trapping subroutine dimensions the array and prints the number of data items on the screen. It isn't really necessary to print it here, but that shows us that the error was successfully trapped. The routine then transfers control back to line 70. The main program issues RESTORE to point back to the beginning of the data, then loads the array.

Notice that an END statement precedes the error trapping routine. If it wasn't there and control fell through to the error routine, the DIM statement is executed again, raising the error Duplicate Definition in 1010. This is trapped also (because the routine is not being executed from ON ERROR GOTO), and control is transferred back to line 1000. This time when the DIM statement is executed, the program is terminated, because error trapping is not in effect in the error routine itself. If that error didn't occur, the RESUME statement would generate an error when control reached it normally. This would be trapped the first time and taken care of in the error-handling routine.

Identifying Data and Program Errors

The program can identify exactly what error occurred in case you might not be able to tell. Two system variables contain information that helps identify it: ERR and ERL.

The ERR variable contains the GW-BASIC error number after any data error occurs. Every error message that may arise has an assigned number, which you won't see when it is displayed on the screen. Typical message numbers are:

3	RETURN without GOSUB
4	Out of DATA
53	File not found

A complete list of error numbers and messages is found in Appendix E. You could use a series of statements of the form IF ERR = 4 THEN GOSUB 900 : RESUME 200 in an error-handling subroutine. The value of ERR isn't changed until another error occurs.

The ERL variable contains the line number in your program that raised the error. You can use it as needed in programs. If a program may get the Out of

```
10 ' Try error trapping
20 ON ERROR GOTO 1000
30 ' initial read loop
40    READ VALUE
50    COUNT = COUNT + 1
60 GOTO 40
70 ' use after counting elements
80 RESTORE
90 FOR X = 1 TO COUNT
100    READ ALLVALUES(COUNT)
110 NEXT
120 END
1000 ' error trap result
1010 DIM ALLVALUES(COUNT)
1020 PRINT COUNT; "data items"
1030 RESUME 70
2000 ' Start SCORE data here, one line per student
2010 DATA 90,87,84,88,76,81,89,76,78,84,94,92
2020 DATA 90,87,84,88,76,81,89,76,78,84,94,92
2030 DATA 87,86,85,84,79,82,86,86,88,94,84,82
2040 DATA 89,100,87,92,90,87,89,90,86,91,93,97
2050 DATA 94,99,96,100,97,89,91,88,87,85,86,88
2060 DATA 90,87,84,88,76,81,89,76,78,84,94,92
2070 DATA 90,87,84,88,76,81,89,76,78,84,94,92
2080 DATA 87,86,85,84,79,82,86,86,88,94,84,82
2090 DATA 89,100,87,92,90,87,89,90,86,91,93,97
2100 DATA 96,99,96,97,87,89,91,88,87,95,96,98
```

——————————— Figure 12.2. Resuming Program Execution

DATA message on line 90 or on line 350, you might use IF ERR = 4 AND ERL = 90 THEN GOSUB 500 to specify processing for one specific situation.

Testing the Error

When you put an error-trapping routine into a program, you want to be able to test it carefully. GW-BASIC lets you insert errors into your program by number with the ERROR statement, so you don't really have to generate actual errors. To see the effect of an Out of DATA error, for example, include the statement ERROR 4 in your program. This will trigger error trapping exactly the same as a real error will. Figure 12.3 shows the effect of inserting error 4 into a program.

```
10 ' Test specific error
20 ON ERROR GOTO 800
30 DEFINT H-L
40 DIM HITEMP(20), LOTEMP(20)
50 FOR I = 0 TO 19
60   IF I = 18 THEN ERROR 4
70   READ HITEMP(I)
80   READ LOTEMP(I)
90 NEXT
100 FOR I = 0 TO 19
110   TOTHI = TOTHI + HITEMP(I)
120   TOTLO = TOTLO + LOTEMP(I)
130 NEXT
140 AVGHI = TOTHI / 20
150 AVGLO = TOTLO / 20
160 PRINT "Average high temperature: "; AVGHI
170 PRINT "Average low temperature:  "; AVGLO
180 END
800 ' error handling routine
810 PRINT "line ", ERL
820 RESUME NEXT
1000 ' Start DATA lines here
1010 DATA 87,58,85,57,82,52,90,61,85,62,83,57,79,59
1020 DATA 74, 53, 78,54,75,59,79,61,81,60,84,58,82,59
1030 DATA 79, 56, 75, 54, 77,53,76,54,76,53,72,56
```

Figure 12.3. Inserting an Error

Line 60 includes the ERROR statement; it is executed late in the loop. The error-handling routine in lines 800 through 820 is invoked and prints a constant and the line that invoked the error. In this case, "line 60"appears on the screen before the output from lines 160 and 170.

You can also use ERROR n in direct mode to see the text of the message that n refers to. If you type ERROR 15 in direct mode, for example, the screen shows the message String too long.

1. Load the program you wrote in Chapter 11 and saved as 11SELF.BAS. If you didn't do (or save) that program, try the same exercise with any program that uses an array.
2. Add an error trapping routine starting at line 800. In it, print the error number and the line that generated it, then continue processing.

3. Add a statement to set up error trapping. Test the program. If it worked before, it should still be fine if END is before the error routine.
4. Add an ERROR statement to cause the Out of DATA error to appear between the two loops. Test the program again.
5. Remove the ERROR statement. Then insert a real error by increasing the upper limit of the last inner loop by 1. Change the error routine to transfer control to the END statement.
6. Test the program again. You should get error number 9 in a line in the last inner loop.

Here's how our program looked after item 4:

```
10 ' test error trapping
20 ON ERROR GOTO 800
30 DIM PAYROLL(11,2)
40 FOR X = 0 TO 11
50    FOR Y= 0 TO 2
60       READ PAYROLL(X,Y)
70    NEXT
80 NEXT
90 PRINT "error here" : ERROR 4
100 PRINT "Salary   Dependents   Class
110 FOR X = 0 TO 11
120    FOR Y = 0 TO 2
130       PRINT USING "#####,##"; PAYROLL(X,Y),
140    NEXT
150 PRINT
160 NEXT
170 PRINT "End of program"
180 END
800 ' error trapping routine
810 PRINT
820 PRINT "Error number"; ERR,"Line with error"; ERL
830 RESUME NEXT
1000 ' start data stuff here
1010 DATA 24000, 5, 1, 22000, 4, 1, 25000, 2, 2, 36000, 1, 2
1020 DATA 18500, 1, 0, 32000, 3, 2, 31000, 4, 1, 29000, 1, 2
1030 DATA 20000, 1, 1, 36000, 4, 2, 28000, 3, 2, 40000, 3, 1
```

For item 5, we deleted line 90, changed line 120 to read FOR Y = 0 TO 3, and changed line 830 to read RESUME 180. The message reported error 9 in line 130.

Your program may be somewhat different, depending on how you originally coded the program. If it prints the error code you specified and the line number you inserted, it works correctly.

DOS 3.0 Features

If you are running GW-BASIC under DOS 3.0 or later, you can use some additional features. You can identify more specifically any errors originated from devices attached to your system and you can get extended error information. These features are covered in this section.

Identifying Device Errors

A device error occurs when some piece of hardware is not able to handle the function the program asks it to do. Device errors are identified by number, but the number doesn't tell you which device is the problem. For example, these messages may not give you all the information you need:

57	Device I/O error
68	Device unavailable

Your program may need more information to deal with such situations adequately. The ERDEV and ERDEV$ functions help you do this. To understand them, you need to know a bit more about devices.

Device Types. Devices are either character or block. The screen, the keyboard, the printer, and the modem are character devices. They have a name of up to eight characters, such as SCRN, CON, LPT1, AUX, or COM1. Disk drives are block devices; they have two-character names such as A: or C:.

Device Variables. After a device error, the value of ERDEV$ is always the name of the device, such as LPT1 or C:, depending on the device. You can print it just like any other string variable.

If the device that generated the error is a character device, the value of ERDEV is a negative number; if it's a block device, ERDEV is positive. That may be enough information for you. The value of ERDEV points to two bytes in memory. Locating the contents of those bytes requires several GW-BASIC features we haven't covered. However, if you want to try it, use a set of statements in this form:

```
DEFSEG: A%=ERDEV:B=VARPTR(A%):PRINT PEEK(B);PEEK(B+1)
```

Two bytes from memory are printed. The first byte indicates the exact error, while the second gives more technical information.

Identifying Extended Error Codes

DOS 3.0 (and later) provide extended error information; this isn't available in earlier versions. Some GW-BASIC statements use DOS to perform their actions; if you use LOAD, SAVE, or LPRINT, for example, DOS provides extended information if the operation fails.

The function EXTERR(n) returns whatever extended information DOS makes available in four different codes, ranging from 0 to 3. The values are handled entirely by DOS. But if they're available, they are always returned if the DOS actions are performed. The EXTERR function just makes them available to the program. Your DOS documentation contains details on the meanings of all the function results.

EXTERR(0). The value of EXTERR(0) is a code that identifies the error; it's not the same as the ERR value. These codes range from 1 to 88. Code 2 is File not found, 88 is a network data fault.

EXTERR(1). The value of EXTERR(1) gives the classification of the error; it returns a value from 1 to 13. Class 5 is a hardware failure, for example, and class 10 indicates that something was locked.

EXTERR(2). The value of EXTERR(2) gives a suggested action; it returns one of these values:

1	Retry
2	Delay retry
3	Ask user to reenter input
4	Abort
5	Immediate exit
6	Ignore
7	Retry after user intervention

The action suggested, of course, depends on the error. The statement PRINT "Line ";ERL;" Action ";EXTERR(2) can give you help in deciding what to do next.

EXTERR(3). The result of EXTERR(3) can help you narrow the error location down even more. It can have any of these values:

1	Unknown
2	Disk
3	Network

4   Serial devices
5   Random access memory

Using Extended Error Information

Suppose the user is asked to input a path and name for saving a file created by your program. The program has to deal with the fact that an invalid path might be entered. If the program uses an error trapping routine, it can get the information and use it. An invalid path error returns these values:

ERR	76
EXTERR(0)	3
EXTERR(1)	8
EXTERR(2)	3
EXTERR(3)	2

Notice that the GW-BASIC error message number (ERR) is not the same as the DOS error number (3). The classification 8 indicates that the entity was not found. The suggested action is to ask the user to retry the input. And the additional information indicates that it is related to a disk problem.

The information provided by the EXTERR function can help you in debugging a program and preventing abnormal termination. Once you know what errors may occur, you can test values of these functions and perform the necessary action within error-handling subroutines.

1. If you use DOS 3.0 or later, add a line in the error-handling routine to print all four values returned by EXTERR. Test the program. Notice that all four values are 0.
2. Modify the program you just used to save the current program to a drive that you don't have. Remove the ERROR statement, then test it again.

We added line 30 SAVE "E:TRYEXT"*, which printed 76 for the GW-BASIC message number and 3 8 3 2 for the DOS extended information.*

Summary

This chapter has covered the fundamentals of error handling in GW-BASIC programs. An error-handling routine can be included in any program to handle trapped errors and prevent inconvenient program termination.

The ON ERROR statement sets up error trapping. It transfers control to the specified line when any error occurs while trapping is in effect. The error-trapping routine can handle various errors you expect the program may encounter. To turn off error trapping, use ON ERROR GOTO 0.

The RESUME statement marks the end of an error-handling routine and sends control back to the statement that caused the trapped error. Other options of RESUME transfer control to the line following the statement that caused the error or to a specified line number.

The ERROR statement inserts an error of the specified number into a program; this is usually done just for testing purposes. You can also use ERROR in direct mode to see the text of a numbered message.

The ERR and ERL system variables contain the error message number (ERR) and the program line number (ERL) that caused the error.

The ERDEV and ERDEV$ system variables contain information about the devices that caused errors. ERDEV$ always contains the name of the device (in a form like LPT1 or C:). These functions are not available prior to DOS 3.0.

The EXTERR function returns one of four values that give extended information about DOS errors; it returns 0 if GW-BASIC is running under a version of DOS earlier than 3.0.

This chapter has no special exercise. You have already tried the commands and features covered in this chapter. You'll find that you use error handling more and more as your programs get more sophisticated.

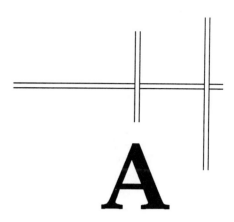

A

GW-BASIC Reserved Words

ABS	CSNG
AND	CSRLIN
ASC	CVD
ATN	CVI
AUTO	CVS
BEEP	DATA
BLOAD	DATE$
BSAVE	DEF
CALL	DEFDBL
CDBL	DEFINT
CHAIN	DEFSNG
CHDIR	DEFSTR
CHR$	DELETE
CINT	DIM
CIRCLE	DRAW
CLEAR	EDIT
CLOSE	ELSE
CLS	END
COLOR	ENVIRON
COM	ENVIRON$
COMMON	EOF
CONT	EQV
COS	ERASE

ERDEV	LOCK*
ERDEV$	LOF
ERL	LOG
ERR	LPOS
ERROR	LPRINT
EXP	LSET
EXTERR*	MERGE
FIELD	MID$
FILES	MKDIR
FIX	MKD$
FNxxxxxx	MKI$
FOR	MKS$
FRE	MOD
GET	MOTOR
GOSUB	NAME
GOTO	NEW
HEX$	NEXT
IF	NOT
IMP	OCT$
INKEY$	OFF
INP	ON
INPUT	OPEN
INPUT#	OPTION
INPUT$	OR
INSTR	OUT
INT	PAINT
INTER$	PALETTE*
IOCTL	PCOPY*
IOCTL$	PEEK
KEY	PEN
KEY$	PLAY
KILL	PMAP
LEFT$	POINT
LEN	POKE
LET	POS
LINE	PRESET
LIST	PRINT
LLIST	PRINT#
LOAD	PSET
LOC	PUT
LOCATE	RANDOMIZE

READ	VAL
REM	VARPTR
RENUM	VARPTR*
RESET	VIEW
RESTORE	WAIT
RESUME	WEND
RETURN	WHILE
RIGHT$	WIDTH
RMDIR	WINDOW
RND	WRITE
RSET	WRITE#
RUN	XOR
SAVE	
SCREEN	
SGN	
SHARED	
SHELL	
SIN	
SOUND	
SPACE$	
SPC	
SQR	
STEP	
STICK	
STOP	
STR$	
STRIG	
STRING$	
SWAP	
SYSTEM	
TAB	
TAN	
THEN	
TIME$	
TIMER	
TO	
TROFF	
TRON	
UNLOCK*	
USING	
USR	

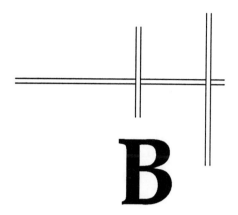

B

ASCII Collating Sequence

!	>
"	?
#	@
$	A
%	thru
&	Z
'	[
(	\
)	]
*	^
+	_
, (comma)	´ (apostrophe)
-	a
.	thru
/	z
0	{
thru		
8	}
9	~
:	
;	
<	
=	

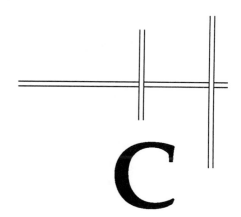

C

ASCII Character Listing

Decimal	ASCII		Decimal	ASCII
000	NUL		023	ETB
001	SOH		024	CAN
002	STX		025	EM
003	ETX		026	SUB
004	EOT		027	ESC
005	ENQ		028	FS
006	ACK		029	GS
007	BEL		030	RS
008	BS		031	US
009	HT		032	SP
010	LF		033	!
011	VT		034	"
012	FF		035	#
013	CR		036	$
014	SO		037	%
015	SI		038	&
016	DLE		039	'
017	DC1		040	(
018	DC2		041	)
019	DC3		042	*
020	DC4		043	+
021	NAK		044	,
022	SYN		045	-

Decimal	ASCII	Decimal	ASCII
046	.	087	W
047	/	088	X
048	0	089	Y
049	1	090	Z
050	2	091	[
051	3	092	\
052	4	093	]
053	5	094	^
054	6	095	_
055	7	096	'
056	8	097	a
057	9	098	b
058	:	099	c
059	;	100	d
060	<	101	e
061	=	102	f
062	>	103	g
063	?	104	h
064	@	105	i
065	A	106	j
066	B	107	k
067	C	108	l
068	D	109	m
069	E	110	n
070	F	111	o
071	G	112	p
072	H	113	q
073	I	114	r
074	J	115	s
075	K	116	t
076	L	117	u
077	M	118	v
078	N	119	w
079	O	120	x
080	P	121	y
081	Q	122	z
082	R	123	{
083	S	124		
084	T	125	}
085	U	126	~
086	V	127	DEL

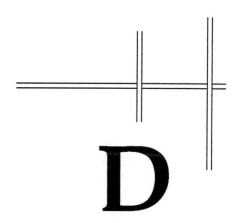

D

Additional GW-BASIC Statements, Functions, and Options

There is much more to know about GW-BASIC. This appendix lists statements, functions, and variables that are not discussed in this book, as well as some that have significant features we did not get to. Your GW-BASIC documentation will have additional details on the format and use of these features.

ATAN	A trigonometric function that returns the arctangent of the numeric argument.
BLOAD	Places the contents of the named file in memory, starting at a specific byte location in the current segment. It is useful for loading graphics or machine language programs.
BSAVE	Copies values from a specific range of bytes in the current segment to a file on disk. You can use it to store graphics or machine language programs.
CALL	Transfers control to the named file, which contains a machine language subroutine. Control will be returned

to the current program when the statement RET *n* is encountered.

CHAIN Transfers control to another GW-BASIC program and terminates the current program. It works much like GOTO.

CHAIN MERGE Transfers control to another GW-BASIC program, much as GOSUB transfers control to another line. When it ends, control returns to the current program.

COM(n) Controls trapping of a signal from the specified serial port during communications activity.

COMMON Specifies variables to be passed to another program if CHAIN or CHAIN MERGE is executed. Similar COMMON statements must appear in both programs.

COS A trigonometric function that returns the cosine of the numeric argument.

DEF FN Defines and names user functions that can be used in the program. The FN becomes the first two characters of the function name.

DEF SEG Specifies which GW-BASIC segment is to be current; this is the data segment by default. It affects the action of BLOAD, BSAVE, CALL, PEEK, POKE, and USR.

DEF USR Specifies the starting location of a machine language routine that may be called from memory by the USR function.

ENVIRON Specifies a string to be added to your system's environment. This function can be accomplished under DOS with the SET command.

EXP A function that returns the value of the natural log (*e*) to the power of the argument.

GET An additional format transfers graphics from the screen to a named array for holding in memory.

HEX$	A function that converts the decimal numeric argument into a hexadecimal string.
INP	A function that returns the byte just read by the specified input port. This function is most useful in communications.
IOCTL	Sends a "control" string to a character device driver after the driver has been opened as a file. IOCTL$ reads a string from the specified driver.
LINE	Additional option lets you style individual lines, so they appear dotted, dashed, or a combination.
LOG	A function that returns the natural logarithm of the numeric argument.
MERGE	Specifies a program to be loaded and added to the current program in memory; if any program lines match, incoming lines replace the existing ones.
MOD	An operator that returns the remainder of integer division (performed with \). It is expressed as *dividend* MOD *divisor*.
OCT$	A function that converts the decimal argument into an octal string.
ON	Additional formats can trap COM (communication ports), PEN (light pen), PLAY (music buffer), STRIG (joystick), and TIMER.
OPEN "COM	Sets up a buffer for asynchronous communications (RS-232)
OUT	Sends a byte of data to the named output port.
PAINT	Additional option lets you style the color, to create patterns on the screen.
PALETTE USING	Expands PALETTE to let you use an array to reset many colors at once.

PCOPY	Copies one screen page to another.
PEEK	Gets the value at the specified single byte.
PEN	Tells the program to recognize and interpret light pen input.
PLAY	Plays musical notes through the computer, using a macro language similar to the DRAW statement.
PLAY(*n*)	Controls trapping of a signal when the number of notes stored in the music buffer is less than *n*.
PMAP	Maps expressions to logical or physical coordinates. It is used to transfer a graphic from one set of coordinates to another.
POINT	Reads the color or attribute of the specified pixel on the screen.
POKE	Puts the specified value at the specified memory location.
PRESET	Displays a point at the specified location on the screen. Differs from PSET in how it handles a default color.
PSET	Displays a point at the specified location on the screen. Differs from PRESET in how it handles a default color.
PUT	Additional format transfers graphic images saved earlier with GET back to the screen.
RESET	Closes all open files.
SCREEN	Additional options let you create and store several screens for use in such effects as animation.
SIN	This trigonometric function returns the sine of the argument.
SOUND	Generates an audio tone based on the frequency (pitch) and duration specified in the statement.

STICK   This function returns the x and y coordinates of two
                  joysticks. It tells the program to recognize and interpret
                  lever movements on a device controlled by a game con-
                  trol adapter.

STRIG   This function returns the status of the joystick triggers. It
                  tells the program to recognize and interpret button pres-
                  ses on a device controlled by a game control adapter.

TAN   A trigonometric function that returns the tangent of the
                  argument.

USR   This function calls a machine language subroutine
                  pointed to by a DEF USR statement.

VARPTR   This function returns the address in memory of a par-
                  ticular variable or file control block.

VIEW   Lets you define a viewport as a specific rectangle and
                  place graphics and colors only within it without affect-
                  ing the rest of the screen.

WAIT   Tells the program to do nothing until the specified input
                  port receives the specified value.

WIDTH   An additional argument that lets you specify a device
                  and control line length on your printer.

WINDOW   Sets up a physical space not limited by the screen. It can
                  also change the coordinate system so that the 0,0 point is
                  in the lower-left corner, so the program can use actual
                  Cartesian coordinates.

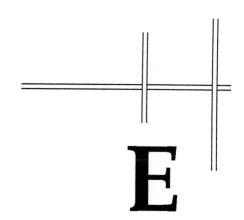

E

GW-BASIC Error Messages

Number	Message
1	NEXT without FOR
2	Syntax error
3	RETURN without GOSUB
4	Out of DATA
5	Illegal function call
6	Overflow
7	Out of memory
8	Undefined line number
9	Subscript out of range
10	Duplicate Definition
11	Division by zero
12	Illegal direct
13	Type mismatch
14	Out of string space
15	String too long
16	String formula too complex
17	Can't continue
18	Undefined user function
19	No RESUME
20	RESUME without error
21	Unprintable error
22	Missing operand

Number	Message
23	Line buffer overflow
24	Device Timeout
25	Device Fault
26	FOR Without NEXT
27	Out of Paper
28	Unprintable error
29	WHILE without WEND
30	WEND without WHILE
31-49	Unprintable error
50	FIELD overflow
51	Internal error
52	Bad file number
53	File not found
54	Bad file mode
55	File already open
56	Unprintable error
57	Device I/O error
58	File already exists
59	Unprintable error
60	Unprintable error
61	Disk full
62	Input past end
63	Bad record number
64	Bad filename
65	Unprintable error
66	Direct statement in file
67	Too many files
68	Device unavailable
69	Communication buffer overflow
70	Permission Denied
71	Disk not Ready
72	Disk media error
73	Advanced Feature
74	Rename across disks
75	Path/File Access Error
76	Path not found

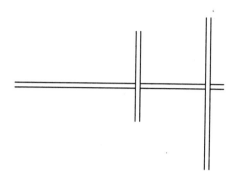

Glossary

Access The process of reading, locating, or writing a record in a disk file.

Accuracy The degree of freedom from error. This is not the same as precision.

Argument A value that is required to find the result of a function.

Array A set of values in which the position of each item is significant. Also a collection of data items all referred to by the same variable name and varying subscripts.

ASCII (American Standard Code for Information Interchange) A standardized 8-bit code used in most computer systems for recording character data.

Asynchronous communication A way of transmitting data serially from one device to another. It is also called start/stop transmission, since each character sent has a start bit and at least one stop bit.

BASIC (Beginner's All-purpose Symbolic Instruction Code) A programming language supported by most personal computers. It was originally developed at Dartmouth College and is considered the easiest language to learn.

Baud A measure of data processing or transmission speed. It is the number of signal elements per second. A baud is not quite the same as a bit-per-second, since a signal element can represent more than one bit. Common baud rates are 300, 1200, 2400, and 9600.

Binary A number system that uses only two digits (0 and 1) and is based on powers of 2.

Bit A contraction of binary digit. A bit is either 0 or 1; it is the smallest piece of information that the computer can recognize.

Block An amount of storage space or data, handled as a unit.

Bps (Bits per second) A measure of transmission speed often used erroneously to mean baud.

Buffer A temporary storage space that holds data when it is transferred to or from various devices.

Byte Eight bits of data handled as a unit. A byte represents one character in string data or part of a numeric field.

Character Any single letter, number, or symbol that the computer can store in one byte.

Command Something that tells the computer to perform a specific action to start, stop, or continue an operation. It is not the same as a statement, although the terms are sometimes used interchangeably.

Compiler A program that translates a program from its source into a form that can be executed.

Concatenate Joining together end to beginning. GW-BASIC lets you concatenate strings. DOS lets you concatenate files.

Configuration A group of interrelated hardware devices that make up a system.

Constant A value or data item that never changes.

Data All the basic information elements that a program can produce or process.

Debug The process of checking and correcting the logic of a program to make sure that it works correctly.

Default An action or value that takes effect if you don't specify otherwise.

Delimiter A character that marks the beginning and end of a piece of data. Commas, semicolons, spaces, and periods are all used at times.

Device A piece of hardware that performs a function. A printer, disk drive, and modem are all devices.

Directory A record of the files on a disk, including the location, size, and last revision date for each.

Diskette A removable disk for a computer, often called a "floppy disk."

DOS (Disk Operating System) A collection of programs that enable you to start up and use a computer and its disks.

Double precision The use of twice as much space (two computer words) to store a number. This allows use of twice as many significant digits as are normally available.

Drive A device that holds a disk or diskette and can access any part of it for storage and retrieval of data.

End-of-file mark (EOF) A symbol or magnetic mark that enables the program to detect when the last record has been read from a file. It is placed there automatically when a new file is closed.

Execute To perform an instruction or carry out a statement or command.

Exponent A value that tells how many times the base factor is repeated. It follows the E or D in floating-point numbers.

Extension Up to three characters following the period in a file name.

Field A portion of a record that stores one item of data, such as a first name or an account number.

File A collection of related data or programs stored under a single name.

File name The unique name that identifies a file; it can have up to eight characters plus an extension.

Fixed point A form of numeric value or arithmetic that includes the actual position of the decimal point and all significant digits.

Floating point A form of numeric value or arithmetic that is based on the location of the decimal point as expressed in the exponent and specification of only significant digits in the mantissa.

Function A computer action invoked by a single instruction, such as SQR, to calculate the square root or RIGHT$ to extract characters from the right of a string. Functions generally have arguments to supply further information.

Function keys Keyboard keys that are preprogrammed to perform a specific action.

Graphics The display of pictures rather than words on the screen.

Hardware The physical equipment that makes up a computer system.

Hexadecimal A number system based on 16, which uses digits 0 through 9 and letters A through F.

Input/output (I/O) Any data going into or out from a computer.

Interpreter A program that reads, translates, and executes statements in a program without going through a separate compilation step.

Instruction Another term for statement; a single program step.

Integer A whole number, with no fractional part.

K (kilo or 1000) In computer use, this actually refers to 2^{10}, or 1024.

Loop A series of statements in a program that are executed repeatedly.

Mantissa The significant digits in a floating-point number. It precedes the E or D.

Memory The area of a computer that can hold data temporarily. Data can be worked with more quickly in memory than on a disk.

Modem (modulator/demodulator) Device that connects a computer to telephone lines; used to transmit data.

MS-DOS (Microsoft Disk Operating System) Software distributed by Microsoft Corporation that lets you start up and use IBM PC- compatible computers.

Network A system that enables several computers to communicate and share equipment through the use of cables and communication lines.

Null Empty. A null string is represented by "".

Numeric Containing only digits, a decimal point, and a sign.

Octal A number system based on 8. It uses only digits 0 through 7.

Operand A general term for a quantity or data item involved in a calculation.

Operating system A collection of programs that manage the operation of a computer.

Operator A symbol that represents an operation and indicates the process being performed.

Option A part of a statement format that can be used or not, depending on the program's needs.

Parameter A variable in a statement that has a value for the current purpose.

Pixel (picture element) A single point on a monitor that can be referenced by the program.

Port The location where a device is connected to the computer. Some ports are solely for input, some just for output, and some for both.

Program A series of instructions to the computer in the form of statements and commands.

Prompt The message that appears on the screen to tell you the system is ready for input.

RAM (random access memory) The part of the computer's memory that can be used by programs.

RS-232 A standard interface between a modem and a computer or terminal; this is a serial interface.

Single precision The use of a standard amount of space (one computer word) to store a number. In GW-BASIC, this allows up to seven significant digits.

Software Programs and instructions that control the computer.

Statement An instruction to the computer that causes it to perform the specified action or sequence of actions.

Switch An option that can be used on a command or statement to cause a special effect.

Syntax The structure of a statement or program element.

Variable A quantity that can have any of a set of values as a program is executed.

Word A computer word is the amount of space the computer takes to store one single-precision number. In PC-compatible systems, a word is four bytes long.

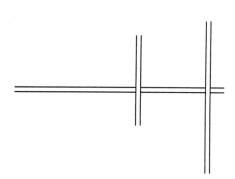

Index